Clothing and Landscape in Victorian England

Working-class Dress and Rural Life

Rachel Worth

BLOOMSBURY VISUAL ARTS

LONDON • NEW YORK • OXFORD • NEW DELHI • SYDNEY

BLOOMSBURY VISUAL ARTS
Bloomsbury Publishing Plc
50 Bedford Square, London, WC1B 3DP, UK
1385 Broadway, New York, NY 10018, USA

BLOOMSBURY, BLOOMSBURY VISUAL ARTS and the Diana logo
are trademarks of Bloomsbury Publishing Plc

First published in Great Britain 2018 by I.B. Tauris & Co.
Paperback edition published 2019 by Bloomsbury Visual Arts

A catalogue record for this book is available from the British Library.

A catalog record for this book is available from the Library of Congress.

ISBN: HB: 978-1-7845-3396-0
PB: 978-1-3501-2284-0
ePDF: 978-1-7867-3345-0
eBook: 978-1-7867-2345-1

To find out more about our authors and books visit
www.bloomsbury.com and sign up for our newsletters.

Rachel Worth is Professor of History of Dress and Fashion at the Arts University Bournemouth. She is the author of *Dress & Textiles* (2002), *Fashion for the People: A History of Clothing at Marks & Spencer* (2006) and *Fashion and Class* (2018).

'There is a great deal of original evidence and analysis here, as well as insights into the often-contradictory impulses at play within Victorian art and literature in its depiction of ways country people dressed. It is particularly fascinating to read about the symbolic and mythic status of landscape over this period, and to have dress foregrounded as a crucial element within both debates about and visualizations of the countryside during a time of rapid industrialization.'

— Rebecca Arnold, Oak Foundation Senior Lecturer in
History of Dress & Textiles, The Courtauld Institute of Art

'I was lucky enough to see this volume when it was little more than a pattern; when the author's initial ideas were being measured against a complex fabric of historic artefacts, period photographs, and other archival sources from the Museum of English Rural Life and elsewhere. The finished monograph holds nothing back. It goes to great lengths to capture the complexity of the period under investigation, delivering through its outerwear a balanced and detailed sense of the many changes to the countryside that occurred during this time. A multifaceted and nuanced narrative underlies these robust garments. The text deftly and expertly contrasts and explores the layers of social hierarchy, cultural influence, economic reality, and material uncertainty that make this such a compelling field for investigation. For my own part, as a curator and interpreter of rural material culture, it offers a reference text that is both subtle and challenging, and one that confronts the enduring paradox of apparently precious collections that are comprised of seemingly unimportant, disposable, and outmoded things. Not unlike the smock-frocks it so carefully unpicks, this volume is a hard-wearing must for the specialist and an accessible way in for those trying on the English countryside for the very first time.'

— Oliver Douglas, Curator of Collections, Museum of
English Rural Life, University of Reading

CONTENTS

ILLUSTRATIONS

BLACK-AND-WHITE ILLUSTRATIONS

COLOUR PLATES

ACKNOWLEDGMENTS

This book developed out of research undertaken for my doctoral thesis, which I completed in August 2002, a couple of days before the birth of my son, who most considerately(!) arrived 12 days 'late'. I am very grateful to my PhD supervisor Aileen Ribeiro, who wholeheartedly supported my early research focus on working-class dress, a topic that was considered a little unusual at the time.

Later, Aileen's successor at the Courtauld Institute of Art, Rebecca Arnold, made suggestions for a choice of publisher, and I am indebted to her for steering me towards I.B.Tauris, and also for discussing with me alternative ways of organizing the research material. Giorgio Riello offered generous feedback on early chapter drafts.

Thank you very much to Philippa Brewster at I.B.Tauris for her sustained enthusiasm for the project and invaluable insights into successive drafts of the manuscript, along with suggestions on how it could be improved. My copy editor Mary Chesshyre did so much more than her role implies, questioning assumptions and suggesting clarifications in my arguments, and patiently editing the text with scrupulous attention to detail. Any errors or inconsistencies that remain are of course mine.

This research was supported by the Museum of English Rural Life, University of Reading, with the award of a Gwyn E. Jones Research Fellowship (2012–13) enabling me to access the wonderful object and archival collections. Heartfelt thanks to the curator Oliver Douglas for facilitating my research and making my many visits so enriching; to Caroline Benson for tirelessly assisting me in my searches through the photographic archive; and to Laura Bennetto who took many of the beautiful photographs (reproduced here) of the museum's collection.

Finally, I extend my gratitude to the Arts University Bournemouth for financial help with the cost of colour reproductions.

INTRODUCTION

... the largest secular change of a thousand years: from the life of the fields to the life of the city. Nine out of ten families have migrated in three generations.

(C. F. G. Masterman, *The Condition of England*)[1]

This book is an exploration of literary and visual representations of working-class dress in the context of Victorian rural life and landscape. Until the mid-nineteenth century, England can be described, in generalized terms, as a rural society, with the majority of the population living in the countryside, and an economy based essentially upon agriculture, rural industries and crafts. By the close of the first decade of the twenty-first century, however, England was the most urban of the three countries comprising mainland Britain. Over 90 per cent of the population lived in just 8.3 per cent of the total land area.[2] It is therefore hard for us now to imagine that a child living at the very beginning of Victoria's reign – the last years of the 1830s – was more likely to have been born in or near a hamlet or village than in a town or city. But just two or three decades later, by the 1850s–60s, the converse was true: statistically, a child was more likely to have begun life in a town or city, or to have moved from a village to a larger (urban) centre during the course of a lifetime. Given that this transition was so rapid, it must have affected both the individual's and the community's experiences. It had implications for occupational patterns, which, in turn, impacted on traditional clothing styles and perceptions of 'fashion'.

The representation of clothing chronicles, sometimes in complex ways, this transition from a predominantly rural society at the beginning of our period to an urban one by its close. Dress as visual signifier may be a coded message for class, status or 'place' in society, and often all of these. In the examples I discuss over the course of the chapters that follow, dress also became a focus for debates about tradition versus modernity. Although the distinctions between these two ideas were not as crude or simplistic as this opposition suggests, the association of the past with stability and perceptions of traditional modes of dress came to be contrasted with the evolution of newer, fashionable styles. In other words, dress was an indicator of cultural change. And of course, it was not only about the aesthetics of clothing, though for many this was crucial, but also about changes in the way in which clothing was made and manufactured over the Victorian period. Hence, the perceived merits of, say, an individual smock (or smock-frock) that was hand-embroidered and made 'at home' (although many were in fact made on a commercial basis) could be contrasted with the anonymity and apparent uniformity of clothing that was ready-made. Such changes served as a perfect foil for debates about the role of technology, mass production and sweated labour that featured so prominently in the Victorian period. From this point, it was only a small step to making value judgments about the efficacy and suitability of new styles in relation to those that were displaced, and vice versa.

In this study, 'landscape' means both the rural landscape, its fields and woods and rivers and heaths, and the wider 'landscape' of Victorian society and culture. Clothes, both as objects and as representations, became embedded in the metaphorical landscape of memory and nostalgia. This book is about how the representation, in its many forms, of clothing assumed a significant role in the depiction of the rural worker in this period, and ultimately in the construction of Englishness. Notwithstanding the developments in ready-made clothing over the 60-or-so years of Victoria's reign that for some meant increased availability of cheaper items of dress, for many labouring families it was still in painfully short supply. Working-class clothing, often ragged and threadbare, but also prized and beautiful, was constantly mended, as some of the examples discussed in this study attest. Recognition of this fact lifts the viewer out of a twenty-first century fast-fashion mind-set. The mends and darns on the clothing that survives from this period are sometimes executed with care and skill, but elsewhere reflect the owner's desperate, time-starved attempts to keep a garment going for just a little longer before it became, literally, a rag according to our own modern definition.

In this context it is enlightening to consider a case, documented in the Annual Register of 1802, so some years prior to the start of our period, of child abduction that came before the Middlesex Sessions, in which one

Elizabeth Salmon was indicted for feloniously receiving (knowing them to have been stolen) a child's cap, gown and other articles of wearing apparel, the property of Elizabeth Impey. What Salmon had in fact done was to arrange for the abduction of the child and then try to pass the child off as her own. The chairman of the bench informed the jury that the law did not take cognizance of the theft of the child, but only of the clothes that the child was wearing.[3] While this example provides a shocking illustration of the perceived un-importance of the rights and status of a child from a working-class background, it also exemplifies clothing as property; for those who had so little, it had a high value. Little wonder then that, for this reason alone, the representation of clothing should feature prominently in literature, paintings and photographs.

The descriptor 'working-class' in the context of rural life is used here inclusively. In his classic reference manual, *The Book of the Farm* (first published in 1844, with subsequent editions printed until 1908), which promoted the latest farming techniques, Henry Stephens set out his purpose in the book's long title: 'Detailing the Labours of the Farmer, Farm-Steward, the Ploughman, Shepherd, Hedger, Cattle-man, Field-worker and Dairy-maid'. Although based on nineteenth-century farming in Scotland, these occupations also represent general agricultural practice in England. Apart from the first two on this list – who, other than in the case of farmers of very small farms, cannot as general categories be described as working-class – the remaining six provide a good starting point for identifying the rural and agricultural labourer. However, the labouring workforce in the countryside encompassed a multitude of possible occupations, the nomenclature often confusing for contemporaries. 'Even the census reporters', Alun Howkins explains, 'were aware of problems in distinguishing between what they call "agricultural labourers" and "general labourers".'[4] Yet problems of terminology are only the tip of the iceberg. The terms 'labourer' and 'field worker' hid a multitude of different occupations and social relationships. A whole range of occupations was not covered by the census enumerators, because, individually, they were either too local to show up in national statistics or too short-lived to rank as an occupation at all.[5] Employment in a large number of local industries supplemented income earned from occupations more directly associated with agriculture, and the necessity for the rural poor to earn money from a number of sources at different times of the year means any attempt to categorize them by occupation is an over-simplification.

The distinction made by contemporaries throughout the nineteenth century between clothes worn for work and Sunday best makes the appellation 'rural working-class dress' more inclusive than the terms 'labouring' or 'working' dress. Despite the potential pitfalls of the word 'class' – either as a general term or as applied to rural workers in the countryside – the term 'rural working class' has value in encompassing great diversity of work. It does not assume that all rural workers' economic conditions were alike, but is used here to include, for example, shepherds and carters, agricultural labourers, women working in agriculture (from dairying to fieldwork), and those engaged in a variety of rural crafts. It does not assume that there was a common class experience among the rural working population, but describes a large disparate group whose members, nevertheless, had something in common through their economic circumstances and their living in the countryside. Significantly, too, contemporaries sometimes used the names of garments to distinguish one class from another, for example, 'landlords' were 'frock-coats' and 'labourers' were 'smock-frocks'.[6] Furthermore, over the Victorian period as a whole, the rural working class came increasingly to be singled out in relation to its urban counterpart, in terms of occupation, identity and dress. In Dorset, for example, significant occupations were 'buttony', glove-, rope- and net-making for much of the nineteenth century, and attempting to group workers who combined this type of work with agricultural work (for example, harvest work) complicates the picture. Mick Reed confirms this impression of occupational diversity in rural areas whereby the 'production of a range of agricultural produce would be carried on alongside various trade, craft, or service activities', thereby revealing that the distinction sometimes made by historians between, for example, 'small farmers' (including labourers who managed their own allotments) and rural trades and crafts people may in many cases be a false one.[7] While farm workers living either in, or in close proximity to, maritime communities may have combined agricultural work with fishing, for the purpose of this study, the clothing of fishermen as a separate category is not specifically included (other than in the brief discussion of images of Newhaven in Chapter 5). Cornwall was dominated by mines and the fishing, china clay, slate and granite industries. With its own distinctive clothing styles, it lies beyond the range of this study.

In 1851, it was estimated that there were 1,077,627 agricultural workers in England and Scotland, of whom 70,899 were female (though many more than this during harvest time: the question of female labour is discussed in Chapter 2).[8] In spite of variations in these figures, depending on the complexity of occupational nomenclature and difficulties arising from interpretation of the census returns, as the nineteenth century drew to a close the proportion of the total workforce employed in agriculture as defined by the census enumerators was in decline. It has been calculated that in 1851, agriculture employed more than 20 per cent of the occupied population, whereas by 1901 the figure had decreased to less than 10 per cent.[9] On the other hand, notwithstanding the long-term decline in its importance from the mid-nineteenth century, agriculture in all its many forms remained the largest single employer of labour in 1851, both in the countryside and generally, and indeed at every census until 1901.[10] Thus even though the proportion of the population engaged with agriculture was in decline, it remained a significant occupation over the Victorian period as a whole.

For William Cobbett in his *Rural Rides* (first published in 1830), the diverse economies of rural England constituted a highly political issue. A decade prior to Victoria's accession to the throne, Cobbett drew attention to the contradictions of rural England, noting the contrast between the aesthetic beauty of the landscape and the reality of labour and consequences of low wages: 'If I had told him [his servant with whom he was travelling] that the buildings and the labourers' clothes and meals, at Uphusband [in Hampshire], were the worse for those pretty roads with edgings cut to the line, he would have wondered at me.'[11] As the large number of surveys and resultant reports attest, we encounter in the Victorian period what historian Mark Freeman has described as 'an underlying unity' and a 'generalized importance' of the rural in political discourse of the period.[12] In much documentary and fictional literature, the enduring contradictions of the nineteenth-century English countryside were frequently alluded to: its extraordinary variety and aesthetic beauty fuelled the imaginations of writers and artists alike, contrasting sharply with the reality of labour and economic hardships of those who lived and toiled in it.

In underlining the importance of clothing to poor people during the Victorian period, this study explores how and why certain items achieved iconic status in the construction of a particular view of England and the English landscape. Clothing provision was a significant factor in debates about child and female labour, and about the competing claims of earning a wage and contributing to the family economy on the one hand and acquiring an education on the other. Clothing and its 'place' in the landscape became a point of reference for the concerns and contradictions of Victorian England, including the hotly debated topics of poverty, education and urbanization.

In Chapter 1, the social and economic background contextualizes a discussion of the historiography of rural working-class dress. Not only was it hugely challenging for the poor to eke out a living and provide adequate food and shelter for themselves and their families, but the acquisition of clothing was a significant aspect of their struggle, and as the century progressed it increasingly fell to women to provide clothing and to oversee its maintenance – making, washing and mending – as a 'respectable' alternative to working outside the home as field workers or in domestic crafts and industries. In Chapters 2 and 3, this topic, and the acquisition of clothing more generally, is discussed in relation to a variety of literary evidence: parliamentary commissions of enquiry and surveys along with a selection of working-class autobiographies and biographies. While the impact of urbanization in the second half of the nineteenth century was expressed most obviously through the loss of rural land to urban building, the urban and industrial processes that were in many cases so destructive of the countryside also had the effect of stimulating intense interest in rural life. Never before had the idea of rural life been as cherished as it was by the industrialized and urbanizing society that had done so much to destroy it.[13] 'Ironically, as "agriculture" began its slow decline as a part of the national economy, so a mythologized version of its remnants became desirable to the urban élite.'[14] Jan Marsh observes how 'the visible decline of the countryside prompted a sudden rush of nostalgia for rural life', and while the countryside held an ambivalent position in English cultural attitudes, sometimes seen as the abode of joy and tranquillity, but also often regarded as dull, the values it appeared to represent were reasserted with intensity just as it was apparently disappearing forever.[15] However, David Matless has counselled caution in describing all cultural expressions of ruralism in terms of a nostalgic and conservative longing for a past rural idyll.[16] So, whether considering images in paintings, photographs, literary texts or, indeed, garments in museum collections, I have tried to avoid reducing the ruralist material in this study to simple categorization.

This 'mythologized version', discussed in relation to clothing depicted in painting and photography (Chapters 4 and 5), has been pervasive and arguably remains very much with us today. The urban demand for, and consumption of, literary and visual representations of the rural form a leitmotif in this book, exemplified by, say, the patronage of the naturalist artist George Clausen by the manufacturer Sharpely Bainbridge (Chapter 6), and by Thomas Hardy's observation that 'the townsman seeks what he finds in novels of the country' (Chapter 7). While both Clausen and Hardy may have satisfied the middle-class demand for everything rural in the period, both also evolved images of the landscape that questioned the idealization of the rural. They did this in part through their representations of clothing.

In Chapter 8, a selection of the garments found in museum collections, in particular that of the Museum of English Rural Life at the University of Reading, are considered both for the fascinating insights into rural life that they can offer, but also for the ways in which they themselves perpetuate a particular view, which emphasizes and privileges a world that was lost rather than the one which superseded it: the garments that replaced specifically rural items of dress are mostly absent from the displays of museum collections. Meanwhile, the dialogue between the rural and the urban both complicates and, at the same time, illuminates the ways in which the representation of clothing can be understood, offering a new perspective on how we might describe and chronicle cultural change in the Victorian period.

A NOTE ON CHRONOLOGY

While I have sketched a broad chronological framework, the historical logic of each chapter, alongside its respective focus in relation to the different source material, gives also to each chapter its own discrete chronology.

1

CHANGE AND TRANSITION IN VICTORIAN ENGLAND
The rural context

The changes that took place in England in the decades from 1840 to 1900 were profound. While we must not over-generalize in considering their effects, we can be certain that the impact on social and economic structures, and on people's lives, of the transition from rural to urban living over the Victorian period was enormous. Indeed, England was so dramatically transformed during these six decades that historians have written of 'complete breaks with the past'.[1] The move from village to town could be perceived as something to be aspired to, with its apparent promise of employment and perhaps greater freedom, but simultaneously, and subsequently, rural life would be seen as something that was being lost. As Mark Freeman observes, the realities of rural life were 'hidden behind a series of pastoral conceptions of the countryside that accorded rurality a status superior to that of urban cultural life'.[2] This chapter sketches the broad social and economic context out of which emerged the representations of working-class dress that are the subject of this book.

The 1851 census provided the quantitative evidence that, for the first time, the English population was more urban than rural.[3] However, this point needs some clarification: Alun Howkins points out that the census returns show the population as divided almost exactly between 'urban' and 'rural' areas, but, since an *administrative* definition of 'town' was used, rather than one based on size, the 'urban population' included many people in towns like Lewes in Sussex or Aylesbury in Buckinghamshire that were predominantly rural in character.[4] But if the balance in the 1850s was only just tipped in favour of an 'urban' population, by 1911, a decade after Victoria's death, 80 per cent of the population of England and Wales resided in towns, however defined. While the population of England and Wales rose from 17.9 to 36.1 million in the period from 1850 to 1914, the number of people living in rural districts fell from 8.9 to 7.9 million.[5] However the term 'rural' was defined, a story of great change is revealed.

As the title of Raymond Williams's *The Country and the City* reminds us, the dichotomy between rural and urban values, often represented so vividly in literature and the visual arts, was not new in the second half of the nineteenth century: the 'contrast between country and city, as fundamental ways of life, reaches back into classical times'.[6] In eighteenth-century England, as new ideas about 'landscape' and 'nature' were being formed in terms of aesthetics on the one hand and agricultural 'improvement' on the other, poetry and prose, for example, were preoccupied with both realistic and mythologized consideration of the relationship between the rural and the urban. However, in the nineteenth century it was the *scale* of social change that fuelled well-known radical critiques of industrial society, such as those of Thomas Carlyle (1795–1881), A. W. N. Pugin (1812–52) and William Morris (1834–96). For many, including Morris, this became a quest for an idyllic rural society: the frontispiece of his *News from Nowhere* (1890) was an image of his own rural retreat from the urban chaos of Victorian London, Kelmscott Manor in Oxfordshire. The idea of the countryside as an escape from the pressures of modern life is familiar to us in the twenty-first century, but in the nineteenth century it was the reality of their own lived experience that, for so many people, added a particular poignancy to representations of the rural.

The census enumerators found it challenging to define precisely the boundaries between the rural and the urban, and there is no easy demarcation in geographical or cultural terms, partly because these boundaries were shifting so rapidly. Contemporaries, however, offer fascinating glimpses of their own experience of change from around the middle of the century, and of the ways in which, more and more, the countryside offered refuge in a rapidly changing world. Nowhere was this more apparent than in the increasingly industrialized north of England. In her novel *Mary Barton* (1848), Elizabeth Gaskell describes the way in which the growing industrial town of Manchester rubs shoulders with its still rural environs:

> There are some fields near Manchester, well known to the inhabitants as 'Green Heys Fields', through which runs a public footpath to a little village about two miles distant. In spite of these fields being flat and low, nay, in spite of the want of wood (the great and usual recommendation

of level tracts of land), there is a charm about them which strikes even the inhabitant of a mountainous district, who sees and feels the effect of contrast in these common-place but thoroughly rural fields, with the busy, bustling manufacturing town, he left but half an hour ago.[7]

If you could walk from the middle of Manchester to a landscape of 'thoroughly rural fields' in half-an-hour in the 1850s, things had altered dramatically by the latter years of the nineteenth century in areas where the tentacles of cities, and of a growing suburbia, spread forever outwards, drawing in any hitherto isolated rural pockets that remained. As a counterpoint to this process, however, the 'countryside' became increasingly accessible to the town- and city-dweller, if not by foot, then, as the railway network expanded, by train. So as Tim Barringer observes, ideas about 'nature' changed radically as early as the 1840s and 1850s, as a result of increasing urbanization on the one hand and the new accessibility of the countryside by rail on the other, and this was expressed in the renewed demand for agrarian landscape paintings and a shift in cultural values among the urban middle class – to which artists and the majority of their patrons belonged.[8] It was arguably this proximity between town and countryside that fuelled an awareness of the contrasts between them, so that they were frequently perceived precisely in terms of their respective 'otherness'. Published just after the end of the Victorian period, and set in the places where he himself grew up on the Nottinghamshire–Derbyshire border, D. H. Lawrence's novel *The Rainbow* (1915) repeatedly contrasts the beauty of the countryside with the 'corruption' of the urban and its 'modern' buildings: to him, 'it was a violation to plunge into the dust and greyness of the town'.[9]

By the 1850s, the countryside had earned an identity entirely distinct from that of the urban and increasingly industrial centres that is reflected, for example, in Elizabeth Gaskell's *North and South* (1855).[10] In *Mary Barton*, Gaskell had focused on the conflicts between factory owner and factory worker, arguing that these could be resolved if it were recognized that their interests were actually the same. In *North and South*, she turns to another conflict that was created in industrializing society – that between the new, thrusting urban–industrial class and the older, rural–agricultural communities. She represents this as a conflict between the north and south of England. Gaskell's world is framed in terms that might not stand up to the historian's scrutiny.[11] Nevertheless, she provides a contemporary perspective that has influenced our own and still has a resonance today. Likewise, in the writing of Thomas Hardy, whose Wessex is both a literal and a figurative representation of 'a vanishing life',[12] the urban and the rural are juxtaposed in a way that recorded and at the same time shaped a particular vision of that dichotomy. For Gaskell it is the *northern industrial* city that is the antithesis of the southern rural village, and of the countryside in which it nestled. In southern England itself, as we shall see in Hardy's novels, the urban, as well as being intimated through a brash 'northern' character such as Alec d'Urberville (whose real family name is of course 'Stoke'), is also associated with the metropolis of *London*, geographically not so far away and anyway now linked to his Wessex by the railway, in stark and sprawling contrast to what appeared to be a disappearing rural England.

A SOUTHERN LANDSCAPE OF ENGLISHNESS

The construction of the railway network from the 1840s, combined with rapid developments in agricultural technology, led to large-scale rationalization of the English landscape into the two broad regions that broadly persist today: a more arable and intensively farmed south and east and a largely pastoral north and west.[13] Published in the year after the 1851 census, James Caird's *English Agriculture in 1850–51* (1852) defined what has become the classic geographical division of England and Wales. This division was the result of many factors, including climate, topography and geology, which have all played a part in determining settlement and farming patterns over thousands of years. In this context it is useful to be reminded of W. G. Hoskins's thesis in *The Making of the English Landscape*, his pioneering account of the historical evolution of the landscape: 'everything is older than we think'.[14] Caird's division followed an imaginary, roughly diagonal north-east to south-west line from the Scottish border in West Northumberland to the river Exe: the area north and west of this line (including Wales), which has a more maritime climate, he described as upland and largely pastoral, given over to grazing and dairying, while the area south and east of the line, with a drier climate, he defined as lowland and largely arable – the chief corn districts of England; these geographical 'zones' therefore determined different types of farming. Caird's divisions in fact conceal many regional variations and are therefore something of an oversimplification.[15] Even so, the upland areas were, predominantly, areas of scattered homesteads, while the lowland regions were characterized by village settlements.

The type of farming and land-use in turn corresponds to distinctive patterns of settlement and social organization. While 'living-in' farm servants were a regionally important occupational group, in most of arable England the land was worked by men and women who were hired for relatively short periods and who lived away from the farm where they worked, either in villages or small towns: 'farm labourers' made up about 80 per cent of those who worked the land in England.[16] These groups of workers were more mobile and therefore arguably more receptive to new ideas, for example with regard to clothing styles and the adoption of what some contemporaries would have termed 'fashionable' – often synonymous with 'urban' – dress. Significantly, it was the adoption of such 'new' styles that from the 1870s and 1880s drew attention to the fact that the more traditional, 'rural' styles were vanishing.

The 'southern' landscape identified by Caird became the 'landscape of Englishness' – the world of village England, and this is frequently the landscape represented in literature.[17] Regional variation notwithstanding, the dominant cultural image of rural England was a southern one.[18] The poet Edward Thomas used the idea of 'The South Country', a term he borrowed from Hilaire Belloc, in his prose-poem of that name (1909). For Thomas, the South Country included the counties of Kent, Sussex, Surrey, Hampshire, Berkshire, Wiltshire, Dorset and parts of Somerset. The focus on the south was reiterated by social commentators in the Victorian period.[19] Furthermore, the tendency by historians to concentrate their attention on southern England is partly explained by the particular economic patterns of farming prevalent in the south and south-east: these areas were associated with low wages in the nineteenth century as well as deep-seated agricultural unrest arising out of poor and depressed conditions of employment. As a result, there is a greater body of evidence of the activity of the agricultural labourer. For example, the Swing riots of 1830 took place predominantly in the corn-growing areas of Norfolk, Suffolk, Essex, most of Cambridgeshire, Bedfordshire, Huntingdonshire, Hertfordshire, Middlesex, Kent, Surrey, Sussex, Berkshire, Wiltshire, Hampshire, parts of Northamptonshire, Buckinghamshire, Oxfordshire, Gloucestershire, Somerset and Dorset. In many of these counties, an increasing pool of agricultural labour had the effect of depressing wages, and what alternative employment there was in local rural industries was adversely affected during the second half of the nineteenth century by mechanization and a consequent decline in the number of workers required for these occupations. Conversely, economic and social conditions for those working in rural and/or agricultural employment in areas with alternative employment opportunities resulting from industrialization and urbanization (generally speaking to the north of that same imaginary line that runs from the mouth of the river Exe to that of the river Tees) were better. Social commentators at the time, and historians subsequently, have tended to concentrate on the counties of Devon, Somerset, Dorset and Wiltshire, where wages were particularly low and the condition of the labourer appeared to be in most urgent need of redress.[20] Indeed, it was the Wiltshire labourer in the Avon valley near Salisbury that William Cobbett described so despairingly as 'the worst used [...] upon the face of the earth'.[21]

It is true that 'agricultural historiography in Britain has always been shot through with southern English insularity',[22] and it is therefore this southern contextual landscape that frames here the representation of dress – both the garments found in museum collections and the clothing represented by artists and writers in a variety of literary and visual media. And together they cast refracted light on perceptions of a vanishing world, alongside an emergent urban and suburban culture.

THE DECLINE OF AGRICULTURE

Interest in rural issues between 1840 and 1900 was informed by concern not only that, as a proportion of the total national income, agriculture was declining, but that, not unrelated to this decline, by the 1870s the plight of the agricultural labourer was particularly acute. Despite this overall pattern, however, England supported a diversity of regional economies, each with their own distinctive social structure. To complicate matters further, change over the period was uneven: during the six decades covered by this study, the 'decline of agriculture' was gradual at some points and more rapid at others. For example, the late 1840s and early 1850s were relatively prosperous decades, often referred to as a period of 'high farming'. There then followed 20-or-so years of agricultural depression from the 1870s and, finally, a slight upturn towards the end of the century. Over this period as a whole, there was a sharp decline in the proportion of the population employed in agriculture. And to this can be added a corresponding downturn in the proportion of the national income accounted for by agriculture, decreasing from 20 per cent to less than 6.6 per cent.[23]

The 'decline' in agriculture that characterizes the period was primarily a decline in *arable* farming, combined, from the 1870s onwards, with increasing mechanization, and associated migration from rural to urban centres. Together, these factors had a profound impact on agricultural employment. As the areas given over, traditionally, to arable farming, the south and east of England were the most severely affected. The 'great depression' of the 1870s was predominantly the result of the repeal of the Corn Laws in 1846, the impact of which was felt acutely some 30 years later, and of increasingly cheap wheat imports from the United States and Canada.[24] In the decade 1870–80, wheat imports increased from 28,827,000 to more than 44 million hundredweight. In 1870, 52 per cent of this wheat came from the US and Canada; only a decade later this proportion had increased to about 90 per cent.[25] The blow to England's arable farming caused by foreign competition was exacerbated by a series of cold, wet summers and poor harvests; in 1879, for example, the rains lasted all summer with the corn being carried in from the fields soaking wet.[26] High levels of rainfall in the years 1879–82 led to widespread outbreaks of pleuro-pneumonia among cattle and liver-rot in sheep.

The long-term decline in arable farming resulted in many farmers switching where they could to dairying and specialist farming production: the sale of milk, fruit and vegetables was often more profitable than arable. Those areas that could substitute wheat-growing with other agricultural activities, such as fruit- and hop-growing (for example in Kent, parts of East Sussex, Herefordshire and the Vale of Evesham) or dairying, fared quite well.[27] However, overall, whereas farmers in northern England generally did better, for example, in parts of Lancashire where the countryside had a close relationship with urban centres because of the demand for milk,[28] much of the arable, wheat-growing south of England suffered severe agricultural depression. In some cases the effect on landowners and farmers was devastating: in the marginal wheat-growing lands, tenant farmers suffered catastrophic drops in profits and landlords' rents fell dramatically. In trying to save money, farmers dispensed with casual tasks for which they had predominantly (though not exclusively) employed women, such as weeding, stone-picking, hedging and ditching. The decline in the employment of casual workers (both men and women) from the 1870s made a significant contribution to the poverty and desperate plight in which large numbers of rural workers found themselves at this time.[29] Unsurprisingly, rural depopulation was a notable feature of the history of the south of England in the second half of the nineteenth century, with the principal occupational losses borne by farming and rural industries.[30]

THE 'CONDITION' OF THE AGRICULTURAL LABOURER: WAGES, INCOME, POVERTY AND CLOTHING

The material condition of the agricultural worker bore a direct relation to his or her ability to afford or acquire clothing. From at least the middle of the nineteenth century, the farm worker was described as 'among the worst paid and worst treated of all male English manual workers'.[31] But there is also much evidence of the plight of the agricultural worker in the decade-or-so before Victoria's accession to the throne. For example, William Cobbett gives us a fascinating and detailed account of the struggles experienced by labouring families in southern England in the 1820s. A reliance by historians on wages and income as primary measures of relative wealth or poverty can obscure the fact that there were alternative ways in which families could, and had to be, resourceful about maintaining a livelihood and securing the basic necessities of food, shelter and clothing: wages on their own were generally inadequate. Unsurprisingly, the majority of such creativity is undocumented. Of course, definitions of poverty are different for each generation, but by the rather vague Edwardian definition of the word, the majority of wage earners, argues Mark Freeman, could be described as 'poor'.[32]

Bronislaw Geremek defines the technical limit of poverty as the point at which survival of the individual and of the family becomes threatened. Less precise but more useful is a definition of *relative* poverty determined by particular social conventions that evolve with time. For B. Seebohm Rowntree, for example, in his classic study of poverty in York, the primary poverty line represented the minimum sum on which physical efficiency could be maintained – a standard of bare subsistence rather than living. But this is only approximate, because it is subject to regional and cultural variation. Furthermore, it is difficult to separate poverty from its extra-material aspects, such as lack of educational opportunities, which meant poor qualifications and job prospects.[33]

Therefore one – but by no means the only – measure of the condition of the agricultural labourer is an assessment of wages. The average weekly wage for farm workers in England was 9s 7d in 1850–1, rising to 13s 9d in 1879–81, although, unsurprisingly, there were wide variations between north and south and between one district and another.[34] For example, the economic circumstances of a Northumberland hind, Isaac Atkinson (who, in 1865, earned 16s 6d per week, had a house and garden rent-free and coals brought to the house at cost price), may be contrasted with those of James

Wallis, senior carter on Home Farm on the Courthope estate in Sussex, in 1861 earning only 15s a week, out of which he had to pay the rent for his cottage and garden, and receiving no 'perks' such as cheap coal.[35] A comparison between these and industrial wages reveals an even greater differential: at virtually no point after 1850 were agricultural wages more than 50 per cent of the average national industrial wage.[36]

Since cash wages varied so much from region to region and within counties, the usefulness of citing average wage figures is limited. As the above examples illustrate, the issue is further complicated by whether the labourer received benefits such as a cottage for himself or herself and his or her family, or whether he or she lived-in, that is, when the employer provided food and basic accommodation on the farm as part of a worker's 'wages'. This continued to be quite common as late as the 1880s and 1890s in the south, and well into the twentieth century in parts of northern England. There could also be allocations of fuel such as coal or wood, and beer, a not insignificant contribution given that, along with tea, it was the principal beverage for labouring families; such 'perks' could add substantially to the balance of the family economy. It is therefore important to distinguish between cash wages and total 'earnings', although it is difficult to calculate non-cash payments in kind since they were frequently undocumented: while sources such as the reports of two parliamentary commissions of enquiry into the employment of women and children in agriculture (1843 and 1868–9), considered in detail in Chapter 2, provide detailed figures on wages, as the commissioners themselves pointed out some labourers received supplementary earnings and the receipt of goods in kind. (And, as we shall see, clothing too was sometimes a supplementary 'extra', or one element of charitable provision.)

And it becomes more complicated. There was a clear differential between male and female agricultural wages, with women receiving lower wages than men. For example, in 1843 the parliamentary commissioners recorded that, in Dorset, women received around 8d per day but more during harvest time.[37] In Wiltshire, actual wages for men amounted to 8s to 10s per week, but, as the commissioners pointed out, this did not take into account the following: the possible provision of beer, straw for keeping a pig or a cottage at a low rent or rent-free. A labourer, they pointed out, sometimes had an allotment, or else the 'master often allows him a small piece of ground rent-free called the potato ground'.[38] The earnings of wife and children almost invariably supplemented a married man's wage: in Dorset, occupations such as button-making were followed by 'nearly all the labourers' wives and children above six years old'.[39] 'Buttony' was concentrated in and around Blandford and Wimborne, while netting and rope-making were important sources of employment in the Bridport area. Thus, apart from formal wages, supplementary, *ad hoc* work brought in much-needed extra money. As we shall see, one of the topics hotly debated by the parliamentary commissioners was the economic roles of members of a family, in particular the relative 'utility' of women earning cash by working outside the home as against the consequent 'neglect' of domestic chores, including the provision of clothing. And then there was the question of whether children of agricultural labourers should go to work rather than attend school. (The argument seems to have been less over the question of the benefits of education than over the question of the wear and tear on children's clothing if they worked as agricultural labourers!)

Meanwhile, there is the difficulty of quantifying the payments in kind referred to by the parliamentary commissioners. In his study of social investigation into rural England in the period 1870–1914, Mark Freeman points out that different informants disclosing information about such perquisites would have valued these differently.[40] Undocumented systems of barter between families are difficult to quantify in any meaningful way for our purposes here, although they may have been crucially important in the context of precarious family economies. Household producers in rural England mostly produced for direct consumption, exchange within neighbourhood networks and exchange through the market. The precise combination of these elements varied enormously geographically, chronologically and according to the nature of a particular enterprise.[41] Evidence provided by probate inventories suggests the widespread availability of rural credit.[42] Furthermore, clothing clubs, charities and the provisions of the Poor Law also furnished a source of clothing for many needy families. As in any period, it is therefore difficult to determine precisely what being 'poor' meant and important to avoid projecting twenty-first-century living standards on to the past.

Not surprisingly then, the relation between economic status and dress/appearance was not straightforward. In Dorset, for example, the agricultural labourer was frequently singled out as one of the worst-paid in the country. And yet some contemporaries were quick to note his 'neat' appearance. According to the social observer and commentator Richard Heath:

It is, I suppose, an undisputed fact that the Dorset labourer has worked for generations at a lower money wage than any other member of the agricultural community [...] There can be little doubt that the labourer in Dorset has been, and still is, notwithstanding the rise in wages which has taken place in some districts, worse off than in any other part of the land.[43]

Yet Heath continues: 'It is perhaps in dress and behaviour one sees more than in anything else the gentle breeding of the Dorset peasant. On Sunday the men mostly wear tidy coats of black or blue, with tall beavers, while the women are simply but neatly attired.'[44] While, in the majority of cases, ragged clothes or no shoes were a clear indication of dire poverty, the converse – a 'neat' appearance such as that described by Heath – did not necessarily indicate a sufficient income. The importance of maintaining a 'respectable' appearance even in the face of dire poverty could act as a thin veil for very real need.

RURAL DISCONTENT AND TRADE UNIONISM

In spite of what we would regard as the desperate poverty endured by many families for much of the Victorian period – low wages, poor living conditions and periodic unemployment – and notwithstanding substantial evidence of discontent, historians have noted the relative acquiescence of rural labourers.[45] The Hammonds, in what became a classic account – though not without bias – of the condition of the 'village labourer', argue that it was because conditions were so dire and oppression of the agricultural labourer so total that any kind of resistance was impossible.[46] However, there were pockets of extreme unrest manifested by rick-burning and machine-breaking, especially in the rural south. The historiography of the Swing riots of 1830,[47] and of the unrest that preceded them, reveals some of the complexity of economic conditions and deep-rooted rural discontent in the south of England. Inaccurately also described as the 'last labourers' revolt', the riots marked the culmination of a series of disturbances that had erupted sporadically throughout the first half of the nineteenth century: rapid population growth meant a labour surplus and low wages, and, alongside the misery caused by poverty, villagers' ancient rights had been eroded as a result of the process of enclosure. During the Napoleonic wars, the process of enclosure was particularly energetically pursued; large tracts of common land were taken for arable farming in the quest for greater efficiency and, specifically, in response to rising wheat prices. Even small farmers benefited from the high prices of wheat during this period. Labourers, on the other hand, found it difficult to manage their already fragile economies with rapid increases in the cost of wheat and bread, caused partly by the price distortion of a wartime economy. And then many lost a number of traditional rights such as the right to graze livestock and collect fuel from the common land. In this context of widespread rural poverty, the Speenhamland system was introduced in 1795; this calculated a family's poor relief according to the price of bread and the size of the family. Conditions did not improve substantially over the next 20-or-so years, with wages remaining low and rural unemployment widespread. At the same time, the introduction of machinery, in particular the steam-powered threshing machine, provided a visible symbol of oppression, associated as it was with the loss of traditional winter employment.

Between 28 August 1830 and 3 September 1832, it is thought that 387 steam-powered threshing machines and 26 other agricultural machines were broken in 22 counties. Machine-breaking and rick-burning, and other forms of incendiarism, were the principal expressions of discontent in 1830, and spread throughout the low-wage arable counties of southern and eastern England.[48] There was an appreciable rise in wages as a result of Swing, although once the riots were over wages tended to slip back to their former level, and it is impossible to know for how long any wage concessions following the Swing riots were maintained.[49] But the riots were largely successful in halting – at least temporarily – the use of steam threshing machines over a substantial part of the country up until at least the 1850s.[50] However, in the eastern counties in the 1840s there is evidence of the prevalence of machine-threshing, and by the middle of the nineteenth century most large farmers were hiring steam-driven machines to thresh their corn.[51] The annual visit of the travelling steam threshing machine became as much a part of the farming year as the harvest itself.

Little is known about the pattern of agrarian unrest in the aftermath of Swing until the emergence of agricultural trade unionism in the 1870s, other than that sporadic outbursts of incendiarism characterized the period. An isolated attempt at rural trade unionism took place in 1833 in the village of Tolpuddle in Dorset; for some months, local farm labourers had been in dispute over wages with their employers, and two delegates of the newly formed Grand National Consolidated Trades Union (GNCTU) visited the area. The Tolpuddle Lodge of the Friendly Society of Agricultural Labourers was founded. But harsh repression followed with six of the leading trade unionists arrested, found guilty of illegal oath-taking and sentenced to transportation to Australia. In the 1840s, political activity was resurgent in some areas, connected as it was with the spread of Chartism: for example, in Dorset there was activity around the Blandford area, which, significantly, is near to Tolpuddle.[52]

Unrest bubbled up too with the passing of the Poor Law Amendment Act in 1834, which established the system of poor relief for the rest of the century. Assistant commissioners were appointed by the Poor Law Commission in London to organize over 15,000 parishes into 600 Poor Law unions, thus taking the administration of poor relief out of local hands. The direct result of the 'new Poor Law' was that, for the able-bodied poor, outdoor relief was abolished in favour of indoor relief. Thus, under the new system, the poor were to be given aid primarily in the form of entry into the workhouse, which was made as unpleasant as possible. The act thereby established a principle of deterrence, with the explicit purpose of eradicating pauperism by invoking the principle of 'less eligibility'.[53] However, the threat of unrest was sufficient to provide a check on the complete implementation of the new measures; in some areas they were introduced only cautiously and hesitantly. Despite the pressure from London for uniformity, there remained a degree of local variability. Outdoor relief, for example, was never completely eliminated, if only because it turned out to be cheaper under certain circumstances than consigning families or individuals to the workhouse.[54] The Poor Law turned out to be less harsh in practice than many have supposed, at least until the 1870s.[55]

The form of rural unrest changed over the course of the nineteenth century, and by the middle of the century had become more overtly political in terms of labourers' demands and the ways in which discontent was manifested. Incendiarism – by now a well-established expression of rural unrest – continued well into the 1850s, even when the condition of the labourer improved slightly with the tightening of the labour market.[56] Evidence of other forms of rural protest may be found in unexpected sources. Ian Dyck's study of cottage songs from the period after 1850 reveals that farm workers were becoming ever more specific in their demands. While songs of the 1820s articulated some of the grievances characteristic of the 1830 Swing riots, condemning compulsory parish labour, unemployment and threshing machines, and those of the 1840s and 1850s were about low wages and exploitation in the workplace, the songs of the 1870s and 1880s (for example, 'Three Acres and a Cow' and 'Wake Up Hodge') mirrored the demands of the National Agricultural Labourers' Union (NALU), founded in 1872 by Joseph Arch: extension of the suffrage, prohibitions against lock-outs and a living wage.[57]

Although the period 1850–70 is often described as a 'golden age' for agriculture and for farmers (before the onset of the depression of the 1870s and the impact of cheap grain imports), it was a different story for the agricultural labourer. According to Joseph Arch, by the early 1870s 'things were going from bad to worse with the bulk of the labourers in our neighbourhood [Barford in Warwickshire]'. By 1872, exclaimed Arch, there seemed to be two doors open to agricultural labourers: either the 'degradation of the poorhouse' or 'the narrow door of death which perchance would lead to a freer and happier life beyond the grave [...] Their poverty had fallen to starvation point and was past all bearing.'[58] Although Arch's polemic was no doubt used to strengthen his message and the cause of the NALU, there is little doubt about the reality of the pitiful plight of many rural workers.

Over the course of the nineteenth century as a whole, the most successful attempt at raising the level of wages was indeed accomplished by the NALU – the first rural trades union. In 1874, there were over 86,000 members, although numbers began to dwindle as successful lock-outs organized by the farmers near Newmarket in Cambridgeshire spread not only across East Anglia, but also as far afield as Dorset and Gloucestershire. By 1889, membership had fallen to 4,000, and the NALU was finally dissolved in 1896.[59] Nevertheless, contemporary observers attributed the gradual improvement in agricultural wages during the 1880s to its work. Howkins has shown that, as a result of strike action, a gain in wage levels of up to 20 per cent may have been made by the spring/summer of 1874.[60] Thomas Hardy claimed a greater increase in his 1883 essay about the condition of the Dorset agricultural labourer:

> The result of the agitation, so far, upon the income of the labourers, has been testified by independent witnesses with a unanimity which leaves no reasonable doubt of its accuracy. It amounts to an average rise of three shillings a week in wages nearly all over the county. The absolute number of added shillings seems small; but the increase is considerable when we remember that it is three shillings on eight or nine – that is, between thirty and forty per cent.[61]

RURAL–URBAN MIGRATION

Apart from short-distance movement, rural–urban migration was not very widespread until the second half of the century.[62] However, from the 1850s the general and long-term depressed state of the countryside became both symptom and cause of large-scale migration to the towns, gaining momentum as the century drew to a close. The causes of this urban migration are complex and cannot be explained solely by changes in agriculture, although this was a primary reason. Changing work patterns both reflected, and helped bring about, changing cultural aspirations, especially for women. The gradual decline of field work as either a viable or an acceptable occupation for women and, at the same time, the shift towards domestic service made the countryside less attractive as a place of work. As Pamela Horn observes, most of those engaged in domestic service had been born in rural districts and many were very young.[63] Moral and cultural precepts on the question of female employment in agriculture informed legislation such as the 1867 Agricultural Gangs Act, which had the effect of making it more difficult for women to engage in certain types of outdoor agricultural work, thus effectively pushing women towards alternative employment.

The passing of the Agricultural Gangs Act in 1867 followed a number of scandals over the exploitation of women and children in agricultural work: it prohibited the employment of children under eight years of age in public gangs and forbade the licensing by magistrates of gangs of mixed sex (which, it was believed, led to licentiousness and promiscuity). However, even by the 1860s and the *Second Report from the Commissioners on the Employment of Children, Young Persons and Women in Agriculture* (1868–9), the commissioner for Northamptonshire stated that 'on the whole it is quite clear that it is the exception rather than the rule for a woman to go to work in the field'.[64] The prospect of declining opportunities in female agricultural work encouraged the shift into domestic service, but there were other incentives too; migration to the towns or overseas reflected not only dissatisfaction with rural poverty and the lack of material goods, but also what Howard Newby has termed a 'cultural aspiration'.[65] From the perspective of the village with its rural hinterland, urban life was increasingly viewed – sometimes naïvely – as richer materially, socially and culturally, with greater opportunities for employment, education and social advancement. In fact, by the early 1890s, there was widespread comment that the large-scale migration of village girls to posts as domestic servants in the urban areas was encouraging the men to move also.[66] Improvements in communications, especially in the railway network, contributed to this process.

So the changing role of agriculture in the English economy – and all that this entailed – colours the history of the second half of the nineteenth century. The changes and developments described in this chapter were to influence directly the styles of dress adopted by those who moved into domestic service and away from a predominantly rural environment, making all that had been left behind in the village and surrounding countryside seem old-fashioned. In a longer historical perspective, what was actually happening here was not only a profound change in the English agricultural system, but the demise of the English agricultural labourer: since at least the eighteenth century, rural society had been divided into landowners, farmers and labourers; by the 1990s the farm labourer had all but disappeared.[67] This complex process took place over more than a century, but what happened in the Victorian period constitutes a crucial landmark. Meanwhile, for contemporary middle-class observers of the process of change, there was a subtle reappraisal of the role of agriculture: the 'traditionalism' of the countryside, its very 'old-fashionedness', became idealized:

> There were those, coming out of the towns, who wanted to hold the process [of rural depopulation] still [...] and to do that created a nostalgic and idyllicized view of a world that was vanishing before them, giving it a permanence in élite and even popular culture which it never had in reality.[68]

RURAL HISTORY AND THE HISTORY OF WORKING-CLASS DRESS

With the recognition of the implications that the social changes described in the first part of this chapter had for the study of nineteenth-century history, and for the study of the 'separate' experience of working-class people, historians in the early twentieth century turned their attention to rural history as a distinct area. Paying particular regard to the importance of the agricultural or 'village' labourer, rural historiography was pioneered by J. L. and Barbara Hammond in their 1911 study *The Village Labourer 1760–1832*. As they explain in their preface:

> Many histories have been written of the governing class that ruled England with such absolute power during the last century of the old regime [...] One history has only been sketched in outline: it is the history of the way in which this class governed England. The writers of this book have here attempted to describe the life of the poor during this period. It is their object to show what was in fact happening to the working classes under a government in which they had no share. They found, on searching through the material for such a study, that the subject was too large for a single book; they have accordingly confined themselves in this volume to the treatment of the village poor, leaving the town worker for separate treatment.[69]

The divide between the rural and urban working-class experience already alluded to thus encouraged separate histories. Furthermore, the title of the Hammonds' book, with its identification of, and focus on, the *village labourer*, offered an alternative to the usual equation made between the *rural labourer* and the *agricultural labourer*. Thus while agriculture remained the principal 'industry' in rural areas throughout the nineteenth century, we have seen how the wives and children of agricultural labourers – as well as those men engaged in agriculture directly – supplemented agricultural earnings by working in local industries: straw-plaiting in Bedfordshire, lace-making in Devon, button-making in Dorset, to name just a few examples.[70] The journal *Rural History* – first published in 1990 – set out to unpick the generalizations made about the subject. In particular, it encouraged an interdisciplinary approach in order to deflect discussion of the rural away from, as the journal editors put it, an exclusively 'economistic' (agricultural) agenda.[71] Even without an overly 'economistic agenda', the historian of dress must acknowledge the primacy of agriculture as the principal economic pursuit – even while in crisis; in the Victorian period it is positioned as the determinant of individual livelihoods and provides the occupational context for a study of clothing and of how clothing was represented. And in ideological terms, the defining characteristic of the rural 'vision' is in its perceived difference from that of the town and city – a distinction that became more marked as the nineteenth century progressed, and which is highlighted by the literary and visual representations of clothing discussed in these pages.

Until the early twenty-first century, the majority of dress historians sought to describe and explain the history of broad shifts in Western fashion by focusing on élite clothing (partly, at least, because it survives in the greatest quantities), thus neglecting working-class dress and marginalizing the clothing of the poor. 'Fashion' histories tended to be exactly this: histories of *fashion*, with the term relatively narrowly defined. As Phillis Cunnington and Catherine Lucas explained in 1967, 'little has been written up to the present on the costume worn by people at work, since compared with high fashion, its documentation has always been scanty.'[72] Pioneering in the context of its time, their study considers dress in relation to trade and occupation, while also addressing the subject of rural labouring dress – including the historical evolution of the smock – and makes reference to a wide range of 'alternative' sources, including paintings and photographs. But surprisingly, given their reputation for the methodical collection and analysis of examples of surviving dress, Cunnington and Lucas rarely refer to these in the context of *occupational* dress. Furthermore, their treatment of fictional literature lacks a critical perspective, a shortcoming Anne Buck later addressed in her work: when asking the question, 'how far can we accept the evidence of novels on the dress of their time or the time they portray?' she insists that there are important interpretative and methodological issues at stake.[73]

Like Cunnington and Lucas, Alma Oakes and Margot Hill in *Rural Costume: Its Origin and Development in Western Europe and the British Isles* (1970) adopt a largely descriptive approach and, although they reference a variety of different sources, they do not worry particularly about issues of accuracy and representation. They discuss rural dress – in particular the smock[74] – in the context of a European folk tradition, and, while this provides a useful comparative dimension, it ignores the particular pattern of industrialization, rural depopulation and depression in Britain in the second half of the nineteenth century that I argue is so crucial for the meaningful contextualization of the subject. By placing the clothing of the rural poor within the context of classification by trade, occupation or else as part of a broader European folk tradition, Oakes and Hill avoid consideration of the relationship between working-class clothing and fashion, or what the latter might actually have meant to working-class people. Consequently, it is often assumed that working-class clothing only became 'fashionable' in the 1960s with the expression of self-consciously anti-fashion statements and through the medium of distinctively urban sub-cultural styles.

Anne Buck, on the other hand, attempts to trace relationships between élite and non-élite fashion. She analyses the complexity of the evolution of dress worn by working people in the eighteenth and nineteenth centuries and, in so doing, has helped to modify the view of dress which mostly concentrated on 'the fashionable sequence of changing style'.[75] She has also considered the distinctions between working and Sunday dress as well as sartorial variety among and between the old and the young. In summary, Anne Buck's work illustrates the ways in which, for a relatively under-researched topic, studies that concentrate on specific garments, regions and types of sources can be extremely informative. The work of Alison Toplis exemplifies such a case-study approach.[76]

Investigation of late eighteenth- and early nineteenth-century dress represented a shifting focus, away from the study of the dress of the élite in favour of non-élite clothing. Peter Jones's work concentrates on the provision of clothing during the first third of the nineteenth century, the period prior to the Poor Law Amendment Act of 1834, Jones observing that 'the provision of clothing under the poor laws remained one of its most important and significant functions right up to the period of transformation ushered in by the Poor Law Amendment Act of 1834.'[77] Jones cites Steven King's work, which had demonstrated that both the evidence and methodology were readily available to historians who wished to engage with this neglected area of study.[78] Important work by John Styles on 'plebeian' clothing in the eighteenth century has contributed much to consolidating the focus on non-élite clothing for this earlier period.[79]

Nevertheless, the dress of the poor in the period of Victoria's reign remains relatively under-researched, with the focus of much scholarship once again on fashionable, middle-class styles, and, where working-class clothing is considered, it is often in relation to its increased availability as a consequence of the mechanization of textile manufacture and the development of ready-to-wear clothing. The work of Vivienne Richmond aimed to redress this imbalance.[80] Her pioneering study of 'clothing the poor' draws on a wide range of hitherto untapped sources, and considers not only what it meant to be poor and the implications for the provision of clothing, but also notions of identity and 'respectability'. Although in this book I focus on the rural working-classes, the perspective adopted by Richmond strikes a chord with my own: like her underclass, the agricultural workers in the south of England were often the poorest of the poor and their wages much lower than those of Victorian industrial workers.

So rather than viewing the history of dress as peripheral to our understanding of the past, in fact social and cultural history is more fully and richly described when clothing becomes a part of its narrative. Social historian Margaret Spufford remarked in 1984 that 'the social historian does not normally look at histories of costume with a serious analytical eye', and, what's more, 'the sources used by historians of costume have been almost entirely noble ones'.[81] Spufford discussed her work with historians of dress, and, unusually, examined a number of garments in museums. The acknowledgement by a social historian of the importance of looking at extant examples as 'evidence' was significant, and Spufford's rigorous approach offered a model for the critical assessment of sources. Even so, discussion of the role of clothing by historians researching the nineteenth century has mostly considered its relevance only obliquely.[82]

In 2002, a conference at the Humanities Research Centre at Oxford Brookes University took as its starting point 'the topic of the dress of the poor', an area that 'held great potential for research across disciplinary boundaries'.[83] There was lively discussion of why the topic had been 'unjustly neglected'. Following the conference, *Textile History* devoted a special issue to the subject, referencing the work of researchers united by their common interest despite working from within different disciplines.

Contributions from social, economic, art and literary historians illustrated the diversity of research being conducted in the field, but also revealed the ways in which the subject had frequently been located on the academic margins. Their respective approaches have influenced the one adopted here.

2

WOMEN'S WORK, EDUCATION AND THE DOMESTICITY OF DRESS

Surveying and documenting the rural (I)

As we have seen, in the Victorian period the number of agricultural labourers in England declined.[1] The fall in the number of women employed on the land contributed to that decline, and this and other changing patterns of female employment had a significant impact on clothing worn in the countryside, and on the ways in which clothing was represented in the visual arts and in documentary and fictional literature. By the 1860s, strong views had emerged on the 'morality' and the appropriateness of the idea of women working in agricultural pursuits outside the home, and one of the dominant arguments against it that can be gleaned from the documentary sources considered below emphasizes the domestic role of women, including the provision and maintenance of 'decent' clothing. This and the following chapter will explore the reports that were produced by the 1843 and 1867 parliamentary commissions of enquiry into the employment of women and children in agriculture, touching also upon the *Daily News* survey of 1891; all three, in their different ways, imply ideals of femininity and female domesticity in relation to women's employment outside the home, as well as considering the competing demands of child labour as against educational provision. In Chapter 3 the reports will be considered specifically in relation to the question of the provision of clothing among agricultural working families.

Between 1750 and 1843 there had been a striking reduction in the number of agricultural jobs open to women.[2] And by the 1880s, it was becoming quite rare to see women engaged in field work in winter, although some helped tend the threshing machine or spread manure on the meadows, or spent long hours trimming roots from vegetables such as turnips.[3] In fact, some historians have argued that the numbers of women in paid and unpaid farm work did not fall as radically as the censuses suggest.[4] Throughout the nineteenth century, women were expected to help on the land at the busy seasons of the farming year in most rural communities, and there is a need for caution against a literal reading of the census returns.[5] Women in part-time work, for example, were grossly under-enumerated, often because their jobs were casual and seasonal (for example hop-picking); householders were often asked about 'occupation' rather than about work.[6] So while there undoubtedly was a decline in women's employment in agriculture, why was the trend exaggerated?

Ostensibly factual accounts such as census returns and parliamentary reports were authored by men who appear to have assumed 'a woman's place, and especially a married woman's place was in the home, not in the factory, shop or office',[7] or, we might add here, the field. By the 1860s, the large-scale employment of married women, who were expected to remain at home to look after the family, was deplored in some circles.[8] Dairy work, however, was one of the few branches of agricultural employment considered acceptable for single women. This was partly because of economic demand (in proportion to the shift from corn-growing to dairy-farming over the Victorian period), but also because dairy work often involved women living-in and doing a range of jobs which could, more or less, be equated with domestic service. With its long and relentless hours, dairy work must have been exhausting, yet it was mostly constructed as one of the most pleasing metaphors for industrious (female) domesticity.[9] In the hierarchy of acceptable and less-acceptable types of work for women, both dairymaids and field women 'were judged by their clothes, bodies and features as much as by their skill as wives and mothers, or the paid work they did'.[10] Certain other rural industries in which women and children participated were approved of if they conformed to a female domestic ideal, as was to some extent the case with the plaiting of straw for the hat industry. In the 1820s, the revival of village industries, and in particular the making of Leghorn bonnets out of ordinary wheat straw, had been strongly advocated by William Cobbett in his *Cottage Economy* (1822). Practised by thousands of skilled women and children in their homes, by the mid-nineteenth century straw-plaiting became solidly concentrated in the south-east midland counties of Bedfordshire, Buckinghamshire and Hertfordshire. Until cheap straw began to be imported from the late 1870s, straw-plaiting also supplemented the income of families in some southern counties where the main breadwinner was on a meagre agricultural labourer's wage.[11]

Domestic service in its many forms became one of the few acceptable female occupations in the Victorian period. Certainly, there was a real decline in opportunities for field work, but it was also the middle-class demand for servants that explains this shift, which in turn helps to account for changes in clothing and its representation. By the 1880s, around one-third of all young women aged between 15 and 21 were likely to be in service.[12] Employers generally preferred girls from the country to urban young women, 'who might be aware of alternative possibilities, more independent in their lifestyle'.[13] Regional differences, however, qualify what might otherwise be assumed to be a national trend: broadly speaking, in the south, there was greater competition for agricultural jobs between men and women, where neither had the alternative of industrial employment and where an impoverished labour force resulted in a clearer division of labour between the sexes.[14] In the districts of the north of England where there was arable farming, women's employment in agriculture on a full-time basis persisted the longest.[15] Pamela Horn observes as evidence of half-a-century of changing female work patterns that, by 1901, women comprised under one-quarter of the workers in rural areas, compared with almost one-third of the total in the country at large, concluding that 'throughout the Victorian years, it was domestic service rather than agriculture which was the major employer of working women in country districts, as in the nation at large.'[16] In the final decade of the nineteenth century, the *Daily News* survey of 1891 cited an Essex farmer and his difficulty in finding women to work in the fields, and noted how, increasingly, the departure of women – who in the 1860s were paid an average of 9d per day as opposed to men who received 2s per day – from the village to the town was encouraging the men to do likewise:

> 'We get no women to work now […] Some of the old ones'll do a day now and again, but we get no young women in the field now. They all go into the town to service. While ladies'll give thirty or five-and-thirty pounds for a cook, and sixteen and eighteen pounds for a housemaid, of course we can't keep 'em here.'
> 'And no doubt when the lasses go, the lads soon begin to follow?'
> 'Of course they do.'[17]

On face value the census returns (of 1851, 1861, 1871 and 1881) record the largest single category of paid women workers to have been in domestic service. In terms of numbers this was followed by textile workers and

then those in the clothing trades. These three groups made up 80 per cent
of all women in recorded occupations in 1851. By contrast, the number of
women recorded in agricultural work was halved in this same period (falling
from 229,000 to 116,000).[18] However, the census enumerators are likely to
have ignored women's part-time and irregular work of all kinds, including
seasonal agricultural and casual domestic work (such as washing, and working
in family businesses). In effect, they exaggerated the decline of documented
female employment in agriculture and underplayed women's roles in the
workplace in general. 'Such activities', observes Rendall, 'were not necessarily
perceived either by women themselves or by others as an "occupation".'[19]
On the other hand, both indoor and outdoor farm service for women was in
decline, although that of the former was slower. But these changes were often
to do with ideology, with what a job was called, and therefore its status and
respectability, rather than real changes in employment patterns.

> Thus 'indoor service', often, indeed usually, included a good deal of out-
> door work, yet 'indoor' has domestic associations. One step further is to
> slide indoor service into 'domestic' service, thus removing any 'unwom-
> anly' association from it, even though in rural areas domestic service,
> especially on farms, often meant outdoor agricultural work.[20]

Such views reflect an 'ideology', and influenced evolving perceptions of
Victorian female domesticity.

Of the many types of literary account relating to the condition of the
agricultural labourer in this period that refer either directly or obliquely
to the provision of clothing, some contenders are the 'official' (bluebook)
parliamentary commissions of 1843 and 1867 investigating the employment of women and children in agriculture and, of a very different genesis,
the correspondence relating to the *Daily News* survey of 1891 enquiring into
'Life in the Victorian Village'.[21] But any assumption that these 'documents'
reveal an uncomplicated narrative is misplaced. As Raphael Samuel astutely
observes, there is an enormous amount of value to be gleaned from the parliamentary bluebooks, 'but only if the historian works against the grain of
the material, refusing to accept the witnesses' categories as his own, ruth-
lessly winnowing out opinion and harvesting the residue of fact, however
small'.[22] Of the *Daily News* survey, Liz Bellamy and Tom Williamson comment: 'what is revealed here is not so much a collection of facts about the
condition of the countryside, as an account of how these conditions were
perceived and the terms in which they were analysed in Victorian Britain.'[23]

Knowing something of the circumstances of origination of these documents is therefore vital. However, my focus is the light these texts throw on the ascribed role of a woman as 'producer' of her family's clothing, and on the ways in which clothing, from a middle-class perspective, could safeguard notions of social respectability, or, conversely, subvert them. Despite their different agendas and authorship, taken together they offer a narrative – incomplete and sometimes inconsistent – of the place of clothing over a 50-year span.

THE PARLIAMENTARY COMMISSIONS
OF ENQUIRY OF 1843 AND 1867

The *Reports of Special Assistant Poor Law Commissioners on the Employment of Women and Children in Agriculture*, 1843 and the *Second Report from the Commissioners on the Employment of Children, Young Persons and Women in Agriculture*, 1868–9 are examples of the proliferating number of official reports of the period on the conditions in which working-class men, women and children were employed in mines, factories and agriculture.[24] In fact, agriculture was more frequently and more thoroughly investigated than any other nineteenth-century occupation.[25] Edwin Chadwick from the Poor Law Commission Office in Somerset House in London, as secretary 'introduced' the 1843 report in a letter (7 December 1842), requesting that the commissioners, who were barristers, look into 'the sorts of labour at which they [women and children] are respectively employed, the wages received, the hours of work, and any other similar facts which may tend to throw light upon their physical and moral condition'. The commissioners justified the selection of the counties that would be the subject of their enquiries: 'it appeared to us that these four districts, being exclusively agricultural, and distinguished from one another by marked peculiarities, would afford a field of inquiry sufficiently wide for the objects contemplated by Her Majesty's Government.'[26]

Geographically, the counties covered fall more or less south and east of that same imaginary Exe–Tees line – the area roughly encompassed by James Caird's 1851 definition of lowland and largely arable land introduced in Chapter 1. Alfred Austin, for example, spent seven days in each of four counties (Wiltshire, Dorset, Devon and Somerset), and a similar pattern emerges in the other reports. Arguing that the findings from one area were fairly representative of the whole, the commissioners thereby justified their limited focus on one district: for example, in Dorset, it was the market town of Blandford. Nevertheless, the scope of the reports is impressive, with the two reports for England alone consisting of over 1,500 pages of (frequently subjective) comment and supporting 'evidence'. The commissioners clearly encountered difficulties in pursuing their field of enquiry and referred to the ways in which both labourers and employers 'misled' them over facts they wished to become acquainted with, a statement left tantalizingly unexplained.[27] However, if nothing else it hints at the mismatch between the agendas of commissioners and the respective concerns of employers and labourers.

In his investigations, Austin interviewed 39 people (rather than basing his findings solely on an informant method of enquiry); in so doing he had contact with the following: four labourers and 12 labourers' wives, while also recording written communication from 15 people including six vicars or curates, three medical officers of health, a farmer, a manufacturer and the clerk of St Thomas's Poor Law union in Exeter.[28] The needs of the labouring poor were rarely reported directly, but they can be seen here 'within a middle class interpretive framework'.[29] Clearly an understanding of the authors' agendas and of the methods by which the information was obtained influences any conclusions that might be drawn.

Nevertheless, the reports that resulted from the 1843 and 1867 commissions of enquiry offer valuable and often detailed insights into the agricultural work performed by women and children (and sometimes also by men), the hours and general conditions of work and the perceived effects on the female constitution of outdoor work. In 1840s Wiltshire, Dorset, Devon and Somerset, jobs included 'working in the hay and corn harvests or in the dairy; hoeing turnips; weeding and picking stones; planting and digging potatoes; pulling, digging and hacking turnips; attending the threshing machine and winnowing corn; beating manure; filling dung-carts; planting beans and so on'.[30] Women worked from the age of 15 to 70, with the majority of field work performed by women over the age of 30.[31] The views expressed by the commissioners – purportedly reporting those of the women themselves and of the 'medical men' ('surgeons and apothecaries') – were less condemnatory of field work than those of the 1868–9 report that came out of the 1867 commission would prove to be, the commissioners concluding that outdoor work does not injure the health of grown women, except when the weather is cold and wet, and that the benefit gained from such earnings 'outweighs any of the mischiefs arising from such employment'.[32] However, for younger girls undergoing puberty, the effects were thought to be harmful.[33]

Unsurprisingly, the 1840s commissioners alluded to huge regional differences, especially in relation to 'wages'. In Wiltshire, for example, male agricultural labourers received relatively low wages (8s to 10s per week), but these could be supplemented by 'goods' in kind.[34] Meanwhile, the wages of a wife and children constituted a valuable addition to the family's income, either earned through agricultural pursuits or in local industries. As well as investigating data on wages, the commissioners were also interested in 'qualitative' issues such as the state of cottages, which, in many counties, were in poor repair and overcrowded, and the diet of labourers, 'mostly bread, potatoes, beer, a little butter, tea; occasionally some cheese and bacon'.[35]

They also commented upon the quality and acquisition of clothing. As we have seen, hard work and poor working conditions did not necessarily result in the worst clothing: Austin reported that the 'severest labour is often on dairy farms', but wages were better here, and, because many dairymaids were single women and lived in the farmhouse with food provided for them, they were 'amply sufficient to supply them with clothing'.[36] Field women, on the other hand, were for the most part married and had to consider their well-being in the context of the earnings of their husbands.[37] They probably had much less to spend on clothing. The fact of better wages earned by unmarried dairymaids probably contributed to the idealized manner in which they were often represented.

The 1843 enquiry was relatively limited in its aims, and its findings were never actually discussed in parliament.[38] Some 25 years later, the rural 'agenda' had changed and investigation is best understood against the backdrop of concerns about agricultural trade unionism, the rural franchise, rural depopulation and the land question, in addition to wages and housing.[39] The Second Commission on the Employment of Children, Young Persons and Women in Agriculture (appointed in May 1867) had been prompted by public outcry following Hugo Seymour Tremenheere's report on agricultural gangs in March 1867, which resulted in the 1867 Agricultural Gangs Act. The latter, in the words of commissioner Mr Tufnell, 'effectually remedied the chief disorders complained of as regards gangs'.[40] Developing in the wheatlands of Norfolk, Cambridgeshire and Lincolnshire, the gang system was a way of sub-contracting in which a 'gangmaster' took a particular job for a price and then employed women, young men and children to work for day rates. 'Travelling from place to place, "immodestly" dressed, young men and women "indiscriminately" mixed together, but above all, public and visible, the agricultural gang embodied all that the Victorian élite attacked in women's field work.'[41]

The 1867 commission was especially concerned with regulating the employment of children in agriculture for the purposes of educational provision. It covered the whole of England, with the exceptions of Middlesex and the manufacturing districts of Lancashire.[42] With a much broader scope than its title suggests, the commission sat for three years, published four reports and several volumes of evidence, and was arguably the 'most impressive rural manifestation of the growth of the official enquiry in the early to mid-Victorian period'.[43] The enquiry's stated purpose was to ascertain 'to what extent, and with what modifications, the principles of the Factory Acts can be adopted for the regulation of [rural] employment, and especially with a view to the better education of such children'.[44] Some insight into the methods used by the commissioners in obtaining their evidence was provided by E. B. Portman (for Hampshire, Devon and Cornwall):

> I have endeavoured as far as possible to obtain a just estimate of the real condition of the agricultural labourer, not only through the medium of his employer, or his minister, but also from the mouth of his wife, his children, and himself, and from the experience of the school teachers in many villages.[45]

The commissioners clearly wanted to prove the accuracy of their findings. The report by F. H. Norman is particularly detailed in this respect, stating how long he stayed in each county – between 27 days (in Worcestershire) and 46 days (in Wiltshire) – and the methods he employed to obtain his information. The greater part of the evidence, as he explained, consisted of verbal statements obtained in conversation with persons of all classes. In addition, he claimed to have 'distributed a considerable number of the printed circulars of questions with which I was provided to gentlemen who I was informed were able and willing to supply the information asked for'.[46] The commissioners relied heavily upon the information they were given by farmers and clergymen, although they also interviewed some male and female labourers. Although some of the original questions are printed in *Appendix* II of the report (discussed below), if we only had a complete account of all the questions asked we could better ascertain the agendas of those involved. In spite of the claims made for the inclusion of evidence from members of 'all classes', the investigation was conducted within a consciously established methodological framework that excluded the rural labouring population from involvement in the representation of its own condition.[47] Although Rev. James Fraser's report on

East Anglia, Sussex and Gloucestershire was perhaps the most sympathetic to the labourers, the information he gleaned from them was not used in the final compilation of the report.[48]

Notwithstanding the class bias inherent in the framing of the report, the 1867 commission led to wider public discussion of the position of the agricultural labourer partly because of the effective work by independent journalists and propagandists in distributing its findings. Thomas Kebbel's *The Agricultural Labourer* (1870) was written partly in fulfilment of his self-appointed task of spreading the commission's findings to a wider audience than would otherwise be inclined to read the parliamentary papers; Charles Whitehead's *Agricultural Labourers*, published in the same year, was driven by a similar motivation.[49] Nevertheless they also advanced an 'essentially optimistic assessment' of the position of the agricultural labourer.[50]

As in 1843, so the commissioners in 1867 were particularly concerned with the general pattern of agricultural activity within their designated counties, with conditions of employment, and, specifically, with the state of cottages and the provision of education. According to the commissioners, one issue beyond dispute was the 'deplorable conditions of cottages'.[51] Their 'verdict' is greatly at odds with the visual representations of picturesque cottages a decade or so later that are a common feature in the paintings of Helen Allingham (see Chapter 4). However, opinions were more varied with regard to whether field work performed by women required legislative intervention, although the general opinion was that it was unnecessary because women were becoming less inclined to undertake field work and so the practice was declining by itself. Even so, there were instances of women engaged in farm labour in all the counties visited, most regularly in Dorset.[52] One of the concerns expressed by the commissioners was the physical effect on women of working for long hours out-of-doors, in particular on the turnip lands during inclement winter weather.

The most immediate physical danger said to be facing women was presented by machinery, in which they might so easily catch their clothing.[53] Reassurance was provided by Mr Neville of the Staffordshire Chamber of Agriculture, who stressed that women working on the 'thrashing' machines was 'not objectionable' and that he knew of no cases of accidents caused by their dresses, while Rev. A. C. Talbot knew of a steam engine attended by an elderly woman 'and her petticoats no more interfered than a man's smock frock'.[54] However, there were instances where the smock was specifically blamed for fatal accidents. Whatever the potential and actual dangers of voluminous clothing worn near to machinery, clothing could become the ostensible basis of the case *against* female field labour as mechanization increasingly became a feature of the countryside.

If the dangers of voluminous clothing may have been exaggerated when it suited an argument, the scarcity and poor quality of the clothing worn by field women was genuinely considered to exacerbate the potential for physical harm that field work presented. Mr Culley, commissioner for Oxfordshire, Berkshire, Derbyshire and Hertfordshire, compared the physical effect on women employed in factory work and lace-making with that of field work, concluding:

> There can be no doubt [...] that the effect for good is greatly counteracted by the miserable dress worn by most of the women workers; their husband's coat and an apron cut from an old manure bag may keep out a certain amount of rain from the upper part of their person, but the slipshod feet can rarely remain dry for half an hour on an ordinary winter's day.[55]

One of the worst problems was that poorly ventilated, damp and cramped cottages and the scarcity of fuel meant that it was difficult for clothes to be dried ready for the next day. Labourers and their wives and families sometimes possessed only one set of working clothes. Rev. R. Roberts, vicar of Milborne St Andrew in Dorset, explained to the commissioners that one of the 'evils' arising from field work was that 'the poor people have difficulty in drying their clothes when they come in wet. I have known instances in which they have had to put them on next day just as wet as when they took them off.'[56] The writer and social commentator Richard Heath made the same point, describing people 'so poverty-stricken that they can only afford to light a fire at meal-times; often their wet clothes can never be dried, but are put on damp again the next morning, for fuel is very expensive.'[57]

THE *DAILY NEWS* SURVEY OF 1891

The *Daily News* survey provides a useful 'sequel' to the parliamentary commissions of enquiry. Its 'special commissioner', George Millin, was appointed to investigate 'the present conditions and future prospects of agriculture' in the counties of Essex, Suffolk, Norfolk, Oxfordshire, Berkshire and Buckinghamshire.[58] In some respects the liberal newspaper the *Daily News* (established 1846) thus drew upon the official vocabulary of the earlier parliamentary reports and, as with the evidence provided by the commissioners in 1843 and 1867, Millin enlisted the views of a number of people from diverse walks of life. On the other hand, there was no agenda for legislative intervention behind the survey, which makes it fundamentally different from the earlier parliamentary commissions. Rather it can be likened to the tradition established by social investigators such as Henry Mayhew (1812–87).[59]

There had been a rapid growth in the circulation of the *Daily News* in the decades leading up to the survey, and in particular after the reporter Archibald Forbes's articles on the Franco–Prussian War, the outcome of which was a tripling of circulation to 150,000 in one week.[60] Moreover, the newspaper began to take a particular interest in agricultural affairs. In 1872 it had sent Forbes to Wellesbourne (the centre of the National Agricultural Labourers' Union's activity) to report on the strike two weeks after *The Times* had first reported it in March. Forbes's articles initiated a fierce debate on the agricultural labour 'problem', and prompted other investigations focused on the rural labouring classes, such as those of the civil servant Francis Heath, who made tours of enquiry in his native west country (Devon, Dorset, Somerset and Wiltshire) for the *Morning Advertiser* in 1872 and 1873, on which he based two series of articles and two books – *The 'Romance' of Peasant Life* (1872) and *The English Peasantry* (1874).[61] Fascinating as the parliamentary commissions of enquiry reports are as an untapped source of information about perceptions and ideologies, they had, as we have seen, a limited (direct) readership. On the other hand, the *Daily News* survey both reflected important issues concerning the state of rural life, and communicated them to a much broader audience.

The issues considered included the condition of villages, and the wage levels and general conditions of life (including clothing) of rural labourers. From what was by now a distinctly urban perspective, Millin also discusses the reasons for the steady movement of people into towns which, by the early 1890s, was something akin to mass migration. However, the question of women and children performing field work does not feature; other issues had superseded the concerns of the late 1860s, and in any case by the 1890s the number of women engaged in field work had decreased substantially, while the requirements of the 1870 Education Act had established in principle a system of rate-supported, compulsory elementary education. This, and subsequent legislation relating to educational provision, was both the cause and the effect of changing perceptions of childhood. Although child labour had not been eradicated by the 1890s, the perceived role of children as potential wage earners was becoming increasingly anomalous.

Although Millin provided regular editorials, the interest generated among the newspaper's readers by the reports led to a full-scale debate in which the letters from farmers, parsons and labourers soon outweighed the offerings of the special commissioner, and to this extent the latter's claim that he 'has studied one of the greatest of all national questions from life' and that 'what he has written forms a faithful reflection of the opinions of all classes' could, to some extent, be justified.[62] While Millin used the letters to form a dialogue with his own editorial, he also attempted to let the letters speak for themselves. Thus the specific purpose of the *Daily News* survey was to bring to the attention of its readers crucial issues of the day affecting the state of agriculture. As the historians Bellamy and Williamson observe:

> The interest generated by Millin indicates the importance of rural issues within the liberal agenda of the late Victorian period, despite the increasingly urban nature of society at this time. A healthy agricultural system and happy agricultural workforce were seen as essential for the general well-being of the nation. Yet as both Millin and many of his correspondents noted, the rural economy seemed to be in a parlous condition.[63]

So, even as it declined in relative importance in the English economy, agriculture retained, until at least the close of the Victorian period, a vitally important role both in reality and in the popular imagination.

'A WOMAN'S PLACE IS IN THE HOME': THE CONFLICTING DEMANDS OF FIELD WORK, EDUCATION AND IDEALS OF DOMESTICITY

The evidence compiled by the parliamentary commissioners, and in particular the objections levelled against female (field) labour, reveal the hostile attitude to the idea that working-class women should perform anything other than a predominantly domestic role. Victorian ideals of female domesticity encompassed the acquisition and care of clothing – and 'educational' provision for girls should include adequate preparation for this. Although striking the contemporary reader as extreme, one suspects that Rev. B. Tyrwhitt of Lockinge in Berkshire was not alone in his views:

> It [field work] is the certain ruin of the female character; farmers and farmers' wives admit this; labourers' wives begin to feel it. They become bold, impudent, scandal-mongers, hardened against religion, careless of their homes and children, most untidy, given to drink, coarse minded, debased, depravers of any virtuous girl who works with them; they have

no pride in their home or their children, few home feelings. The children are ragged and quite untaught, and a dirty home often drives the husband to a public house.[64]

Wages earned by women undertaking field work were offset by the fact that it took women away from domestic chores and from looking after children, and from their role in making and caring for clothing. According to the 'Dorset poet', Rev. William Barnes, rector of Came, near Dorchester, working women often came home to 'crockery smashed, torn clothes, the house in disorder, caused by children left locked up in the home'.[65] In Devon, the view of Rev. Canon Girdlestone further illustrates this concern: 'Women have 7d or 8d a day; this scarcely pays for wear and tear of clothes, and not at all for the consequent neglect of household duties, and in reality adds nothing to the welfare of a family.'[66] A similar view was expressed by a former field worker, Mrs Nevill, who told the commissioners: 'I got no good by it [field work], as I had to pay someone to look after the house and children, and things wasn't done, and the wear of clothes was great.'[67] The commissioner for Surrey, Wiltshire, Warwickshire, Worcestershire and Herefordshire, F. H. Norman, claimed the women themselves wanted to stay at home to keep the cottage tidy and attend to domestic chores.[68]

Meanwhile for single women, field work seemed less threatening to the desired social order. Citing the example of a widower's daughter in Staffordshire, Rev. A. C. Talbot told the commissioners that, in ten weeks' field work over the summer, she could earn enough almost to pay for her own clothes.[69] On the other hand, many contemporaries probably shared the view of William Barnes, who described field work as 'a very bad school of refinement', and argued that the 'too often coarse talk of the men tends to tarnish the purity of their [women's] minds and feelings, and [...] make[s] them "mannishly" coarse.' Finally, Barnes asked, 'if the woman, one of whose missions is to refine the man, be made as coarse as himself, how can she refine him?'[70] A similar view is expressed by Rev. J. M. Truman of the Dorset parish of Woodlands, where there were 15 women employed in the fields in the mid-1860s: 'The employment', he argues, 'has a very injurious effect on their morals, and renders them utterly unfit for domestic duties.'[71] These 'domestic duties' constituted the care of children and the preparation of meals for the husband, who was considered the rightful 'bread earner', and the making and mending of clothes.[72] References to the importance of the making and mending of clothes by women, for themselves and their families, and the shortcomings of those women who, for whatever reason, failed to do this, are repeated throughout the evidence provided to the commissioners. The female straw-plaiters of western Hertfordshire were described, for example, as 'very useless for all domestic work; they can't even put a patch on their husbands' clothes'.[73] In Somerset, the story was the same: the 8d wages paid per day to women field workers made little economic sense, according to commissioner R. F. Boyle, when, against these earnings, had to be set 'the wear and tear of clothes, the need of more food [and] the payment to persons employed to make clothes, which she [the field worker] would make herself if at home'.[74]

What was economically viable or morally acceptable were also questions central to Victorian debates on child labour. By the 1860s, the arguments 'for and against' regarding the employment of young children as chimney sweeps and factory operatives were well rehearsed and are evidenced by the agitation focused on the 'climbing boys' and a shorter working day for children employed in factories.[75] The Children's Employment Commission was set up in 1862, the three commissioners – H. S. Tremenheere (the author of the report leading to the 1867 Agricultural Gangs Act and also one of the 1867 parliamentary commissioners), R. D. Grainger and E. C. Tufnell – observing that children needed to be protected against their parents.[76] With regard to the employment of children in agriculture, there was not only concern regarding its physical repercussions, but it was increasingly denounced as the primary cause of children being deprived of an education: the growing recognition by social reformers of the need for children to receive at least a rudimentary education and the necessity, from the parental point of view, of getting those few extra pennies to supplement the family income seemed an intractable conflict. The debate was further complicated by the interests of farmers/employers, who benefited from a cheap labour supply. But it is the educational concerns of the enquiry that stand out from the report: its findings revealed the unevenness in educational provision and played a part in influencing both the 1870 Education Act (which set up local school boards, empowering them to pass by-laws to make education compulsory for children between the ages of five and 12) and the 1873 Agricultural Children's Act (prohibiting the employment of any child under the age of eight, except on the farm of a parent or guardian). The 1876 Education Act followed, making it illegal for children under the age of ten to be employed, with the minimum age for work raised to 12 in 1901.

Ambivalent attitudes towards children working in agriculture rather than attending school were probably fuelled by the long-held belief that the children of the poor should undergo preparation for their future lives – a life of work. This view partly explains the pressure put on charity schools to instil a work ethic amongst children and, as early as the 1720s and 1730s, to become, in effect, working schools.[77] In Ellesmere in Shropshire, a compromise solution was suggested, whereby children would go to school and work on alternate days, or have half-a-day's schooling followed by half-a-day's work. One of the difficulties raised by the commissioners concerned the arrangements for the washing of clothes, highlighting not only the scarcity of a labouring family's clothing (two sets at most for each member, but more commonly only one), but also the upheaval of washing-day in a small cottage where the lack of space and fuel made drying wet clothing difficult or impossible in all but the summer months:

> Labouring boys' linen is cleaned once a week, shoes are cleaned once a week. If he is to go to school alternate days, he must have his two suits in constant use, and the washing arrangement would be a great difficulty, whereas if he were to go one week to school and another week to work the weekly cleaning of clothes might go on as usual.[78]

The argument that the earnings of children were essential to many families was used frequently to justify child labour, although as with women's field work wages had to be offset by the extra expense and wear and tear on clothing necessitated by outdoor work:

> Henry White, a labourer at Starston, who earns 12s a week, and has 12 children says, 'He is sure there is no profit in a boy's earning 1s 6d a week; it does not pay for the clothes he tears' […] Elizabeth Green (her husband earns 13s a week) says, 'Children that go to work wear out more shoes and clothes and they eat a lot more food and there isn't much gain in their earnings.'[79]

In Tiverton, Devon, evidence was given to the commissioners by 11-year-old Sarah Roe: 'I went out stone-picking with mother at eight years old. I was out a month and earned six shillings. I wore out a pair of new boots in the time, they cost six shillings and sixpence.'[80] As a very real issue for labouring families, wear and tear on clothing was cited as justification for the claim that field work did not make economic sense. But records of a public meeting in Fordingbridge in Hampshire, attended by E. B. Portman for the purpose of obtaining information for his report, illustrates the ways in which the commissioners subtly sought evidence which would confirm or validate their own agendas (in this case the need for better education for young persons). In the following example, the commissioner's view seems to have been in a minority:

> Mr Portman asked if they (the gentlemen present) really thought the earn-ings of a boy under 12 years of age anything like met the wear and tear of the clothes with which he went to work. (Cries of 'Yes'.) Mr Jeans explained that there were clothes clubs established in the various districts, from which, by a weekly payment of from 3d to 6d a week, the children obtained nearly all the clothes they wanted, so that the 2s or 2s 6d a week which they earned left a balance towards the support of the family after the clothes were paid for. Mr Portman urged, however, that as the clothes clubs were supported by charitable institutions of the gentlemen of the neighbourhood, it was hardly fair to take those into consideration.[81]

Portman's argument was as follows: since labourers' clothing was supplied in large part by charity in the form of clothing clubs (see Chapter 3), these should be taken out of the equation when considering whether children's earnings through field work adequately compensated for the wear and tear on clothing which such work inflicted. The commissioners clearly prior-itized children's education, but employers seemed reluctant, unsurprisingly, to relinquish a cheap source of labour. Despite the varying class agendas encountered in reading the reports, the numerous references to clothing are evidence in particular of the latter's currency and value in the finely balanced economy of working-class lives. But what is notable is that even while edu-cational provision for children moved higher up the agenda for reform as the nineteenth century progressed, it only very slowly cast aside a definition for 'education' that included the practical (domestic) role that the working-class child and then the adult would play in his or her later life. Practical and sewing skills for girls were never far from the curriculum and had formed the basis of much educational/industrial provision – where it had existed – since at least the beginning of the nineteenth century.

In 1803 there were an estimated 21,000 children in what were known as Schools of Industry in England where they undertook activities such as straw-plaiting and knitting.[82] Schools in which these activities were taught and promoted had begun to decline with the advent of the new monitorial schools in the early nineteenth century, and by the 1860s the employment of girls in local industries, such as knitting or sewing gloves in Dorset and Somerset or straw-plaiting in Hertfordshire (said in a number of cases to contribute more to non-attendance at school than field work), was singled out for particular condemnation because it prevented women from fulfilling their 'proper' role in life. On the other hand, praise was meted out to the schools that provided 'industrial training', the merit of a school being measured by the extent to which such training was provided. But the term 'industrial' in this context is misleading. The ethos prevailing in many of the village schools endorsed the view that a young girl's prospects lay in the domestic management of the home, including cleaning, preparing meals and making, washing and mending the family's clothes; preparation for these tasks became what was meant by the term 'industrial' – an attempt perhaps to 'professionalize' the idea of domestic service either in one's own or someone else's home. Surprisingly perhaps, even crafts that involved sewing could be considered 'damaging' if they prevented women from repairing their own family's clothes. According to Rev. J. E. Lance of Buckland St Mary in Somerset, gloving made girls into bad wives, 'for it is a kind of sewing useless for needlework or repairing clothes'.[83] The evidence provided to the 1867 commissioners by Miss Kington, the schoolmistress of Milborne St Andrew in Dorset, is indicative of similar attitudes, revealing that women themselves contributed to the prevailing expectations about female domestic roles: 'the attendance of the girls is more affected by gloving and knitting than by field work. We allow knitting to be done one day a week in school [...] I give lessons to all girls over 12 in the theory of cooking, cleaning a house and so on.'[84] The schools where girls were taught *exclusively* needlework (and which neglected the 'subject' of cleaning) are considered 'insufficient', commissioner F. H. Norman complaining that 'schools were very rare in which anything was taught beyond needlework', and suggesting that it would be a good idea if girls were also responsible for keeping the school clean![85] Those schools in which 'ornamental' needlework was taught, rather than 'useful sewing', were also deemed inadequate, thus illustrating the essentially utilitarian and domestic components of education.[86] The gendered bias of education is evident in a number of cases of rural schools: even in more enlightened institutions where subjects such as reading, writing and arithmetic as well as some geography, history and grammar were taught to both sexes, boys might additionally be taught gardening whereas girls were taught needlework, knitting, cookery, baking, washing and domestic economy.[87]

In these years leading up to the educational reforms that began with the 1870 Education Act, repeated references to household chores in the parliamentary commissioners' reports make, for the modern reader, depressing reading, reinforcing the domestic role expected of girls and women. In the parish of Quatt in Shropshire in the 1860s, girls were introduced to 'industrial work' at the age of nine: 'they do the household work, washing and ironing, cooking, baking and dairy work' as well as 'all the mending in the house'.[88] A detailed description of 'industrial training' for older girls at a training school for female domestic servants in Savernake in Wiltshire, established by the Marchioness of Ailesbury in 1852, reveals the way in which there was 'all-through' provision of an essentially domestic 'curriculum' for girls from the age of nine (as seen above) to mid-teens:

> Girls are admitted to the school from all parts (they pay £1 per annum if they belong to Lord Ailesbury's estate and £8 per annum if they do not) at from 14–16 years of age if they can read and write and bear a good character. No girl ever leaves until a suitable place can be found for her. Twenty is the number the establishment can accommodate – two are employed in the kitchen, one in the dairy, one parlourmaid, three housemaids, ten in the laundry. Washing is taken in and conducted under a trained laundress. The girls' clothes are provided by their parents or guardians on their admission; but a stock of underclothing is made and kept at the school and sold to them at one-third the cost-price; and they are provided with a good outfit on leaving.[89]

In state-funded elementary schools in the 1860s the government effectively set the curriculum by making the award of the grant dependent on pupil performance in reading, writing and arithmetic but withholding it altogether if the girls in the school were not taught plain needlework.[90]

The large number of references relating to the provision of 'industrial training' and the emphasis placed on the domestic role of women as described in this chapter are put in context when we consider them as responses to the questions printed in the circular which the commissioners were charged with providing 'evidence' for. Not all the questions asked are listed, but those that are offer some telling insights into a priori – government – agendas. In particular:

> Question 22 (k): 'Have you any observations to make as to the effect of the employment of females in agriculture on morals and on their proper training for domestic duties?'
> Question 29: 'Are any efforts being made for the industrial training of girls, in connection with elementary education, with especial reference to preparing them for their domestic duties?'[91]

The irreconcilability between female field work, an acceptable moral framework and women's expected domestic role is assumed and reinforced in question 22 (k). In question 29 the 'industrial training' of girls – defined here as preparation for their 'domestic duties' – is directly equated with the provision of elementary education. The commissioners thus made explicit the assumption that women are best employed either in the home – looking after children, preparing what meals they can on the meagre earnings of their husband, washing and eking out the life of their husband's and children's ragged clothing. Alternatively, unmarried wage earners should be trained and employed as domestic servants, since this would teach them how to be good managers of their own households.

The commissioners also made interesting comparisons between the relative prosperity of north and south: in Cumberland and Westmorland there is said to exist a 'passion for dress' among the female farm servants:

> No inconsiderable part of the wages of a farm servant girl is expended on her person. At church it would be difficult to distinguish a farm servant from the daughter of a statesman or of a substantial tenant farmer, and a girl whose ordinary costume is a coarse petticoat, pinned close round her body, and wooden clogs, will appear at a dance in a white muslin dress, white kid boots and gloves, and with a wreath of artificial flowers on her head.[92]

The competition of alternative employment provided by manufacturing industries meant that agricultural labour was scarcer in the north, and this factor helped to drive wages up. The point is illustrated by commissioner H. S. Tremenheere, who referred in particular to northern Lancashire where, he observed, the county's 'vast manufacturing development' causes a 'general scarcity of agricultural labour'.[93] However, on the whole, the reasons given by the commissioners for these differences reveal, directly or indirectly, the prejudice against women working outside the home so that in the north of Derbyshire, for example, the 'secret' of the comfort of many labourers' homes is the fact that 'the father brings in 14 or 15 shillings a week and the mother finds work enough at home in managing the cows and house, and *looking after her husband's and children's clothes* [my italics].'[94] Veiled though they may be, the stipulations about women's work outside the home and the requirement of a woman's primary role to be the provision of her family's clothing caused the commissioners to select and manipulate their evidence in order to confirm their own a priori expectations about the domestic role of rural working-class women. What we have here are some telling (middle-class) insights into the significance of working-class clothing provision as a means of maintaining 'order' in a rapidly changing society. So it is no wonder that garments, such as smocks, that demonstrate careful making by women for their husbands took on desirable associations with domesticity and with acceptable 'feminine' skills. In the following chapter, we will turn our attention to a discussion of the acquisition of clothing and fabric by rural working-class households.

3

CLOTHING AND ITS ACQUISITION IN A CHANGING SOCIETY
Surveying and documenting the rural (II)

Clothing and its acquisition were of course aspects of the general 'condition' of working-class men, women and children living in rural areas. In a world where life was spent mainly out-of-doors exposed to the elements, the wear and tear on clothing that resulted from particular kinds of work could seriously undermine that work's earning potential. But, as we saw in the previous chapter, this tension, on occasions clearly articulated by some of the labourers themselves, was cited by the parliamentary commissioners in support of their assumptions about the role of working-class women – that they should be the makers and providers of a 'decent and respectable' home and, as corollary, and evidence, of this, of 'decent and respectable' clothing. The notion that the purpose of a girl's education was to prepare her either to be a good housewife, or, if she was to work outside the home, to equip her with the 'industrial' skills necessary for life as a domestic servant, was expounded not only by the commissioners and repeatedly by the village clergy, but in some cases by the women themselves. In both of these occupations, the making, washing and mending of clothes featured significantly. Ultimately, clothing could reinforce or destroy working-class 'respectability'. How clothing was acquired, and how available and affordable it was, are the subject of this chapter. The parliamentary commissions, as well as the *Daily News* survey, once again offer a middle-class interpretation, but in the second part of this chapter will be added a different voice, muted, partial and insubstantial as it is: that of the poor themselves.

In his 1975 study *Village Life and Labour*, Raphael Samuel observes: 'The village labourer of the nineteenth century remains a curiously anonymous figure, in spite of the attention given to agriculture, Speenhamland and Captain

Swing. We know a certain amount about his movements [...] but very little about his life.'[1] Samuel encouraged historians to take account of the first-hand testimony of social observers and of working-class informants themselves when researching the lives of the rural poor, and to examine more closely the social bias reflected in documentary evidence.

We have seen the inherent bias of surveys enquiring into the condition of agriculture, of rural villages and of the agricultural labourer in the Victorian period, and the ways in which the voices of the labourers themselves were, in the majority of cases, marginalized. The explanation for their apparent 'silence' lies in part with the nature of the specific agendas of those who undertook the surveys, which were, more often than not, as we have seen, constructed from an urban, middle-class perspective, albeit a partially philanthropic one.[2] While recent historical scholarship has sought to embrace the subject of the clothing of the poor in the period leading up to the Poor Law Amendment Act of 1834, contemporary accounts often offered only very unspecific observations, describing working-class clothing as consisting of little more than 'rags',[3] undoubtedly often with justification. We find such observations first-hand in the work of Alexander Somerville, born in 1811, the son of a farm worker and himself a labourer for many years until he found literary success. A commentator might speculate sympathetically about the experience of the agricultural worker: 'What sort of lives these people lead may be imagined,' wrote Friedrich Engels, 'their food scanty and bad, their clothing ragged, their dwellings cramped and desolate';[4] but there were relatively few attempts to delve beyond what 'may be imagined' in order to analyse and describe in detail the accommodation, the food and, in particular, the clothing of the rural poor in the latter half of the nineteenth century.

Published in the late 1940s, the work of G. E. Fussell set out to explore the subject using, as much as was possible, a quantitative survey approach:

> I have tried so far as there is any evidence to determine exactly what goods the rural labourer consumed at different times from Tudor to Victorian days. I have tried to show what house-room he occupied; how many beds and chairs and tables he owned; how much and what kind of food he ate, and how long he had to make a pair of boots last or how many petticoats his wife was able to have. If I have been successful I have been able to define the living of the rural labourer in a physical sense throughout the period and have provided a comparison of the kind of life he led at different times within the four centuries, as well as a basis of comparison with the living of towns-people and the landowning and merchant classes about whom so much more is known.[5]

As an attempt 'to define the living of the rural labourer in a physical sense', Fussell's analysis is limited by his choice of sources. For the earlier period, he relies on the evidence provided by inventories attached to wills: although these generally deal more frequently with the wealthier members of rural society, they occasionally also relate to people who could have been cottagers and labourers.[6] From the eighteenth century onwards, such inventories became fewer, because the few possessions of poorer people were not valuable enough to make it worthwhile to make a will, and so Fussell turned to evidence afforded by 'contemporary engravings and the descriptive passages in contemporary literature'.[7] These, of course, all have varied challenges of interpretation. But at no stage did Fussell refer to collections of extant garments as possible sources, and his work is indicative of a general reluctance on the part of social historians in the past to address clothing as 'artefact' or 'evidence'.

The anonymity of the rural working classes in the Victorian period has partly to be explained by the fact that so few possessions were passed down to posterity, a factor especially significant in the context of a society that was becoming increasingly oriented towards the *acquisition of things*. The survival or non-survival of working-class clothing is key to how it is represented in relation to a past society, an issue that is further complicated by the fact that what does survive is rarely accompanied by a reliable provenance. Poverty, which most labouring families would have encountered at some or several stages of their lives, especially when their children were young, and again when they themselves reached old age, determined the quality and quantity of clothing accessible to the rural working population throughout the latter half of the nineteenth century. Meanwhile, the relatively abundant survival of clothing belonging to wealthier classes has tended to influence and inflect the ways in which we construct a history of dress in general.

POVERTY AND THE SCARCITY OF CLOTHING

Eyewitness accounts from members of working-class communities point to clothing – or, rather, the lack of it – as the principal reason for children's non-attendance at school, highlighting the primary, practical function of clothing as well as its role in maintaining respectability. Recalling the early years of the nineteenth century in his autobiography, Alexander Somerville explains why he did not go to school until he was nearly eight years of age:

But the chief reason for not being sent sooner to school, I believe, was the want of clothes, such as the affectionate feelings of my father and mother wished me to go in – simply something else than rags; and these were not to be had until 1818, when markets fell, and food being cheaper, it became possible to get clothes.[8]

The reports of the 1843 and 1867 parliamentary commissions referred to in the previous chapter cite instances of children not being able to attend school because of the lack of suitable clothing. One of the 1843 commissioners points out that, in the Dorset parish of Hilton, 'many children are [...] hindered in their attendance [of school and church] for want of decent clothes or shoes', while in 1867, in Hentland in Herefordshire, of a total of 55 children who were 'on the school books', nine were absent 'due to a want of money, clothes or food'.[9] References such as one in a school log book for Yalding in Kent in October 1873 point to similar deprivation, and in particular the importance of shoes and the consequences of having none: 'Opened School today after the Hopping Holiday. Attendance rather small, children not quite ready to come. Some are waiting to buy shoes.'[10] Meanwhile, Rev. W. Pidock of the parish of Addlestone in Surrey was more cynical and cited the want of clothes as 'the ordinary *excuse* [my italics] for keeping the children away from school'.[11]

The agricultural trades union leader Joseph Arch, born in 1826 and a shepherd's son, describes how he began to earn money at the age of nine in order to contribute to the family economy. He recalls how the money he earned 'was not enough to keep me, let alone buy clothes [...] My clothing was of the coarsest. I had to go to school in a smock-frock and old hob-nailed boots and my work-a-day garb was the same.'[12] Arch may have wished to underline the poverty and deprivations he suffered in his early years to put himself on a level with the workers for whose cause he was fighting and, at the same time, to add weight to the rural agitation for higher wages for agricultural labourers, but there is no evidence to suggest that he was not describing the reality of his childhood. W. H. Hudson, describing the appearance of a poor young shepherd at the end of the nineteenth century, sardonically points to the very different impression he might make if seen in another kind of clothing and another setting:

If this poor fellow, washed and clean and clothed becomingly in white flannels, had shown himself in some great gathering at the Oval or some such place on some great day, the common people would have parted either side to make way for him, with a kind of worship – an impulse to

kneel before him. There, on the downs, his appearance was almost grotesque in the dress he wore, made of some fabric intended to last forever,
but now frayed, worn to threads in places, and generally earth-coloured.
A small old cap, earth-coloured too, covered a portion of his big, round
head, and his ancient, lumpish, cracked and clouted boots were like the
hoofs of some extinct large sort of horse which he had found fossilised
among the chalk hills. He had but eleven shillings a week, and could not
afford to spend much on dress.[13]

Other documentary literature affords evidence of a perception that conditions were improving and clothing was becoming more affordable for
agricultural labourers by the second half of the nineteenth century; such
optimistic accounts should be treated with as much caution as Hudson's
hyperbole. But the expense of clothing in the context of so many competing
demands on the family budget meant that some agricultural workers towards
the last decades of the nineteenth century were happy to take advantage of
the availability of cheaper, ready-made items and this change goes some way
in explaining the casting aside of what is to us that most distinctive item of
rural dress, the smock (see Chapter 8).

According to Joseph Arch, the first priority for any family was 'keep' before
clothing, and, as Fussell points out, 'when saving in any form proved impossible what boots and clothes that were bought had to come out of extra earnings
at piece work, or out of the harvest money, if that was not already earmarked for
rent.'[14] Clothing was of course a necessity, because without it a labourer could
not work or even seek work, and raggedness implied a lack of respectability
while nakedness was tantamount to destitution,[15] but it was rarely included in
nineteenth-century calculations for the spending of wages, perhaps because it
was an irregular cost: the *regular* spending was for rent, fuel and food, whereas
clothing was bought when there was money left over. A number of contemporary comments regarding the purchase of clothing are for one-off purchases
when families had the opportunity to earn extra income, for example out of
harvest earnings. This pattern seems to have continued into the early twentieth
century: Pamela Horn cites a hop picker in Kent who remembered 'with the
money we had earned, mother fitted us out with new clothes for the winter.'[16]
The oral historian George Ewart Evans describes an East Anglian shepherd,
born in the decade 1885–95 and one of the last generation of the 'old culture',
using the money earned at lambing sales to buy shoes for his family.[17]

The poverty that loomed on the horizon must have been a constant fear in
the lives of the rural working classes. New clothes – let alone considerations

of 'fashion' – may not have featured significantly or at all in their lives, and yet the distinction made between working dress and best or Sunday dress serves as a reminder of the importance of suitable attire as a requirement of respectability. Indeed, having suitable Sunday clothing was a question not merely of respectability, but could also be one of morality: one of the objections levelled at farm apprenticeships at the time was focused on the issue of dress. According to commissioner Austin in 1843, these apprenticed lads – generally indentured at the age of nine – did not always attend church because 'although they are sufficiently clothed for their work, they sometimes have no better kind of clothing for the Sunday; and their masters are ashamed to let them appear at church in their ordinary dress of the week.'[18] Similar views were aired some 20 years later in the 1867 report. Certain occupations done by boys, such as 'tenting' (which included the scaring of birds and looking after farm animals), were criticized because of their 'injurious moral effects [...] the boy never cleans himself, never puts on his best clothes, loses all reverence for the Sabbath'.[19] So having a second set of clothing was an essential prerequisite for the maintenance of respectability. Indeed, Anne Buck argues that 'there is considerable evidence that one person often had two qualities of smock, one for weekdays and the other for Sundays', the difference being one of colour and fabric and the relative quantity of embroidery.[20] The variety amongst surviving smocks (with their relative status as working or best/Sunday smocks) would support this view (see Chapter 8).

The combination of low wages and large families meant that clothing for working families would have been basic and in short supply, and, in spite of developments in the manufacture and distribution of cheaper ready-made clothing by the last decades of the nineteenth century, the correspondence generated by the *Daily News* survey corroborates the difficulties of obtaining clothing into the 1890s:

> Take the case of a man with wife and four children, and this is something like the way in which his money will be spent: rent, 2 shillings; coal, 1 shilling; bread, 4 shillings; grocery (the term includes tea, sugar, butter, milk, soap, oil or candles, kindling, etc.), 2 shillings 6d.; bacon, 2 shillings 6d.; club, 6d.; total, 12 shillings 6d. In other words, out of his income of £39 per annum he will under the most favourable circumstances have a margin of £6 10 shillings with which to provide himself and his family with clothing and to make provision for old age. Ought any man to be content with this? (Letter from a village parson, 1891)[21]

Until the final decades of the nineteenth century, the majority of garments would have been made at home, bought from local retailers or second-hand, and passed on from one family to another or from one of its members to another – hence the unlikelihood of their survival to this day. One, or at most two, 'outfits' per family member would have been the general rule. There is some evidence to suggest that conditions were better for some southern labouring families by the 1860s – a farmer from the Devonshire parish of Cadbury commented that 'the labourers are better fed, better housed and better clad than I ever remember';[22] while the comments of farmers, as employers of labour, must be treated with caution, others were also arguing that conditions for labourers had improved. Of Dorset labourers, Rev. William Barnes observed that 'they are better clad than formerly', although, 'when bread is dear, they are sorely pinched for food and clothing'.[23] The wife of a shepherd living in a parish near Blandford with 12 children reported that clothes were not so dear as they once were: 'When the lads was little, they hadn't a second jacket'; as they started to earn money they could buy their own clothes.[24]

In fact, it was probably only towards the close of the century that conditions in some areas really began to improve, but once again the evidence provided by farmers has to be treated with caution. A letter to the *Daily News* in 1891 from 'one who has lived in the parish [in Berkshire] 60 years and farmed it over 30 years as both tenant and owner' asserts that 'in the parish there has been a revolution in my time amongst the labourers in the way of dress, living, food, education, sanitary matters; and in the village street on a Sunday one would wonder where all the ladies and gentlemen come from':[25] there is perhaps a slightly ironic tone here! Another letter from a Wiltshire landlord comments: 'it is the landlords who have suffered far more from the depressed state of agriculture than the farmers or the labourers. Indeed the latter class are far better off in many respects than they ever were, they have better houses, cheaper clothes, better food and free education.'[26] The availability of ready-made suits for men accounts, in part at least, for the 'cheaper clothes' alluded to. A royal commission on labour (1893–4) commented that 'on the clothes line, instead of rags, good linen is to be seen'.[27] Nevertheless, for the Victorian period as a whole, stories of poverty and the poor state of most labourers' clothes are retold in these and other sources with relentless regularity.

Many labourers were permanently in debt, and relied on the slaughter and sale of their pig, extra harvest earnings, or the wife's earnings and the family's additional field work and gleaning to make it possible to get warm clothes and new boots for the winter.[28] In spite of all the arguments used against the employment of women and children, and the fact that women earned so much less than men, the reality was that, in many cases, without these extra wages many families struggled to survive. According to evidence given by Rev. Charles Sainsbury of Wootton Courtenay in Somerset, women were expected to provide either the money to buy, or the skills to make, the family's clothes while men provided rent, food and boots.[29] Similarly in Sussex 'the general arrangement in the hop districts is that the man's wages pays for rent and food, while that which the women and children earn goes towards clothes.'[30] Thus the problem of finding 'spare' money for clothing was a frequent refrain; it was normally available only at times, such as lambing and harvesting, when families brought in extra earnings. In Dorset, for example, the boot-bill was paid out of the harvest or other extra earnings,[31] while the statement of a shepherd's wife in a parish near Blandford revealed that even the extra money earned by her husband during lambing was not enough to pay for their children's shoes:

> Shoes is very dear; our little children's is 7 shillings or 8 shillings, a man's is 12 shillings 6d.; one of my boys doesn't wear out above one pair in the year, but they must be proper good ones. I expect they'd wear them right out, and they wouldn't last without being soled and mended. That would be when they are shepherds' lads, after that they's wear very much quicker [...] We sometimes pay the shoes when we get the lambing money [...] The lambing money won't pay the shoes; we should want it twice a year for that.[32]

Likewise, the evidence given by a village grocer and draper in 1867 suggests that even the extra money earned at harvest or lambing did not cover the payments for boots and clothing and that harvest time was in fact less profitable than it was sometimes presented as being, taking into account also the extra wear and tear on clothes: 'I doubt if they are much better after it. I always find they pay their bill better in the spring than they do after harvest.'[33] Clearly some shopkeepers and shoemakers were obliged to give credit, since without doing so they would have had little trade and the possibility of being paid at some point in the future must have been preferable to no trade at all. Extra earnings often paid off one debt only to be replaced by another. Giving credit led, as one grocer and draper shrewdly observed, 'to a running account in which there was always a balance unpaid, unless recourse was had to the county court'.[34]

The value of clothing to labouring families and the general problem of acquiring it are topics often referred to in the parliamentary bluebooks. Perhaps the most interesting observations found in these documents are those showing the 'alternative' ways clothing could be obtained – from employers, sometimes through apprenticeships, from schools and in particular from charities and clothing clubs. Some children living-in at farms were provided with limited clothing, normally in lieu of wages: in the parish of Pyworthy in Devon, for example, a farmer reported in 1867 that a boy living-in gets 'meat and clothes in his first year'. When he reaches the age of 21 he gets £13 a year, board and lodging.[35] Elsewhere in Devon, 'lads [...] who live in the farm houses do not at first receive much if any money, but frequently have their clothes given them besides board and lodging.'[36] Similar practices continued until at least the end of the nineteenth century: historian Pamela Horn cites a large farm in the Bromyard area of Herefordshire where, into the 1890s, labourers were provided with a coat, trousers, a blanket and flannel by their employer every other Christmas, and some of the men were also given help with their children's clothes.[37] Prizes of clothing were sometimes given to labourers as gifts for long and loyal service. In the parish of Sturminster Newton in Dorset, the Agricultural and Labourers' Friend Societies awarded clothing to those under 21 years of age who had worked the greatest number of years in succession on the same farm or with the same employer as follows: 'A coat, etc to John Hall, 13 years with Mr E. Rossiter, Child Okeford; A coat, etc to William Cuff, 13 years 4 months with Mr H. Fookes, Whitechurch'.[38] In some trades, apprenticeships still operated and it was not unusual for the indentures binding the apprentice to his master to specify the provision of some article of clothing required in the practice of that trade. An indenture dating from 1844 for Amalek Old from Wootton Glanville in Dorset and apprenticed to William Guppy, blacksmith, provides that Old (aged 17) should be given 'good sufficient and proper diet and lodging together with a proper apron yearly'.[39] Occasionally, schools provided some clothing to their pupils, but the case of Bowood School in Calne in Wiltshire, which provided free education and a suit of clothes annually to its 32 boys in the 1860s, was probably unusual.[40]

POOR RELIEF, CHARITY AND CLOTHING CLUBS

The 1867 parliamentary commission of enquiry provides some fascinating insights into the charitable provision of clothing for the very poor or for those who hit hard times, albeit temporarily. The Speenhamland system was abandoned when the 1834 Poor Law Amendment Act instituted a new system of poor relief. Under the new regime, a harsh utilitarian principle of 'less eligibility' determined the administration of relief; the workhouse, intended to be the last resort for desperate individuals, became the focal point for its distribution. In reality, cost was often the deciding factor determining the form in which relief was to be given, whether inside (indoor relief) or outside (outdoor relief) the workhouse. Following a model adopted in Scotland in the 1840s, some children in the Poor Law unions of Leominster in Herefordshire and Swindon in Wiltshire were boarded out of the workhouse with 'respectable labourers' and an allowance for clothing given.[41] The incentive for the unions may very well have been the financial savings involved rather than the welfare of the children. In the Eton union in Surrey, the relative costs in the 1860s of indoor and outdoor relief show the latter was actually cheaper: 3s 6d per week and an extra 6d for clothing and 2d for education, bringing the total cost to 4s 2d.[42] However, the members of the Wiltshire Society for Befriending Orphan Paupers, founded in 1862 in Swindon, were genuinely altruistic in their concerns, believing that children 'did better' brought up away from the workhouse. They thus provided for children to be looked after by labouring families, donating an allowance of 2s 6d per week for the maintenance of the child and an extra 10s 6d per quarter-year for clothing.[43] Those less fortunate who remained in the workhouse were occasionally given clothing when they left, an attempt perhaps to integrate them into society; this does not seem to have been common practice, but there were exceptional cases, such as in the parish of Lostwithiel in Cornwall, where Rev. J. V. Vivian told the commissioners in 1867 that 'it is almost invariably the custom with the Board of Guardians to supply a boy with clothes if he be sent out from the workhouse'.[44]

Clothing clubs and charity were important sources of clothing for rural working-class families. The diary of Rev. Elton of Wheatley in Oxfordshire shows charity at work in the late 1860s: 'Dec 20th [...] Gave away coals & clothes tickets.'[45] Northern villages contained numerous friendly societies, savings banks, coal clubs and clothing clubs.[46] The last were probably less significant in the north, where there was increasingly easier access to cheap, mass-produced ready-made clothing and retail centres via cheap train and tram, but still important in southern counties in assisting the acquisition of clothing through members' regular (modest) savings contributions.

The parliamentary commissioners of 1843 and 1867 as well as the 1891 *Daily News* survey special commissioner make frequent reference to the provision of clothing to labourers via clothing clubs. These clubs emerged in the late eighteenth century, the number increasing rapidly from the end of the Napoleonic wars, as a new way of financing the purchase of clothing fabric.[47] Vivienne Richmond finds the earliest clothing society in 1796 in Painswick in Gloucestershire, with many operating in the former Speenhamland (southern) counties by the end of the 1830s after the passing of the Poor Law Amendment Act, Poor Law officers being intent on establishing ways of reducing the amount of money spent on outdoor relief.[48] Clothing clubs were essentially parish-based, established and managed by the Anglican clergy, the weekly deposits of the poor (usually between 1d and 6d) supplemented with premiums subscribed by wealthier neighbours. In a number of cases the contributions from the latter clearly left much to be desired. In Hilton in Dorset only one farmer contributed to the clothing club for the benefit of the labourers.[49]

In the Sussex agricultural village of Ripe a clothing club was established in 1854; the majority of clothing club depositors were from households where the head was an agricultural labourer or his widow and where there were dependent children.[50] The motivation behind them was financial, social and moral and endorsed by the concept of 'self-help' as put forward by Samuel Smiles.[51] In the south, they came to form 'the stable and enduring basis of clothing acquisition in the domestic economy of thousands of labouring families in the nineteenth century'.[52] There is plentiful evidence for clothing clubs operating in a number of counties, with anything between 1d and, exceptionally, 6d per week contributed, which was the case for clothing clubs operating in Minehead in Somerset in the 1860s, for example.[53] They were 'generally in the hands of the parson'.[54] In the parish of Prees in Shropshire, membership of a clothing club in the 1860s was linked to attending school: on payment of 1s entrance, children could get a free education and for a further 1d per week, the children could subscribe to a clothing club.[55] The Sussex labourer, according to Richard Heath, contributed in the 1870s on average between just under and just over 2d per week: 'as a rule, the Wealden peasant is provident. Some men subscribe as much as £8 or £9 a year to clubs; £1 for support in illness, and £7 to £8 is expended for clothes.'[56]

While clothing clubs were generally thought to benefit the poor, the control by the clergy was clearly a double-edged sword. Not only did they believe it was within their remit to distinguish between the deserving and the undeserving poor, but, even into the late Victorian period, the clergy made decisions about where clothing or fabric would be bought. The clubs could be a means of controlling the type of clothing and fabric worn by poor families and as such can be seen as a means of social control.[57] This is confirmed by references in the parliamentary reports and the *Daily News* survey. Commissioner Alfred Austin describes the workings of a clothing club in Blandford in 1843:

> Any labouring family of good conduct allowed to belong to it subscribe 1d., 2d., or 3d. per week according to family size and circumstances. At the end of the year (Christmas) these subscriptions are doubled by the donations of persons in a better position of life living in the neighbourhood. The subscribers are then entitled to purchase of the tradesmen appointed to supply the club, to the amount of their respective shares of the funds, any plain articles of dress or household linen.[58]

Austin's reference to 'any labouring family of good conduct', with its implied distinction between those of good and bad conduct (between the 'deserving' and 'undeserving' poor?), begs the question of whose criteria were being applied in making this distinction and is a window on to Victorian morality. We see clothing playing a part in the representation of moral codes and mores. According to Austin, 'the effect of these clubs has been very great in increasing the linen and clothes of the labourers' families since their establishment.'[59] In Somerset, for example, he acknowledges the benefits brought to children by the clothing clubs:

> The outward clothing of a boy appears to be generally good and proper for his work. He has generally a better suit for Sunday for which he is mainly indebted to the establishment of clothing clubs. The deficiency in his clothing is in linen, but in this respect he is much better off than some years ago.[60]

The pattern was similar in schools: in Newbury in Berkshire, schools in the 1860s 'now attracted many children by inducements other than the offer of education, such as shoe and clothing clubs'.[61] Clothing clubs can be seen as tools by which one class was able to pass judgements on another about 'suitable' or 'respectable' social behaviour.

Predictably, it was most likely to be women over whom most control was exercised: for example, in the 1860s, in the parish of Tysoe in Warwickshire, there was a clothing club where, according to the vicar, 'one of the rules is that any parent who keeps an unmarried daughter from domestic service without sufficient reason loses the benefit of the club.'[62] In Winsford in Somerset, Rev. W. P. Anderson pointed out that, for 'women whose children are born too soon after marriage', certain benefits (that is, the clothing club) are stopped, and this is found to have a 'beneficial effect'.[63] Other clergy-men were anxious *not* to try to exercise control over the purchases made by the beneficiaries of clothing clubs. Nevertheless, the rector of Wardley in Rutland, who observed that 'the less people are fenced about by the rules, the better', and who 'let people go to any shop or any town they please [...] to make the best bargain for themselves', was probably in a minority.[64] The priorities of the charitable clothing clubs of the period were that of economy and decency, 'the effect of imposing what amounted to local sumptuary reg-ulations on involuntary consumers', thus denying the poor anything other than what was deemed 'wholesome, durable or practical'.[65]

Despite the evidence for increasing provision – in both provincial urban and surrounding rural districts and villages – of ready-made working-class men's clothing even as early as the first half of the nineteenth century,[66] the importance of clothing clubs into the 1890s reveals their significance as providers of much-needed clothing in rural parishes, even if such need was 'determined' by those who controlled their operation. A letter to the editor of the 1891 *Daily News* survey observed that 'in most agricultural neighbour-hoods the wages are totally inadequate to supply the necessaries of life, and as a result, charities, so-called, exist in abundance in the form of clothing and other clubs.'[67] In a letter from 'E. C. H.' to the editor (who was in general much more sceptical about the 'benefits' of clothing clubs than were the ear-lier parliamentary commissioners), the correspondent disclosed the way the vicar, or, in another case, the widow of a clergyman, prescribed exactly from which draper those who had contributed to a clothing club should obtain their goods.[68] In a Suffolk village 'there was a clothing club, to which they all contributed, but everybody who went to town to buy clothing had to take the parcel from the shop straight away to the parson's wife, who would minutely inspect them to see if they were suitable for persons in their state of life.'[69] The level of control exercised over clothing in this way is nowhere better illus-trated than by the following example, in which a whole scene is recreated:

> One of these clubs [...] was called a National School Clothing Club, into which the children of the school, or their parents through them, paid their weekly pence, receiving at the year's end certain additions from 6d. or 1 shilling, to 2 shillings 6d., according to the amount represented, leaving the tradesman and the vicar to settle accounts. Finding that several of the people were anxious to obtain their clothing elsewhere, the vicar was expostulated

with, and replied that he had a perfect right to do what he would with his own. He was asked by what means money became his which had been deposited week by week by the members of the club, upon which he curtly declined to enter into any further correspondence on the matter.[70]

Over the Victorian period as a whole, the majority of villagers were supplied with clothing and drapery by village shops (supplemented by the travelling pedlar), while boots and shoes were made by the local bootmaker and shoemaker; customers effectively bought on credit until they could afford to pay the bill. With regard to shoes, Giorgio Riello has shown that the polarization of shops into different social categories should not be exaggerated.[71] Linen and woollen drapers such as William Corbett of Ombersley in Worcestershire – also a grocer, tea dealer and tobacconist – supplied goods to a range of customers in terms of social class.[72] In some villages, new retail outlets and practices were also developing. In the 1860s there was a co-operative in Whitchurch in Dorset whose business was specifically drapery and grocery.[73] Later, in 1891, the *Daily News* survey described co-operative outlets, such as those in the Berkshire villages of Ardington and Lockinge, 'managed on the Rochdale principle [...] on profit-sharing terms'.[74] The co-operatives supplied drapery, clothes, boots and shoes as well as the other necessities of life – bread, groceries, meat, other household provisions and coal – and encouraged customers to save via their dividend schemes.[75] A Lincolnshire landlord wrote to the paper to say that there was a 'flourishing co-operative society turning over an average of £20 a week, where the women spend their club money or not, and as they please'[76] (free, presumably, from the influence of the vicar or his wife!). While the 1867 parliamentary commissioners made relatively few references to co-operatives, by the 1890s there is mention of one in Chipping Norton in Oxfordshire[77] and of one in Royston in Hertfordshire, where calicoes, shirtings and flannels could be bought:[78] retail practices in rural areas were undergoing some significant changes by the close of the nineteenth century.

Much of the concern at all levels of village society regarding the provision of suitable clothing for labouring men, women and children was to do not only with economic necessity, but, just as, if not more, important, with maintaining a decent and respectable appearance – throughout the working week, but particularly on Sundays. William Cobbett commented in the 1820s that, in the village of Tenterden in Kent, 'shabbily-dressed people do not go to church'.[79] Seventy years later, certain villagers could not live up to the ideal of having Sunday 'finery' to wear to church; the *Daily News* special commissioner in 1891, commenting on the neighbourhood of High Wycombe in

Buckinghamshire, sees the irony and pathos of their predicament: 'What matters that some of their bits of finery are threadbare, and that some of their shoes turn up at the toe because they are two inches too long, and may properly belong to their mothers?'[80] In response to a landlord who had claimed 'the lot of the labourer [...] to be well-nigh all beer and skittles', the retort was that, as well as the lack of these and other comforts that could have made life tolerable for a labourer in the area of the counties of Berkshire, Buckinghamshire and Oxfordshire, 'respectable clothing' for the labourers' children was an 'impossibility'.[81] Maintaining a respectable appearance was, arguably, as important for the labourers themselves as it was for middle-class onlookers who cast judgment when poverty pushed it beyond the former's reach.

FINDING A VOICE: WORKING-CLASS PERCEPTIONS OF RESPECTABILITY

In spite of the claims made by the 1867 parliamentary commissioners that their reports reflected the views of all classes of society, the opinions of agricultural labourers were in fact rarely heard other than obliquely via the agenda of others, whose interests were, for the most part, alien to the concerns of labourers' daily working lives. While the special commissioner for the *Daily News* survey claimed that 'we know what all classes of the rural population, from the squire to the ditcher on the road, think of the agricultural question', and that 'taking the letters [...] together as a whole, it may be said that we have here one of the fullest and most realistic representations that could be given of a most important branch of English social life',[82] the letters actually written by working-class people engaging with the survey constituted a minority. Unsurprisingly, a number of accounts written by agricultural labourers that have come down to us were written by those who had, in some way, removed themselves through their work, or, in the case of Joseph Arch, their political career, from the day-to-day experiences of their fellow workers.[83] Two such examples of the working-class perspective are Alexander Somerville's first-hand *The Whistler At the Plough* (1852), and a second-hand account, a biography of Joseph Ashby of Tysoe (1859–1919) written by his daughter, not published until 1961.

Alexander Somerville (1811–85) was the eleventh child of a family living in a one-roomed hovel in East Lothian, Scotland. The accommodation was windowless except for a single pane of glass, owned and treasured by the farm-labouring father who reputedly moved it with him every time he moved.[84] As a youth, Alexander worked in a number of different occupations – farm helper, ploughboy, sawyer, limekiln labourer, stone breaker, sheep shearer, drainer, quarryman and dock labourer. A meeting with the Anti-Corn Law leaguer Richard Cobden, following letters Somerville had published in the Morning Chronicle in 1842 on the Corn Laws, led to his being supported by the League to travel the English countryside (which he did between 1842 and 1844) to report on its general condition and on the possible effects of Corn Law repeal.[85]

Like William Cobbett's observations on the state of agriculture in Rural Rides, which have as their context the debates about political electoral reform that culminated in the Reform Act of 1832, Somerville's writings can usefully be seen against the background of a political agenda. His support for the cause of Corn Law repeal informs and colours his descriptions of the countryside: while we can hear in his voice the resounding echo of that of an agricultural labourer, he frequently explains the plight of the agricultural labourer and of agriculture itself as the results of protectionism, and was an advocate of free trade and the immediate repeal of the Corn Laws. Even so, The Whistler at the Plough is much more than a treatise for the Anti-Corn Law League: in the course of his travels, Somerville interviewed at length farm labourers and the poor. As Keith Snell points out:

> Some of the most remarkable features of Somerville's literary style are his versatility, the way in which poetic vision and pastoral embellishment are juxtaposed against harsh realism to considerable effect, his imaginative use of different literary devices to persuade his readers, and the persistent humanity and empathy of his sentiments.[86]

Approaching the subject primarily from his own experience as an agricultural labourer rather than setting himself up as an impartial observer, Somerville intended to persuade his audience by arousing sympathy for the poor. On the one hand, it is precisely this subjectivity that renders his work so valuable. On the other, in his frequent use of verbatim, oral evidence, he enables the labouring poor and farmer unmediated 'speech'. It is possible that he was aware of the parliamentary commissions investigating the conditions in mines and factories, and may have known something of the research being conducted more or less at the same time as his own that concluded in the report of 1843 (see Chapter 2):

> I proceeded to examine into the physical and moral condition of the people [...] more minutely than I had at first designed; for I was surprised (a commissioner, if examining into the state of the colliery or

factory workers would say shocked) at the extreme depression under which each family, each principle of independence, each feeling of humanity struggled.[87]

Meanwhile, the biography of Joseph Ashby written by his fourth daughter Margaret (born in 1892) is of a different genre of writing. Born in the village of Tysoe in Warwickshire, Joseph was the illegitimate son of a domestic servant, Elizabeth Ashby, and her employer. Margaret goes to some lengths at the beginning of the biography to emphasize her father's high-ranking ancestry, together with the fact that Joseph becomes not only a successful writer on the condition of the agricultural labourer for the *Leamington Chronicle* and a prominent figure in local politics, but, by the end of his life, the tenant of a substantial 200-acre Cotswold farm. It is likely that the motivation behind the biography was to record the successful life of a working-class man who 'made good' and who thereby recovered his more 'lofty' ancestry. But the biography also records not only Margaret's recollections of her childhood in the 1890s, but also those of her father, which, Margaret points out, are 'sweetened' somewhat but at the same time devoid of nostalgia:

> Many of these experiences of my father's early days come back to me in his own voice, but of murky stories and the uglier hardships I heard nothing directly from him. He kept them in his mind to correct what might otherwise have become a rose-coloured vision, and though not to be recounted in his home, they could be charmed from him in outline by my brothers working with him out in a field.[88]

Given the tendency towards nostalgia that plays like a leitmotif through the representation of rural life in art and literature, it is interesting to note that Margaret articulates this 'rose-coloured vision' of the past.

Both Somerville and Ashby offer their personal experiences of clothing – of the problems of acquiring and maintaining it, of keeping abreast of wear and tear and, above all, of its importance not only as protection for working outdoors but as an indicator of respectability. So, alongside the reports arising out of parliamentary surveys and the *Daily News* survey of 1891, they provide a complementary narrative with a parallel chronology: the 1843 parliamentary commission coincides in time with the travels of Alexander Somerville, the 1867 parliamentary commission with the teenage years of Joseph Ashby, and the *Daily News* survey just predates the childhood of Margaret Ashby. There is of course a considerable difference of perspective evident in each of these sources: all documentary accounts describe the scarcity of clothes and difficulties in acquiring them; the personal experiences of Alexander Somerville and Joseph Ashby make the descriptions three-dimensional. Somerville recreates the years when, as children, he and his siblings were 'decayed into rags, and almost to bare-footedness, in the depth of winter', and his mother would stay up night after night 'to mend and re-mend, to set patch on patch, contending as she did for nine of us against the united attacks of winter, nakedness and famine'.[89] He remembers having just one 'chief garment' – a pinafore, which, 'made up of the best parts of several that had fallen to pieces [...] was ingeniously shaped and extended in size to hide the poverty of the clothing beneath it. When it was washed I had to stay indoors.'[90] The recollection clearly affected Somerville, less in terms of his own deprivation than, as he points out, in terms of 'the unequal contest which my mother held with famine and decaying clothes'.[91] Later, on his journey around England in the early 1840s, he empathizes with those whose conditions strike him as similar to his as a child and those of his mother:

> In a great majority of cases the wives of farm-labourers introduce the subject of their incomings and outgoings, which I am unwilling to speak of first, because I am speaking to a child whose toes are out of its shoes, whose pinafore is torn, or whose clothing is otherwise scanty and much worn; and, unhappily, we may go over many miles of country, and across some entire counties, and not alight on a family where this is not the condition of the children's clothes. In these cases, the mother very commonly makes a remark on the difficulty of getting clothes for them. Seeing you notice the children, she says, 'Ah, poor dears, I had intended all summer to get some new things for them after harvest; but now winter is coming on, and I have not got them yet.' Then she says she owed some rent, and that had to be paid out of her husband's harvest wages. It grieved her much to see her children going barefooted; but it was all they could do, even by selling the pig, which they should have kept for themselves, to pay the shoemaker for her husband's shoes, for he must have them to work in; and to pay for some other small things which they could not possibly do without, unless they went naked altogether.[92]

Somerville often refers to the mending and patching done by labourers in order to eke out the life of inadequate clothing. He describes a Sussex labourer's wife who is expecting a baby and preparing articles of baby-linen: 'her slender stock, of even the merest fragmentary rags, was collected, from which to patch up one or two of those indispensable articles required for new-born babies.' He then adds, ironically, that 'all that "over-production" of clothing, which ill-informed politicians sometimes complain of as coming from the factories, afforded nothing to her'.[93] On occasions Somerville even mentions children by name when describing their tattered clothes or lack of shoes, thus making his examples personal in order to achieve extra impact: 'little Josh Something, with his little smock-frock all in tatters, and his toes, cold day as it is, bare and red, through the old shoes he has on', and 'young Jem Rice', who lends his shoes to 'young Bill Masterton' because the latter has none.[94]

In spite of claims that conditions had improved, some decades later, in about 1860, Joseph Ashby left school before his eleventh birthday in order to help his mother with the harvest because they 'depended on these harvest moneys, as did many folk, to buy boots and the like for winter'.[95] Even so, he laments 'the insufficiency of the harvest when gathered – the low feeding, the lack of clothes, the draughty houses'.[96] And after the harvest, Margaret writes, her grandmother Elizabeth would count her money and survey the family's gleanings: 'She tidied the house for normal life to be resumed, and paid her small debts. Shoes must be bought for the three children, pattens for herself, and some unbleached calico, stout and cheap and warm – you could make almost any garment with it, if you must.'[97]

Despite the supposedly greater availability of ready-made clothing by the latter half of the nineteenth century, clothes were, nevertheless, rarely new. Here is part of the record of a detailed conversation between Somerville and a labourer, who lived on the border between Hampshire and Berkshire, talking about his wife:

> 'She have more nor enough to do at home to contrive how we be to get somewhat to put on us, and how we be to get somewhat to cover us. It ben't easy out of our income to get a bellyful for so many, be it?'
>
> 'No, I fear not, nor clothes either, when you need them.'
>
> 'Clothes, bless you! We never have no clothes, not new – not to speak on as clothes. We thought to have something new as bread was getting cheaper, but wages came down, and we ben't better nor afore; it takes all we earn to get a bit of bread, and not enough of that.'[98]

Margaret Ashby recalls the rare 'treat' of new dresses for herself and her sisters on the death of an aunt. The fact that she remembers the details so clearly ('new black dresses, ruffled and gathered along the yokes and at the wrists') hints at the importance of the event; 'their other dresses had hardly ever been new throughout'.[99] George Sturt (1863–1927), more usually known as George Bourne, after the Surrey village of which he wrote, makes a similar observation:

With regard to clothes, it is doubtful if anything new is bought, in many families, from year's end to year's end. At 'rummage sales', for a few pence, the women are able to pick up surprising bargains in cast-off garments, which they adapt as best they can for their own or their children's wear.[100]

Rent and food were regular expenses; clothing, despite being a necessity, was not: 'The only important thing which is still not bought regularly is clothing. The people get their clothes when they can, and when they positively must.'[101]

A single woman who worked as a domestic servant might be the best off in terms of the quantity and quality of clothing she could obtain, but if she married an agricultural worker not only did her economic circumstances change but also her priorities. Margaret Ashby relates Joseph's mother Elizabeth's story of Hannah (Elizabeth's daughter-in-law and Margaret's mother), who worked as a domestic servant in the late 1870s in Ryde in the Isle of Wight: before her marriage to Joseph, Hannah bought for her trousseau enough calico, cambric and flannel to make three of everything, and also managed to save for a sewing machine, 'a Jones made of iron and steel, which fifty years later was still capable of use', and with which, as a newly-wed, she made clothes for the women and children of Tysoe.[102] Hannah married Joseph in 1885 and, according to Margaret, remembered in detail her wedding outfit – a grey jacket and skirt of 'finest serge', the jacket trimmed with cherry-red velvet ribbon, and a hat decorated with cherry and grey ribbon. 'Never again', observes Margaret, 'would [her mother] Hannah be so well-dressed; life became so full that minor questions of beauty and taste were crowded out.'[103] Such precise descriptions of clothes that were saved up for, lovingly made and worn on a special and memorable occasion remind us of the significance of clothing and why people's attachment to it is more than just a practical one, and are all the more moving when we know how scarce and precious such clothes must have been.

The struggle to get adequate clothing, and to make it last, 'justified' the emphasis given by, for example, the parliamentary commissioners to the domestic role demanded of women – to make, mend and generally care for their family's clothing. The fact that girls in the 1860s were kept away from school on the weekly washing day reveals the enormity of the task. Moreover, the conventions of Sunday dressing required a considerable amount of time and ingenuity on the part of mothers and children: 'everyone who could must dress in Sunday clothes on rising.'[104] Those who could not were the poorest members, the tramps (described by Margaret Ashby in her biography of

Joseph) trudging along the country roads from town to town in their 'flap-
ping ragged top-coats and shuffling shoes, with great cuts to let out a toe
or swollen joint'.[105] For the better-off, Sunday leisure hours had an 'unrestful
preliminary', with one of the biggest jobs being the cleaning of everybody's
better pair of shoes.[106] In 1884, all the Tysoe children had Sunday clothes; these
were rarely new:

> Who shall say how much these added to the set-apart quality of the day?
> Mothers were showing a degree of that divine, 'amazing love' of which
> the hymns sang – laundering the little girls' white bonnets of starched
> and goffered muslin, making them Sunday frocks for summer out of old
> petticoats of machine-made broderie anglaise, or winter ones from old
> cloth garments rendered new by blue or scarlet braid. Even the little boys
> had Sunday coats.[107]

Respectability meant dressing in decent clothing, mended painstakingly so
that it was not falling to pieces, and it also meant dressing appropriately for
the occasion and according to class and status. Margaret Ashby describes
a scene in Tysoe in 1872 when a meeting was to be attended by Joseph
Arch. The opening address was made by a Primitive Methodist lay preacher
who asked: 'And did y'ever hear o' the red ribbon took from a little gal's
hair, and her told to tell her mother not to dress her above her station?'[108]
While both Somerville and Ashby discuss its importance, 'charity' could, as
we have seen, be repressive and have a demoralizing effect, as Somerville
points out: he describes a savings bank in the Dorset village of Wimborne
St Giles, established by the vicar's wife and members of the local gentry, 'in
which a penny a week is deposited, to be drawn out at Christmas, at which
time they, the patronesses, double the amount of each deposit, and bring
a travelling haberdasher to the village, who exchanges certain kinds of
goods for the money in the bank.' Somerville adds, 'Yet with all this charity,
the people were no better provided than they ought to have provided for
themselves without it. The comfort is not wholesome which is promoted
by charity.'[109]

Parliamentary reports might extol the virtues of clothing clubs and charity, but personal accounts reveal the sentiments of the agricultural labourers
themselves, and the stigma that might be attached to charitable provision.
More light-heartedly, but nevertheless with a hint of irony, Margaret Ashby
describes how a labourer's wife received a parcel from the 'Charity Estate'
consisting of several yards each of unbleached calico and scarlet flannel:

She had wanted to cut up the calico, which must first be well washed, but then she had to put the red flannel through the water too, and hung it on her line just where the neighbours and passers-by must see it. 'Sarah Ann, what ha' you bin doin',' they asked, 'washin' that new flannel?' 'Why, I bin washin' the charity out on it,' she said. And there it hung, a long scarlet banner, pure of charity.[110]

The attention given to literary sources in this chapter touches the tip of an iceberg; there is much potential for pursuing this field of enquiry with other texts. Encounters with such sources make clear the dual function of clothing for agricultural labourers, whose jobs involved much walking and working out of doors in all weathers. First, clothes provided protection, and, hard to come by as they were, they were also, paradoxically, a 'luxury': clothing was rarely a regular purchase and would be acquired only after rent, food and fuel had been paid for, and much of it would be worn and mended until it was ragged, and so particular garments – those made and worn for a wedding, for example – might be memorialized. Second, clothes and how people acquired them – home-made or obtained via a clothing club, or both – became significant measures of respectability and of how, in the eyes of labourers themselves as well as in those of their employers and the clergy, this could be won or lost. The employment of women and children in agriculture, the education of children, the state of cottages, the merits of Corn Law repeal – these were 'agenda items' for the 1843 and 1867 parliamentary commissioners and for the special commissioner appointed to undertake research for the *Daily News* survey of 1891. But the condition of the clothes worn by the rural poor, and the various means by which they managed to clothe themselves, or not, were never made an explicit focus of enquiry. Neither was it, apparently, a principal concern of labourers, such as Alexander Somerville and Joseph Ashby, who had 'made good', even if only temporarily. But repeated references in the sources discussed in this chapter to some aspect of clothing are testimony to its economic and cultural importance; that clothing is discussed so often in reports and in texts that are not specifically *about* clothing shows how powerfully it can reveal attitudes to working-class people, and their social and economic status, and what Victorian society regarded as 'acceptable'.

4

PAINTING NOSTALGIA
Dress and the vision of a vanishing rural world

England had not produced a Millet or Courbet, but the profound nostalgia of the urban middle classes for their rural past ensured the survival, in however changed a form, of the English landscape in art.

(Rosemary Treble, 'The Victorian Picture of the Country')[1]

Social and economic change in the countryside during the Victorian period was far from consistent over time and place, and, of course, the reality of a rural working life has probably always been at odds with an onlooker's perceptions of it. In the nineteenth century, as the preceding chapters have shown, there was such a disjuncture, between, on the one hand, the countryside as *experienced* by many labourers, and, on the other, what the middle classes believed or imagined it was, or should be, which increasingly came to be represented visually for consumption. For some nineteenth-century artists, Samuel Palmer, for example (1805–81), landscape became the repository of spiritual and religious values. For others, it represented the bounty of God's creation, with representations of harvesting and harvest themes especially popular throughout the nineteenth century. In addition, from the middle of the century onwards, there were increasing numbers of idealizing depictions principally concerned with portraying a rural society that was vanishing, for example in the 'cottage door' paintings of Helen Allingham (1848–1926) and the photographs of Henry Peach Robinson (1830–1901), and in the work of county survey photographers. The significance of particular clothing, often represented out of its 'correct' or original context (that is, represented as current when in fact it had become obsolete in usual day-to-day wear), went beyond the primarily 'physical' or visual nature of the garments worn by people in these images, and became one in which certain types of clothing came to represent a mythologized England. In this chapter, we will explore the relationship between clothing and the (often idealized) landscapes that were created as its setting, beginning with a brief consideration of some of the ways in which the rural worker was depicted in the late eighteenth century, then moving onward into the nineteenth century.

The rural world provided subject matter for the work of a great many artists and photographers, so the selection discussed here is neither exhaustive nor can its interpretation be made straightforward. Rather, it reveals something of the complexity of the visual representation of rural life and rural issues. Clothing is sometimes a specific point of reference for the artist or photographer, but it is frequently 'referred' to only obliquely, or is probably incidental to assumptions the viewer may make about the artist's or photographer's intentions. Here lie interesting methodological issues for exploration: as museum objects, paintings and photographs may be subjected to scrutiny in terms of the 'information' they may be said either to embody or to impart, so we should also ask how 'their nature as cultural products in their own right can be respected'.[2] Of significance is the question of audience: to paraphrase the words of Martin Kemp, we should consider what the painting's 'originator' was aiming to communicate, and 'who was the intended recipient of its message'.[3] Furthermore, as Tim Barringer argues in relation to his study of art and labour in the 1850s and 1860s, the manner of, and the choices made in, a particular representation are critical to our interpretation of it, and here it is taken as 'axiomatic that the full richness of the work of art and the work of art-making can be understood only within the matrix of historical reference'.[4] (While there is much about the photograph of the 1880s that makes it a 'work of art' not dissimilar to a painting, it was, on the other hand, still a relatively new medium at this point, with its own distinctive methods and conventions, and so will be considered separately in Chapter 5.)

So what are the 'particular representations' of rural life that we are looking at? The art historians Christopher Wood and Christiana Payne show how many artists who depicted rural scenes in the late eighteenth and nineteenth centuries were, with some notable exceptions, more concerned with perpetuating myths about the supposed idyllic nature of rural life – and thus with representing ideals threatened by the encroachment of industrialization and urbanization – than in portraying the landscape and labourers in an objective or realistic fashion.[5] Referring to the period 1850–1914, Wood points out:

> Most Victorian artists were painters of pretty pictures first and social historians second. They do not present us with a completely truthful, realistic or comprehensive picture, either of the countryside, or of life as it was really lived by country people. And that, in any case, is not the function of art. Beautiful, evocative and informative their pictures certainly are, but the overwhelming impression they create is one of a rural paradise. This is not because I have deliberately chosen the most idealized and rosy pictures of country life; it is how most Victorian artists saw it, and how their patrons wanted to see it. Victorian landscape paintings, like so much of Victorian art, tell us just as much about the Victorians as they do about the countryside of the nineteenth century. They are a mirror in which the middle-class attitudes and values of the age are clearly reflected.[6]

Likewise, Christiana Payne argues that 'even a cursory glance at images of the nineteenth-century English agricultural landscape shows them to be at odds with the evidence of the social, political and economic circumstances of the agricultural labourer', and that 'in most cases they are vehicles for myth rather than accurate reflections of reality'.[7] Tim Barringer illustrates specifically how Victorian landscape painting 'emerges as a cultural product inherent to urban modernity, profoundly influenced by new urban conceptions of "nature" resulting from the changing relation of the city to the country'.[8] So when trying to understand the realities of rural life, the myths and ideologies associated with it are as important as so-called fact: indeed, it is difficult to separate one from the other.[9] As Daniel Roche observes, 'the conventions and the significations of the image mean that the work of art is a far-from-simple document.'[10] Myths and ideologies as well as 'facts' provide the context within which the works discussed in this chapter are viewed.

This chapter focuses on 'agricultural landscape'. Combining two accepted artistic categories, landscape and genre, the term refers primarily to images of agricultural labourers at work in the fields, although John Barrell, for a slightly earlier period, uses the term 'rural genre'.[11] In the case of the watercolours of Helen Allingham, however, the subjects are, more often than not, women and children working, not in the fields, but either in cottage gardens or on allotments and, as will become clear in the course of the discussion about the clothing represented in such images, this distinction is important. To interrogate the representation of the labourer and his or her clothing, and so to consider methodological issues that arise when using paintings to construct histories of rural working-class dress, helps us to gain a deeper understanding of Victorian country life and attitudes towards it.

THE DEVELOPMENT OF AGRICULTURAL LANDSCAPE PAINTING

A brief chronology of eighteenth-century developments places in context the evolution of the representation of agricultural landscape, highlighting the ways in which, by the late nineteenth century, the work of British rural naturalist artists (Chapter 6) were attempting to redefine the figure of the rural labourer in painting. In the period 1792–1800, pictures depicting a variety of rural crafts and occupations were exhibited at the Royal Academy in London. A number of factors explain the rise in the number of agricultural landscape pieces in 1792, which represented an increase of three times the average for the previous five years. The death of Joshua Reynolds meant the decline of his influence on the attitudes of the Royal Academy, and the visible threat of war with France provided a context for rural subjects acquiring a strongly nationalistic or patriotic appeal.[12] Significant developments in farming techniques and livestock-breeding, which, over the course of the eighteenth century, transformed agriculture into a vital asset in the creation of the country's economic wealth, also contributed to the popularity of rural subjects in art.[13] Furthermore, depictions of harvest scenes were a popular topic throughout much of the first half of the nineteenth century as perennial images of the earth's bounty, bread being the 'staff of life'.[14]

Artists in the late eighteenth and early nineteenth centuries were often acutely conscious of those who might buy their work. For landscape painters, exhibitions were important because few works were done on commission, unless they were views of the patron's house or estate. Rather, most artists painted speculatively and then exhibited in the hope of finding a buyer. In the period c.1780–1820, buyers of agricultural landscapes were usually from the aristocracy or gentry, and although artists were not 'told' what to paint, they had a vested interest in finding subjects that would please prospective patrons.[15] Thus, where the art of the countryside was often associated with national wealth and pride alongside the maintenance of harmonious social relations between the classes, there was rarely a place for images of the discontented or dissolute rural poor, although the work of George Morland (1763–1804) is unusual in this respect (see below). The vision of rural life presented by the paintings of the period can, according to Barrell, 'be understood only by understanding the constraints – often apparently aesthetic but in fact moral and social – that determined how the poor could, or rather how they could *not*, be represented'.[16] So there were few images of abject poverty; those that there were showed the poor in a sentimental light, as, for example, in the well-known *Cottage Girl with Dog and Pitcher* (1785) by Thomas Gainsborough (1727–88), or illustrated the charity of the wealthier classes. Belief in a God-given social order, in which different social classes each had their place and function, persisted into the second half of the nineteenth century. However, in the context of political unrest and discontent in the countryside, William Maw Eagley's *Hullo! Largesse: A Scene in Norfolk* (1862), in which rich and poor regard each other benevolently while a young girl looks in her pocket for a coin to give to her poorer counterpart, appears anachronistic in its subject matter, reflecting a nostalgic longing for a paternalistic social order that was under threat by the second half of the nineteenth century.

The complexities of representation and interpretation associated with paintings of agricultural scenes pointed to by Tim Barringer and Daniel Roche notwithstanding, the increase in the number of agricultural landscapes from the late eighteenth century does make the painting – in terms of sheer numbers – a potentially fruitful source of information; indeed, the fact that these images have complex individual histories and convey social, moral and political messages that may require 'decoding' makes particularly interesting a consideration of their manner of representing clothing. Tattered clothes, heavy boots and agricultural implements distinguish the paintings of artists such as Gainsborough, Morland and Constable from the surviving Italianate tradition in eighteenth-century England which was, in many respects, 'still elaborately Arcadian in its frivolous recreation of the world of Claude and Poussin'.[17] So are the paintings of Gainsborough, Morland and Constable more truthful reflections of actuality than the tradition from which they depart? The answer must be a qualified 'yes'. Of course, artists differed in their treatment of rural themes and might also change their approach to a subject over the course of a painting career, so generalizations can be misleading. The work of Gainsborough provides a case in point. His peasant figures and the landscape in which they are set in earlier paintings, such as *Woodcutter Courting a Milkmaid* (1755), were influenced by rococo themes and inspiration, and belong more to the Arcadian tradition of Italian painting.[18] In the 1760s Gainsborough's daughters were the models for some of his rural themes, as in *Margaret Gainsborough as a Gleaner* (1760). In later work of the

1780s, however, after his children had grown up, he used beggars as models, 'delighting in their melancholy beauty and affinity with the landscape'.[19] Gainsborough's interest in the 'fancy picture' (which, as promoted by the French emigré painter Philip Mercier, had emerged as a recognizable genre in its own right during the first half of the eighteenth century) evolved out of his landscape paintings. The fancy picture 'traded both in fact and fable', even if its subject matter was closely allied to the lives and activities of ordinary rural characters.[20]

While Gainsborough's landscape and genre paintings keep the poor at a distance, his fancy pictures bring them into immediate focus,[21] as exemplified by *Cottage Girl with Dog and Pitcher*. Gainsborough's peasant child is heroically life-size and detailed in execution, down to the torn sleeves of the girl's dress, but the overall effect is towards sentimentality. Ragged clothing and bare feet might be a plausible representation of a poor country girl, given her and her family's economic circumstances, but, in stirring up the sympathetic emotions of the viewer, the portrayal of such clothing makes poverty on a certain level seem picturesque: the balance between fact and fantasy is so finely tuned in such images that their spell as works of art remains unbroken.[22] Gainsborough's fancy pictures were not commissions; based on anonymous character studies (the children of the poor often acted as hired models) rather than on named individuals, they were freer from the constraints imposed by a patron than were commissioned portraits. Nevertheless, they were probably not intended to reflect the reality of the hardships of rural life, but rather 'to engage the spectator's sympathy by their simple expression of charm'.[23]

Where the clothing depicted is detailed, and more than merely generalized rags, as in the work of George Stubbs (1724–1806), complex interpretative issues emerge. Given that Stubbs's reputation rests in large part on the extraordinary anatomical detail of his paintings of horses, the precise representation of the ultra-clean – 'fashionable' – clothing of the 'peasant' subjects of his work has prompted lively debate centred on the question of 'accuracy'. In his well-known pair of paintings *Haymakers* and *Reapers* of 1785, the clothing of the workers is beautifully depicted in terms of level of detail, from the black silk hats, short crossover bed-gowns (an extant example of which is discussed in Chapter 8), aprons and gauntlets worn by the women, to the white shirts, waistcoats, breeches and buckled shoes worn by the men. Although John Barrell argues that the workers are dressed 'well above their station', Neil McKendrick believes that the clothing depicted is an accurate reflection of that worn by agricultural workers at this time: he uses these images to illustrate that fashion had filtered far down the social scale.[24] The existence of drawings for *Haymakers* and *Reapers* (in Stubbs's studio sale of 1807, but since disappeared) suggests that the pictures were based on careful study from nature and direct observation.[25]

Whether or not the clothes themselves are 'real', it is the *context* in which the clothes are being worn, and the extent to which the clothing thus presented is an aspect of the artist's visualization or indicative of a subtext of moral, political or social intent, that are at issue here: there may have been such clothes, but a crucial question is whether they would have been worn by workers for the jobs of haymaking and reaping. The importance of context is a theme to which we shall return and affects how we interpret the work of later artists such as Helen Allingham. But the clothes themselves and the manner in which they are represented are important too – are they clean and without tears or creases (as in Stubbs's *Haymakers* and *Reapers*) or dirty and ragged (as in Gainsborough's *Cottage Girl*)? It would seem paradoxical to present workers during harvest – often the busiest and most profitable time for them (because of extra work and wages earned) – in rags; the clean and rag-less appearance of the haymakers and reapers could reflect the relative prosperity during this period of the agricultural year. It could also reflect the particularly idealizing gaze that was cast on to harvest scenes. And of course, in any case, it is possible that, in reality, by the time winter set in and work was less plentiful, such clothes might have been pawned or sold: the cycle of poverty was influenced not only by the stage of life, but also by time of year. So the appearance of these haymakers and reapers may say as much about the way the business of harvesting was perceived by onlookers as about what it was actually like to participate in it.

Audiences may also respond differently to the same work depending on where they are positioned in time. The paintings of George Morland provide an interesting example: in the years immediately after Morland's death, critics praised, but were disturbed by, what they saw as his representation of the poor without affectation or idealization. However, later reactions in the twentieth century saw the same images as 'positively Arcadian'.[26] Furthermore, those of Morland's engravings that sold in large numbers were altered (both by himself and by other artists) and the figures 'emasculated', in some cases made to look more contented.[27] Although he tried to maintain a degree of independence from the conditions laid down by buyers and dealers by producing works in his own studio at his own expense and by selling them through an agent, Morland seems to have been acutely aware of the demands of his audience, sometimes deliberately using frames of reference that he knew would be acceptable.[28]

A good illustration of the way in which Morland mediated the political and social message of his work through the use of dress and appearance is provided by two paintings. In the tellingly entitled The Comforts of Industry (1790), a well-dressed, white-linen-clad mother welcomes her equally well-dressed and respectable-looking husband home to a tidy cottage. The clothing worn by parents and children is clean and neat and, as contemporaries would have understood it, fitting to their 'station' in life. By contrast, in the painting's companion, The Miseries of Idleness (1790), Morland uses clothing to show the general degradation of a family in which the father is out of work (unemployment in the period was more often than not regarded as the consequence of idleness) and the woman, unlike the 'good' wife, has not mended the ragged clothes of her husband, and neglects her crying baby. Significantly, she is wearing a fashionable black hat, used here to show the result of a woman's indulgence in fashion accessories not befitting her lowly position in life and on which expenditure is at the cost of the genuine domestic needs of the family. Whether Morland himself believed the message conveyed here is of course open to question, but clearly he knew how to manipulate accepted parameters of morality and encoded the clothing depicted in order to convey a message that would be familiar and even very appealing to his particular audience and, most importantly, to potential buyers of his work.

In contrast to both Gainsborough's sentimental depictions of rural figures and Morland's on occasions moralistic paintings, images such as Old Man with a Staff (c.1790) by Thomas Barker (1769–1847) are more convincing in their attention to clothing detail, such as the patched and mended coat with stitching clearly visible. Barker's work anticipates the detailed images of agricultural processes and implements that became typical of the early years of the nineteenth century, as seen, for example, in John Constable's careful Studies of Two Ploughs (1814). But more relevant here are the pioneering studies of rustic figures by William Henry Pyne (1769–1843) and Robert Hills (1769–1844). Founders in 1800 of the Sketching Society, a group of artists who met weekly at each other's houses and made sketching expeditions into the countryside, Pyne and Hills were also among the founding members of the Society of Painters in Water Colours (later the Royal Society of Painters in Water Colours, and now the Royal Watercolour Society), established in 1804. Robert Hills's Farm Labourers and Other Studies (c.1804–10) record a variety of rural figures closely observed from nature and concentrate on clothing and headgear. *Studies of Children Haymaking*, for example, provides wonderful details of the clothing of both child and adult female and male workers, the girls and women in slightly high-waisted gowns, large red neckerchiefs, and black bonnets or white caps, while an adult man wears a shirt, waistcoat and natural-coloured breeches, and a dark hat with a tall crown.[29] These sheets of studies provided records of the artist's observations and could be referred to at a later date in preparation for watercolours for exhibition (see colour plate 1).[30]

W. H. Pyne's *Microcosm* (published in two volumes in 1806) was originally issued as a subscription series in 30 instalments of four plates. Subtitled *Picturesque Delineation of the Arts, Manufactures, etc. of Great Britain*, its purpose was to spread knowledge about the useful arts of the country, and above all to act as a source of figure subjects for use in landscapes.[31] Like Hills's illustrations, Pyne's *Microcosm* gives useful details of labourers in his scenes of mowing, reaping, ploughing, dairying and shepherding. Nevertheless, there is something deliberately fanciful about the images and, even in what seem to be studies taken from observation, 'idealization, didacticism and reassurance are not entirely absent'.[32] Pyne's *Etchings of Rustic Figures for the Embellishment of Landscape* (1815), like his *Microcosm*, were an important aid to landscape artists, and reflected his interest in observing nature and sketching out of doors. However, Pyne saw his figures, as Constable did, as incidental to, and embellishing, landscape rather than as subjects in their own right, explaining that 'these groups have been formed; their costumes, characters and general employments have been attended to, which may furnish subjects to compose groups from, but may also lead the student to select figures of a similar class in nature.'[33]

How close, then, do we get to a realistic or truthful portrayal of the agricultural worker immediately prior to the start of the Victorian period? What, for example, can we make of the work of John Constable (1776–1837), whose depictions of a seemingly peaceful and tranquil countryside provide no glimpses of the underlying social tensions that led to unrest and working-class protest, such as the outbreaks of machine-breaking culminating in the Swing riots of 1830? Based as they are on direct observation of nature and on studies frequently made out-of-doors, Constable's depictions of the Suffolk landscape are full of topographical detail; yet his figures are tiny. His landscapes seem to present a 'new image of harmony between labourer and landscape – a harmony only possible if the labourer is distant or otherwise indistinct'.[34] It is virtually impossible to make out the detail in the clothing of Constable's rural subjects, except perhaps for the red of the boy's waistcoat in *The Cornfield* (1826), for example. Constable's manipulation of colour might have been used for aesthetic reasons to provide a contrast to the otherwise neutral tones of the boy's clothing and the surrounding landscape in general, but it is also a little bit of realism: red flannel, or other woollen cloth, was worn in the countryside at this time, often made into cloaks like those in such paintings as William Bigg's *A Lady and her Children Relieving a Cottager* (1781) and evidenced by the (rare) survival of one such garment at the Gallery of English Costume at Platt Hall in Manchester (Chapter 8).

By the early nineteenth century, agricultural landscape was well established as an acceptable genre for artists. The representation of the rural labourer did not, however, record the hardships of rural life; neither were such details as the clothing of labourers necessarily depicted completely impartially (except, as we have seen, in some of George Morland's paintings and the studies made by Robert Hills and W. H. Pyne). Arguably, the myth of the pleasures and simplicity of rural life became further entrenched as the nineteenth century progressed and as the 'urban problem' became more visible. This thread wove its way into many representations of rural working-class dress, exemplified by the association of particular garments with idealized visions of rural life. How was this myth translated into agricultural landscape paintings in this period, and what were the implications of this for representations of clothing? This question provides the focus for the following section.

ENGLAND'S GREEN AND PLEASANT LAND: DRESS IN AGRICULTURAL LANDSCAPE PAINTINGS

Many of the agricultural landscape scenes discussed above were bought by members of the aristocracy or gentry. But by the 1820s buyers of such scenes were more likely to be from the newly enriched middle classes – merchants, manufacturers and industrialists.[35] Considered in the context of the increasing polarization between town and country, visual representations of the countryside became images touched by a nostalgic longing for the past. Although a 'counter-myth' emerged in response (see Chapter 6), it has been persuasively argued that it was the picturesque aspects that dominated painting:

> This myth was an updated combination of the ancient myths of the greater happiness and virtue of rural as opposed to urban life: its main claim was that the rural working class was contented, industrious, pious, deferential and full of family affection, and thus provided a secure foundation for a stable social system. It appealed particularly to those who supported the social and moral prestige of a paternalistic aristocracy and gentry, but it was also a comforting idea for all members of the middle class who were fearful of revolution. In addition, it could appeal to radicals and socialists attacking the evils of capitalism and industrialization, and to all Victorian town dwellers, rich or poor, who felt that their roots were in the countryside.[36]

There was also the underlying belief that the English countryside lifted humanity above the day-to-day and the mundane, while in some contexts rural labour took on an association with the spiritual. This is illustrated in the work of Samuel Palmer, who in 1824 set up a community of like-minded artists calling themselves the Ancients, based for a short time in the Kent village of Shoreham. Emulating the artistic brotherhood of the Nazarenes in Rome,[37] the Ancients looked to the art of the Middle Ages for both technical and spiritual inspiration. But, unlike the Nazarenes before and the Pre-Raphaelites after them, they failed to win critical acclaim for their innovative pictures and, without the financial backing that the sale of the latter would have afforded them, they gradually abandoned these for more conventional work. Palmer, however, had a small legacy, and, as a result, was able to maintain his more visionary approach for longer, only leaving Shoreham in 1835, whereas his associates had left by 1830.[38]

The landscapes painted by Palmer celebrated the divine in nature.[39] His Shoreham paintings were in the tradition of the spiritual–pastoral, often showing shepherds and sheep and the rural communities to which they belonged protected by enfolding hills. Palmer was well aware of the upheavals in the countryside culminating in the machine-breaking of the Swing riots, but that is not the countryside of his landscapes. He was not trying to depict a literal present in his art, but aiming to evoke a lost, or transcendent, way of life.[40] So it is crucial to consider Palmer's delineation of the clothing of his subjects in this light. In a number of his works of the 1820s, shepherd figures are depicted in generalized flowing clothing. In *Late Twilight* (1825), for example, a shepherd is resting with his sheep in the foreground and a haloed moon in the background (the presence of the moon was a common symbol of Christ), the shepherd not just a shepherd but one with a religious function. However, in *A Rustic Scene* (1823), Palmer presents a heroic image of a plough-man wearing a loose garment with a gathered and 'smocked' yoke – Palmer's interpretation of a smock, perhaps? Palmer here depicts a higher form of reality in which mystery – things intimated, hence the importance of shadows – and transformation are the point. This particular representation of the countryside, in spite, or perhaps because, of being based on a real place and using it as metaphor, perpetuated the idea of a rural idyll (see colour plate 2).

After the unrest of the 1820s and 1830s, in the middle of the century agriculture moved into what has been described as a brief 'golden age'. Visual images of the countryside were still concerned more with the economic and symbolic role played by agriculture than with the unwholesome details of the working lives of its inhabitants in these decades. One of the most popular agricultural subjects for artists into the 1850s and 1860s was the wheat harvest. As we saw in relation to the work of George Stubbs some half-a-century earlier, this period of the agricultural year was potentially the most economically profitable for labourers, when the perennial problem of rural poverty could therefore be most easily ignored even by those with a social conscience. It was also when as many members of the family as possible were expected to take up harvest work, which was now favourably contrasted with the perceived breaking-up of the family consequent upon (urban) factory work. And, of course, the harvest was of national importance as the source of bread, and therefore attractive for its symbolic value in art, while the elements of the process – reaping, threshing, winnowing, gleaning – had long had religious, and specifically biblical, connotations:[41] it was during the 1840s that the annual harvest festival began to be celebrated in English churches.

Agricultural reference manuals such as Henry Stephens's *The Book of the Farm* (1844) promoted the latest farming techniques. Artists, on the other hand, consciously chose to depict methods of farming that were dated or outmoded, celebrating the very practices that were demonized in triumphalist accounts of agrarian improvement.[42] The idealization of particular agricultural processes in art was expressed in a number of ways: for example, machinery was rarely shown in images of the harvest, even though the mechanical reaper began to be used in the 1870s and 1880s, particularly in areas where labour was expensive or in short supply.[43] As the writer Richard Jefferies observed, 'so many pictures seem to proceed upon the assumption that steam-plough and reaping-machine do not exist, that the landscape contains nothing but what it did a hundred years ago.'[44] Similarly, artists chose to represent outmoded agricultural implements in favour of their newer replacements. For example, from the 1850s, the use of the sickle to cut wheat gradually gave way to the scythe, which was more efficient, yet some artists continued to depict reaping by sickle, partly perhaps because of the latter's biblical associations.[45]

Artists also represented clothing in a way that would detract from the dirty and laborious aspects of field work. As we have seen, the employment of women and children in agricultural work was highly controversial in the second half of the nineteenth century, even after its worst aspects had been controlled by the Agricultural Gangs Act of 1867. Many artists therefore chose not to show women working, except in the most generalized and idealized way, and, when they *were* depicted in a working context, this was accomplished without a hint of the moral depravity referred to by some of the witnesses interviewed by the parliamentary commissioners: their clothing was neat, respectable and clean. As late as 1890, Helen Allingham presented in *Harvest Field* a neatly dressed woman reaping, with her child playing happily nearby – worlds away from the images of field work painted by the rural naturalist artists of the 1880s such as George Clausen and Henry Herbert La Thangue (Chapter 6), which exposed labour with much less sentimentalizing or idealizing gloss.

Helen Allingham (1848–1926), née Paterson, became one of the most enduringly popular of artists of rural scenes both in the nineteenth century and beyond. Her early career was as an illustrator for the *Graphic* until 1874 (she also did some work for *The Cornhill Magazine*), when she married William Allingham, poet and editor of *Fraser's Magazine*. In 1875, she was elected to the Society of Painters in Water Colours, although women were not admitted to be full members of the Society until 1890 (at which point she became a full member). As she established herself, Allingham became better known for her watercolours depicting picturesque cottage scenes than for agricultural landscapes such as *Harvest Field*. Intent on recording in her work a rapidly disappearing way of life, she focused her attention on the cottages and cottage gardens of Surrey and Wiltshire. In 1881, she and her husband moved out of London to the village of Witley, near Haslemere in Surrey. Here, at her home Sandhills (see colour plate 3), she became a neighbour of the best-known of Victorian painters of idyllic country scenes, Myles Birket Foster (1825–99). Although Birket Foster's early career was devoted to book illustration, in 1860 he began to exhibit at the Society of Painters in Water Colours, his work selling so well that he was able to give up book illustration. Foster's influence on Allingham's work is thought to have been profound. However, while Foster worked mostly in his studio from memory, Allingham's move to Witley inspired her to paint *en plein air*.[46]

Her two most popular books, compiled from paintings executed in the main from the latter part of the 1880s, are tellingly entitled *Happy England* (1903) and *The Cottage Homes of England* (1909); these helped to establish Allingham as 'the leading exponent of the cottage idyll'.[47] Marcus Huish describes *Happy England* as revealing of 'only a one-sided and partial view of both life and landscape [...] In strong opposition to the tendency of art of the later years of the nineteenth century, the baser side of life has been studiously avoided, and nature has only been put down on paper in its happiest moods and its pleasantest array [...] as regards both life and landscape it is, throughout, a mirror of Halcyon days.'[48] Described as a fair-weather painter, Allingham preferred to paint spring and summer scenes rather than autumn and winter ones: of the paintings she exhibited at the Fine Art Society in 1886, over 50 were of the former and only 13 of the latter.[49] Gradually shifting from painting dominant figures in the landscape, Allingham gave as her reason for this change that she 'could put as much interest into a figure two or three inches high as in one three times as large, and that she could paint it better; for in painting large figures out of doors it was always a difficulty in making them look anything else than they were, namely "posing models".'[50]

Almost invariably Allingham's paintings include a woman or a woman and child/children standing or playing outside a picturesque cottage, as in *A Dorsetshire Cottage* (colour plate 4), or a young woman tending a cottage garden. They are well dressed and neat like the cottages they inhabit; their clothing usually includes a sun-bonnet, even when these garments were going out of fashion. While older women often continued to wear the styles of their youth, it would have been unusual for younger girls such as those depicted by Allingham to be wearing sun-bonnets by the 1890s, especially as the principal job for which women had traditionally worn them – field work – was increasingly being replaced by domestic service. In paintings like *Portrait of a Girl in a Pink Bonnet* (colour plate 5), the sun-bonnet itself, rather than the woman wearing it, seems to become the subject of the work. And in a number of instances, Allingham places the sun-bonnet out of context, associating it with domestic tasks, as in *Cutting Cabbages* (c.1884), or *Washing Day* (colour plate 6) rather than with back-breaking field work. She often uses it to dress models rather than the genuine labourer. She thus depicts 'costume' rather than clothing, and so attaches to this garment a symbolic value.[51] These images offer the viewer a kind of double vision – a particular view of the past recreated as the present. Paradoxically, then, by representing a staged stability, these images throw light on change.

The chronicling of changing styles of clothing may not have been part of Allingham's explicit purpose, but the 'recording in line and colour [of] a most interesting but unfortunately vanishing phase of English domestic architecture' certainly was. 'For the cottages', Huish observes, 'are almost without exception veritable portraits, the artist (whilst naturally selecting those best suited to her purpose) having felt it a duty to present them with an accuracy of structural feature which is not always the case in creations of this kind, where the painter has had other views, and considered that he could improve his picture by an addition here and an omission there.'[52] In other words, Allingham's powers of observation and recording of the cottages were detailed and precise. She even kept in her studio a piece of diamond lead lattice from a cottage window because these were being generally replaced.[53] Whether she collected or owned any sun-bonnets is not known. But their inclusion in her work can be regarded as a kind of collecting. Like the smocks and sun-bonnets collected by individuals and extant in museums today (Chapter 8), those represented in Allingham's painting transforms them from mere clothing into emblems of a vanishing world.

In paintings by other artists depicting harvest scenes, the whole family is often engaged, while the work itself portrayed as pleasant rather than exhausting or back-breaking. Interestingly, although women may be shown in the harvest field, they are rarely doing the harvest work as such, but are tending the children or bringing a midday meal to the male members of the family. This is the case in both John Frederick Herring's *Harvest* (1857) and George Vicat Cole's *Harvest Time* (1860). Such paintings were popular and found a ready market in London.[54] While it was unusual for women to be depicted labouring in the fields rather than in the domestic sphere of cottage home and garden (as in much of the work of Allingham), it was generally more acceptable for men to be represented at work in the fields. Although agricultural labour was tiring on a physical level, some artists treated it as wholesome and rewarding. However, like Constable's miniscule figures in his paintings of the 1820s, Vicat Cole's labourer of more than three decades later is portrayed as too small a figure for the artist to have had to engage with awkward issues of ragged, patched or dirty clothes.

Where the particulars of clothing *are* shown, the garments are often smocks, either generalized, as in John Linnell's *Shepherd Boy Playing a Flute* (1831), or, nearly five decades later, more detailed, as in John Robertson Reid's *Toil and Pleasure* (1879). These two very different images exemplify the way in which the cultural significance of clothing is determined as much by the context in which it is represented, with deliberate choices made by the creator of an image, as by the physical attributes of the clothing itself. In Linnell's *Shepherd Boy* the clothing details – smock, neckerchief and hat – were not drawn from the imagination but were the product of close observation, and provide a fairly accurate representation of a young labourer's clothing in the 1830s, but the painting's composition and its idyllic landscape go beyond that and carry with them the symbolism of the Good Shepherd,[55] thus ushering in a whole panoply of associations for the viewer. Likewise, in Reid's *Toil and Pleasure*, where the 'message' is the contrast between the countryside as a place of work (the labourers take centre stage in the painting) and the countryside as a place where leisure is pursued by the middle and upper classes (seen hunting in the background), the two young boys as well as the older labourer all wear smocks whose details are completely correct. But the choice of smocks, already going out of fashion, as their distinctive attire, rather than what would have been more usual workwear by the late 1870s (jackets and trousers), is an interesting one by an artist not generally known for his idealization of working-class life, suggesting that he saw the smock as the garment that immediately singled out the agricultural labourer from his social superiors. There are connotations of honest, decent, worthy work in contrast to the careless pursuit of pleasure by the rich. To place the smock in a particular context that was more than merely documentary was to attach to it symbolic importance.

Children were often shown wearing smocks even after the latter had gone out of general wear. Not only were smocks and smocking re-popularized by the illustrations of children by Kate Greenaway in *Under the Window* (1878), and subsequently by the smocking on children's 'Kate Greenaway dresses' sold by the costume department of Liberty of London from the 1880s, but their chronology is complicated by revivals of smock-making such as one which occurred in Bere Regis in the early twentieth century. Allingham, too, dresses some of her child subjects, such as the young boy in *Her Majesty's Post Office* (1887), in smocks, so out of their 'correct' historical context, as if smocks were part of contemporary dress when they would, by this time, probably have been unusual attire for young boys.

In asking whether the Victorian artist used accurate details of dress in clothing his or her rural figures, and in considering the context which he or she created as the setting for those details, we are also asking about the preoccupations of that artist, and about the signifying function of clothes – in relation not only to a particular painting, but to Victorian society as a whole. If, say, in Allingham's idealized cottage scenes, sun-bonnets are represented out-side the 'correct' time, place or occasion, this is part of the dialogue between artist and audience in a society in which past and present, and the values associated with them, were perhaps more inextricably and emotively inter-twined than they had ever been, and certain garments, symbols of a way of life that as it slipped into history became ever more available and attractive as myth, could become powerful currency in that dialogue. The photography of this period, the subject of the next chapter, offers some illuminating parallels.

5

PHOTOGRAPHY AND RURAL DRESS
'Work of art' or documentary realism?

Victorian photographs, with a few exceptions, were more or less 'posed'. Those of Henry Peach Robinson (1830–1901), who is the focus of this chapter, were *staged* in a complex process in which 'country' models and clothes were selected to create the image of a rural idyll.[1] In feeling, Robinson's work is similar to some of the paintings of an idealized rural life considered in the previous chapter. Indeed, the photograph was considered by some contemporaries to be as much a 'work of art' as the painting, and the premise on which the previous chapter began – that the work of art is 'a far-from-simple document' – can be as relevant to a discussion of photography as it is to painting.

The relationship between the painting and the photograph in the late nineteenth century was complicatedly reciprocal: while photographs were considered by a number of photographers to be works of art, painters were interested in the visual effects produced by photography. The use of 'photographic effects' by artists such as Jules Bastien-Lepage, Henry Herbert La Thangue and George Clausen was noted by contemporaries: 'One feels', pointed out W. C. Brownell in The Magazine of Art in 1883, 'the painter [Bastien-Lepage] himself as if he were a camera.' However, Brownell went on to ask whether 'the art of painting' was 'to become [...] essentially scientific, and [would] busy itself with collecting facts as the only worthwhile occupation':[2] Brownell might be suggesting that paintings are influenced by photographic techniques, but, unlike many of the photographers themselves, he sees photography as an 'essentially scientific' craft, with the express aim of collecting 'facts'. Clearly, the relationship between the two, and how each was perceived, was not straightforward. Such observations imply a view often taken about the 'factual' or 'realist' nature of paintings that employed 'photographic techniques', but they also imply a view of what is represented by the photograph. John Taylor observes that for writers on photography there seems to have been a shared assumption, which was 'their belief in the authority of what they [photographers] "took" in photographs to be hard evidence or truth. They judged this authority to be derived from the way photographs had a closer, one-to-one relationship to reality than any other system of representation.'[3] As photography emerged as a new medium for representing or 'recording' the visual, it is easy to see why this assumption was made; on the other hand, and, as John Tagg has argued, 'every photograph is the result of specific, and, in every sense, significant distortions, which render its relation to any prior reality deeply problematic.'[4]

Aesthetic and philosophical considerations about whether the photograph of the second half of the nineteenth century was an art-form or a snapshot of 'reality' (or both) have been much debated. But less frequently discussed in this context is the detail of the clothing worn by sitters in so-called British art photography of the period. Commentators such as Phyllis Rose discussing the work of Julia Margaret Cameron (1815–79), in particular her portraits of women, have argued that the latter 'look less beautiful the more the details of their dress are articulated' and that 'Cameron was right to make her models take their hair down and wrap themselves in shawls and turbans. It eternalizes their beauty.'[5] Rose later comments that 'clothing, occupation, class, personality – all these things are transitory and accidental, they did not interest Cameron. She refused to be influenced by mere circumstance.'[6] Rose's observations raise interesting questions about the importance to the late nineteenth-century photographer of what sitters wore: why, and in what ways, might a photographer dictate what was worn? What is the significance of the items of clothing selected? What light do such choices cast on the intentions of the photographer, on possible interpretations of the work itself, and on the way historians later utilize the photographic image as a window on to a past society? These are questions I want to explore here.

The photographic record of the Victorian period is huge, and it is 'difficult [...] to avoid being buried by the sheer weight of the evidence'.[7] As with the agricultural landscape paintings considered in the previous chapter, the selection of photographs and photographers discussed here does not do justice to the thousands of photographs of rural subjects taken anonymously by amateur photographers and kept in national photographic archives, such as that at the Museum of English Rural Life, University of Reading, and in numerous county/local collections. A large number of these photographs can usually be dated to within about a decade, but in many cases the photographer is unknown and their intentions in recording particular people and/or scenes can only be guessed at. The details of clothing recorded in this way are invaluable as illustrative material, supplementing other visual and literary evidence. They may, for example, add to our knowledge of what a garment described in a novel or documentary account actually looked like. In other – rare – cases, where a photograph of an individual wearing a particular garment survives alongside the garment itself, they can bring to vivid life for us the people who actually made and wore the clothes. For example, a kind of smock (it is not actually smocked), with the Prince of Wales feathers and the words 'Ich Dien' ('I serve') embroidered across the chest, survives in the Dorset County Museum along with a photograph of its owner wearing it: we know that his name was Job Green, that he was born in 1814 in the Dorset village of Toller Porcorum, and that he was a shepherd for most of his life.[8] The hand-sewn garment is thought to have been made for him by his wife – and, apart from anything else, is a wonderful illustration of the individuality of working-class clothing.

THE PHOTOGRAPH AS A WORK OF ART AND THE REPRESENTATION OF LANDSCAPE

Even though we know that every photograph actually involves the making of choices, twenty-first century assumptions about the immediacy of photography have influenced our views about the supposed objectivity of the photograph in the nineteenth century. But the early history of photography reveals that the complexity of photographic processes militated against the production of spontaneous images, and this must shape our understanding of photography's relationship with notions of truth and reality. In subject matter, photography took as its model many of the conventions of painting. Indeed, it has been argued that pictorialism, whose specific principles were established in Henry Peach Robinson's *Pictorial Effect in Photography* (1869), was the dominant photographic aesthetic of the late nineteenth and early twentieth centuries. It was concerned with establishing photography as an expressive art medium, aligning its aesthetic potential with the conventions of academy painting, and its subject matter was closely related to the picturesque (landscapes, rural idylls, allegories of life and work) – including the pursuit of the beautiful.[9]

William Henry Fox Talbot (1800–77) is credited with the invention of the 'calotype' process, sometimes called 'Talbotype', in 1840 (patented in 1841). It involved the production of negatives on fine-quality writing paper; each sheet had to be prepared by hand, first brushed with a solution of salt and later sensitized in a bath of silver nitrate. Far from the instantaneity we are accustomed to, exposures made via this process would have lasted half-an-hour even on the brightest days, and each positive from the finished negative took nearly as long to print in the sun. In this process, the image is part of the paper and its fibres, rather than appearing on a coated surface. (The albumen print – the first glossy, coated photographic print, in which thin paper was first coated with a mixture of whisked egg white and salt, then sensitized with silver nitrate – was not in general use until about 1855, and continued to be used until 1890.) Although amateurs could buy a calotype licence for one or two pounds, for photographic professionals the licences could cost anything from £10 to £100 or more, and the patents thus stifled widespread use and experimentation. Meanwhile, in France and America, the daguerreotype, named after its French inventor Louis Daguerre (1787–1851), was favoured over the calotype. While a calotype image could be reproduced, and a daguerreotype was by definition a single image, the latter was highly detailed. It was formed on a sheet of copper thinly plated with silver and then rendered light-sensitive by a chemical reaction with iodine and bromide vapours. The use of the calotype rather than the daguerreotype by photographers such as Benjamin Brecknell Turner thus reflected an aesthetic choice, the former producing 'fuzzier', 'artier' prints while the latter 'seemed to tell the truth, the whole truth and nothing but the truth'.[10]

Despite a number of modifications and improvements, the calotype process still had limited possibilities for reproduction and distribution and was not suited to commercial and popular production.[11] Then, in 1851, exposure times were radically cut and a high resolution of detail achieved when Frederick Scott Archer (1813–57) introduced the wet-collodion process, in which a sheet of glass was coated with a thin film of collodion containing potassium iodide and then sensitized on location with silver nitrate. The plate had to be exposed while still wet and developed immediately. Archer's process of wet-collodion-on-glass negatives successfully combined the precision of the daguerreotype and the reproducibility of the calotype. It allowed exposures that could be counted in seconds rather than minutes, and produced sharp and luminous prints. Although debate over the relative merits of paper and glass was lively in the early 1850s, the future lay with the wet-collodion process. The latter rapidly displaced paper, dominating the medium for three decades.[12]

In the early years, photographers who chose to represent landscape drew upon the artistic conventions adopted within the genre of agricultural land-scape. Benjamin Brecknell Turner (1815–94), for example, was an amateur photographer who travelled widely in the early 1850s, from his native London to Lynmouth in Devon in the west and Whitby in Yorkshire in the north, making highly accomplished images of farm buildings and farm-yards, trees, streams, ruined abbeys and other 'country scenes'; the 60 that he considered his best were included in his album *Photographic Views from Nature* (c.1854–5, Victoria and Albert Museum, London). From the first, Turner was a devotee of the methods of Fox Talbot and the calotype, and owned a copy of Talbot's pioneering publication *The Pencil of Nature* (1844–6). Like many of his upper-middle-class contemporaries, he was familiar with the topographical and picturesque tradition in the visual arts, and he and other early amateur photographers found affinities with their artist forebears such as Thomas Girtin (1775–1802), Cornelius Varley (1781–1873) and John Constable (1776–1837). Depicting humble farm scenes, his work may be compared to that of Robert Hills (1769–1844), and his use of the paper-based calotype, which suppressed detail in favour of a limited tonal range, can be likened to the watercolour effects favoured by Hills, John Sell Cotman (1782–1842) and Peter de Wint (1784–1849).[13] In choice of subject matter, Turner was not unique: his British contemporaries Roger Fenton (1819–69), Frances Bedford (1816–94) and Hugh Welch Diamond (1809–86) dealt with similar imagery, although Turner was consistently praised as being one of the best practitioners of the calotype.[14]

Shunning the contemporary world, Turner's view of the country-side was overwhelmingly nostalgic: in his photos of Bredicot village in Worcestershire, he chose not to acknowledge signs of modernity such as the impact of the railway from Gloucester to Birmingham, which between 1839 and 1840 cut Bredicot village in half. Rarely including working fig-ures in contemporary clothes, it can be argued that this made an image less historically specific, allowing for the possibility of nostalgic projection and a 'timeless quality'.[15] Conversely, for other Victorian photographers such as Robinson, the clothing worn by the figures in the photographs served precisely that nostalgia and timeless quality which Turner, by avoiding it, wanted to represent.

The expense of having one's photo taken limited the number of working-class people who could afford this 'luxury'. References to the commercial sale of calotypes in the 1840s make it evident that they were expensive.[16] Even when, in the 1870s, Robinson and Nelson King Cherrill were running their photography business in Tunbridge Wells, and were forced to lower their prices in order to increase their orders, cartes-de-visite cost 10s 6d per dozen,[17] which would have represented more or less a week's wage for the majority of agricultural labourers and was therefore well beyond their means. Thus, on the whole, photography was something in which they would have posed for the benefit of the photographer. Like the 'second-hand' representations of labourers in the parliamentary commissions of enquiry, these photographs represent the working class as passive subjects of middle-class gaze and enquiry, with little say in how they were represented.

Moving briefly outside our southern English focus, the well-known, albeit short-lived partnership (due to Adamson's premature death in 1848) between the chemist Robert Adamson (1821–48) and the artist David Octavius Hill (1802–70) resulted in some of the earliest images of working-class men and women – the fishermen and fishwives of Newhaven on the Firth of Forth, Scotland, executed in the early 1840s. The village of Newhaven became a natural tourist attraction for summer visitors to Edinburgh who took advantage of the therapeutic effects of dipping into the cold waters of the North Sea. Hill and Adamson's work was seen by a wide audience and its potential influence was considerable.[18] These extraordinary calotypes have preserved a visual record of a working-class community whose women were famous for their beauty. While conveying the 'heroism, the social morality and the distinctive culture of the village', the images are also evidence of Hill and Adamson's fascination with the dress of the fishwives.[19]

The 'picturesqueness' of the Newhaven fishwives' dress derives from the fact that it was based on late eighteenth-century working dress: a short gown, a bodice which came below the waist and short, striped petticoats and skirts, usually kilted up to keep the outer surface clean as well as to show off the interesting effect produced by the pattern thus formed by the stripes. The community's independence from the changing fashionable shape, as well as practical considerations, kept these elements of the costume fixed in time, and, apart from one or two concessions to 'modern' practices – for example, by the 1830s the fishwives normally wore shoes and stockings having previously gone barefoot – dress in the village seemed to remain largely immune from modern developments in fashion.[20] Traditional dress ensured that the fishwives came to represent in the tourist imagination some stability

Fig. 5.1 *Mrs Hall, Newhaven* (1843–7) by David Octavius Hill and Robert Adamson

in an otherwise changing world: as Stevenson observes, whereas 'a sitter in fashionable clothes was fixed to a historical date, the fishwives' distinctive costume took them out of the exact sense of time inherent in more fashionable dress.'[21] On the other hand, Hill's interest was not exclusively in the picturesque: a notable example of this is his depiction of the top hats worn by the fishermen. The stove-pipe hat was fashionable and considered by one contemporary to be 'a mysterious combination of the inconvenient and the unpicturesque'.[22]

Hill and Adamson admired Newhaven for its contemporary reality: Hill was 'not presenting the village as a pastoral ideal divorced from real life [...] he was happy to incorporate such *artificiality* [my italics – the hats were

Fig. 5.2 *Fishermen Ashore* (*c*.1843–7) by David Octavius Hill and Robert Adamson

considered 'artificial' because they were fashionable and represented moder-
nity] and to treat the facts of his own time as part of an ideal'.[23] Significantly,
the pair took their photographic equipment down to Newhaven and may
have set up a working studio there, whereas later photographers invited their
fishwife subjects into their existing studios, providing them with elaborately
painted backdrops of Newhaven or the city streets.[24]

Joseph Gale (1830–1906), another well-known and respected Victorian
photographer, offers a detailed pictorial record of rural England during the
last two decades of the nineteenth century.[25] However, here again, photography does not simply 'record' impartially: Gale, much like Allingham,
deliberately sought out and recorded scenes that he perceived to be fast disappearing. Much of his earlier life was spent in Bedford where he studied

Fig. 5.3 *Village News* (1889) by Joseph Gale

art; later he trained as an architect at the City of London School before taking up photography in the late 1850s, first exhibiting at the annual exhibition of the Photographic Society in 1874. His work continued to be exhibited through the 1880s and he was given a one-man show at the Camera Club in 1889, with more than a hundred pictures displayed. A critic in the *Amateur Photographer* commented, 'Most of them are gems of the first water, and exhibit that attention to *picturesque* [my italics] detail for which this artist's pictures are remarkable.'[26] The notion of the picturesque never seems to have been far away – either in the minds of photographers or indeed in those of audiences and critics.

PHOTOGRAPHY, RURAL DRESS AND THE
PICTURESQUE

The photographs of Henry Peach Robinson offer a contrast to Benjamin Brecknell Turner's rural scenes or Hill and Adamson's images of Newhaven fishermen and fishwives. Described as 'the most celebrated photographer in Britain during his lifetime', dominating the world of art photography for a period of over 30 years,[27] Robinson was particular about the appearance of his models, going to great lengths to collect items of rural clothing and making detailed reference to its function in his work. We also know something of the thinking that informed his art, and it is enlightening to consider well-known composite photographs such as *Bringing Home the May* (1862) and selected later images in the light of his philosophical perspectives published in *Picture Making by Photography* (1884) and *The Elements of a Pictorial Photograph* (1896). In common with the paintings of Helen Allingham, his work presents an overwhelmingly retrospective, nostalgic view of rural working-class life. Comparisons with other photographers who chose similar subject matter, such as Peter Henry Emerson, working in the 1880s, reveal that consideration of the *context* in which particular clothing is represented furthers an understanding of its important role in articulating a society in transition. The portrayal of dress in the work of Robinson and others contributed to the evolution of the concept of a rural idyll in nineteenth-century Victorian culture.

Born in the old Shropshire town of Ludlow, Robinson was apprenticed at the age of 14 to a printer, stationer and bookseller for five years. In his twenties, he began practising photography, although he had held

Fig. 5.4 *Bringing Home the May* (1862) by Henry Peach Robinson

ambitions to be an artist, spending much of the time after his apprentice-ship was completed drawing and painting (as well as during what leisure hours he had in his first job as a bookseller's assistant in Bromsgrove in Birmingham). But he never managed to persuade his parents that he could make a satisfactory livelihood as an artist. His interest in, and approach to, photography, however, can be seen in the light of this underlying interest in painting. Many of his friends were painters and he became connected to some through the matches made by his children: his elder son Ralph, for example, married Janet Spence Reid, daughter of John Robertson Reid, the Scottish painter of genre, landscape and coastal scenes. Robinson viewed the photograph as essentially a work of art, which could convey his ideas about the picturesque. Unsurprisingly, he was an admirer of the work of Myles Birket Foster, whose work also perpetuated images of an idyllic rural England. In *The Elements of a Pictorial Photograph*, Robinson maintained that 'Mr Foster's drawings have been especially worthy of the study of the photog-rapher, his genre and landscape subjects being of the kind very possible in photography.'[28]

While working in Leamington Spa in the early 1850s, Robinson first became interested in photography, subscribing to the *Journal of the Photographic Society* from its commencement in 1853, and successfully practising the calotype process. The friendship and encouragement he received from photographer Hugh Welch Diamond persuaded him to devote his career to the medium and he ran a professional photographic studio first in Leamington Spa, from 1857 to 1864, and then, from 1868 following a period of illness, in Tunbridge Wells. The majority of Robinson's pictures for exhibition were rural in theme. In addi-tion to the photographs, we also have his critique of the medium – a theory of photography based on the aesthetics of the picturesque movement in the arts.[29] Robinson devoted much of his major literary work, *Pictorial Effect in Photography* (1869), to an account of how the real and the ideal could be associated in one photograph, and to emphasizing the importance of the picturesque:

> It is an old canon of art, that every scene worth painting must have some-thing of the sublime, the beautiful or the picturesque. By its nature, pho-tography can make no pretensions to represent the first, but beauty can be represented by its means and picturesqueness has never had so perfect an interpreter.[30]

One of Robinson's best-known photographs, *Bringing Home the May*, demon-strates this ideal – to combine the real, ideal and picturesque. On one level, the photograph conveys the real. 'Truthfulness' was Robinson's intention, although his definition was not a literal one: 'I am far from saying', he wrote in *Pictorial Effect in Photography*, 'that a photograph must be an actual, literal, and absolute fact; that would deny all I have written; but it must represent truth [...] That truth in art may exist without an absolute observance of facts.'[31] In *Bringing Home the May*, approximation to truth is portrayed via the representation of a real country tradition (in which, in his youth, Robinson had frequently participated) when the May blossom was gathered and large branches taken home on May Day. Like many of Robinson's photographs, *Bringing Home the May* is a composite photograph made up of a number of individual negatives – nine in this case – printed one by one and mounted together to form a unified picture. Robinson justified the use of the composite photograph by maintaining that he could 'get nearer the truth for certain subjects with several negatives than with one'.[32] There is artifice in the composition, but the intended finished effect is 'real': 'It is not the fact of reality that is required, but the truth of imitation that constitutes a veracious picture,' Robinson stated.[33] *Bringing Home the May* met with an enthusiastic reception from the photographic press.[34]

From an early age, Robinson took a keen interest in dress and historical costume: between 1849 and 1851 he had produced the designs from which his mother – a skilled dressmaker – made up garments to be worn at the large number of costume balls held in Ludlow in the winter months. Robinson's use of real items of rural dress in *Bringing Home the May* and in other photographs to express the picturesque and a rural ideal is fascinating, and was a practice to which he returned in the majority of his photographs of rural life. The individual elements of the costume in his photographs were authentic. Robinson's view of the importance of 'accuracy' in this respect is illustrated by his own critique of one of his earliest photos, *Mr Werner as Richelieu* (1857), which he regarded as 'desperately bad', not because of the photographic qualities but because the costume was not authentic.[35] The method Robinson used to acquire the clothing that features in his work and the fact of dressing up his models for the compositions (for the sake of 'authenticity') is described in *Picture Making by Photography*:

> It is not always easy to explain what you really mean when you meet a girl in a lonely country lane, and you offer to buy her clothes, but a little perseverance and a good offer usually succeed. A country girl's dress is not often worth more than eighteenpence, and if you turn the pence into shillings, and look businesslike all the time, you may make pretty sure of walking off with the property, or, at all events, getting it sent to you next day.[36]

Fig. 5.5 *The Cuckoo* (c.1900) by Henry Peach Robinson

'My models', wrote Robinson 'may be called to some extent artificial but they are so near the real thing (when dressed in country clothes) as to be taken for it by the real natives.'[37] Robinson urged photographers to acquire a wide range of accessories, as well as dresses, cloaks and aprons. However, judging by the number of different kinds of sun-bonnets that feature in many of his photographs dating from the early 1860s to just before his death (from *Bringing Home the May* to *The Cuckoo*, c.1900), these are the items that appear to have constituted the largest category of clothing he collected. Robinson believed that 'it is the sun-bonnet which is characteristic of the country'.[38]

In his efforts to create authenticity in his photographs, Robinson stressed that the clothes worn by his models should not be new: 'In my practice', he said, 'I always used old clothes.'[39] In *The Elements of a Pictorial Photograph*, he complained of the incompetence of those photographers who mismanaged dressed-up models:

> For instance, we usually find that when a young lady is dressed as a peasant model, she generally looks like one of the chorus in an opera. The clothes are new and very clean, the country clodhopping boots are perhaps represented by patent leather shoes and by some strange dispensation of artistic providence, she is only allowed to appear as a milkmaid or a gleaner.[40]

Robinson was aware then of 'stereotypical' representations of milkmaids and gleaners. However, in trying to avoid the conventions of one genre and attempting authenticity in which he combined real clothes with artificial constructions, he was, ironically, constructing his own version. To this extent his work can be seen as part of the tradition perpetuated also by Helen Allingham and Myles Birket Foster.[41] Allingham repeatedly depicted sun-bonnets in her paintings when they were becoming untypical; Robinson employed them in a similar way.

Although it appears with less frequency in his work than the sun-bonnet, Robinson also used the smock in an interesting way. An elderly man wearing a smock appears in both *When the Day's Work is Done* (first exhibited in the Photographic Society's exhibition in 1877) and *Dawn and Sunset* (1885). These are considered two of Robinson's most successful composite photographs. Both show simple but homely and comfortable – if idealized – cottage interiors. In this respect, *Dawn and Sunset* makes an interesting comparison with Thomas Faed's painting *From Dawn to Sunset (The Full Cycle of Life)* of 1861, the latter 'a somewhat more realistic portrayal of a cottager's home, over-crowded, untidy and drab'.[42] In *When the Day's Work is Done*, an old labourer in his smock reads in earnest (we may assume that the large tome in front of him is the Bible), while his wife contentedly mends stockings, in so doing conforming to the ideal domestic role assigned to working-class women in the Victorian period already discussed. *Dawn and Sunset*, meanwhile, contrasts a woman with her baby – at the 'dawn' of life – with the elderly labourer in his smock at the 'sunset' of his. In both photographs, the association with the smock is one of a reassuring and harmonious cycle of life in which old age and longevity, and by implication, tradition and traditional occupations, are valued and respected; the smock has come to represent an ideal rural existence.

If Robinson idealized the cottage way of life, rather than reveal its harsh reality, he was very different from writers such as Thomas Hardy (Chapter 7).[43] His selection of particular garments to convey this vision is telling. In the case of the smock, it is not so much that it is represented out of its correct period (by the 1880s it would indeed have been mostly confined to the shoulders of old men, as it appears in the photograph *Dawn and Sunset*), but rather that it is now made a symbol of aspects of rural life – its traditions of hand-work and craft – that apparently belong to an age before the onset of mechanization. In the case of sun-bonnets, however, the connotations are more extreme. Robinson believed that these garments were quintessentially associated with the countryside, which explains why he dressed up his young

Fig. 5.6 *When the Day's Work is Done* (1877) by Henry Peach Robinson

models in them to the end of his working life, even when they were by then mostly worn by older women, if at all. The effect of Robinson's work is to attach a symbolism to items of rural working-class dress and to create a vision of 'traditional' country values and culture. In effect these images turn working, functional clothing (that had evolved to help the wearer perform his or her working role) into 'costume', thus attributing to it a different function: worn by 'models', it takes on a performative role for the enactment of authenticity and a particular interpretation of history and the past.

Elizabeth Edwards has debated the nature of photography and its role in the historical imagination of contemporaries, particularly the ways in which the medium could be 'harnessed as a form of collective cultural and historical memory for the benefit of the future'.[44] For example, the idea of the amateur photographic survey was first fully articulated in 1889 when W. Jeremy Harrison, a geologist, science schoolmaster and keen amateur photographer from the Midlands, read a paper at the Birmingham Photographic Society laying out the idea of a systematic photographic survey that would form an archive base for the future, with copies circulated to photographic societies and reprinted in the photographic press.[45] In the Photographic Record of Cambridgeshire, among the long list of subjects to be photographed, were ancient houses (especially cottages, farmsteads and barns), customs and ceremonies and relics of 'characteristic costume' (the sun-bonnet, print gown, smock and breeches).[46] These artefacts were intended to form part of the 'collective and historical memory' to which Edwards alludes. Finally, one further example to conclude this chapter illustrates the strong symbolism that was attached to clothing. The photographer James Leon Williams, in *The Home and Haunts of Shakespeare* (1892), 'aimed self-consciously to use photography and language' in his work to describe – these are his words – 'living links that bind the present to the past'.[47] Williams used an old man as a model in several photos, but returned to Stratford one year to learn that the old man had died. On the latter's death, Williams took comfort in three 'registers of remembrance', which included the bequest of the smock which the old man had worn.

6

CLOTHING AND THE 'COUNTER-MYTH' IN IMAGES OF RURAL ENGLAND

A picture of landscape appeals mainly to the primitive instincts of cultivated people, of people who live in cities, who look from the standpoint of civilization with a sentimental longing towards a more simple state.

(George Clausen, 'Lectures on Painting')[1]

While Henry Peach Robinson dominated the world of art photography in the late nineteenth century, there were other influential photographers expressing different philosophies and alternative approaches. Just as Robinson's images reference themes found also in the paintings of Helen Allingham and Myles Birket Foster (associated, as we have seen, with the sentimentalizing/idealizing 'cottage door' school of painting), the photography of Peter Henry Emerson (1856–1936) appears, at least on first sight, to have more in common with the work of exponents of a 'counter-myth'. Ostensibly offering a more realistic portrayal of Victorian rural life, Emerson's work can be compared to that of the painters Henry Herbert La Thangue (1859–1929) and George Clausen (1852–1944), with whom Emerson maintained close friendships. Together they form the focus of this chapter.

Unlike Robinson, who openly engaged in subterfuge in his pursuit of the picturesque, substituting the children of the gentry for poor children and dressing up his models in the (albeit genuine) articles of rural dress, Emerson attempted objectivity, even if he was ultimately unsuccessful in this endeavour. In more subtle ways than Robinson, he influenced the appearance of the Norfolk 'peasants', including how they were dressed for his photographs, and so exploited the meanings and symbolism that were increasingly being conferred on clothing in the representation of late Victorian rural life. With their accompanying commentaries, Emerson's photographs reveal his preoccupations, principally the desire to record and therefore preserve for posterity a vision of rural England immune to change.

PETER HENRY EMERSON AND 'TRUTH TO NATURE'

So Emerson's photographic record of Norfolk rural life can be paralleled with the paintings of Henry Herbert La Thangue, one of the best-known of British rural naturalist artists, whose paintings *The Return of the Reapers* (1886) and *The Shepherd* (c.1880–9) drew upon the aesthetics of photography. Emerson's training as a doctor, along with his interest in the arts (he admired the work of French artist Jean-François Millet and the British rural naturalist painters),[2] informed his belief that in photography were merged the methods and media of science and art.[3] Unlike Robinson, for whom artistic 'truth' was legitimately achieved through a combination of the real and the ideal (and the possibility of the incorporation of the artificial), Emerson believed in photography's role in conveying the principle of truth to nature, so rejecting Robinson's elaborate photographic constructions and theories as expounded in *Pictorial Effect in Photography*. One of Emerson's main arguments for naturalistic photography was that of differential focusing, whereby parts of the image are sharply focused and the rest less so (likewise, the human eye sees only one part of the subject it is viewing in sharp focus, while the rest of it is softened).[4] In his book *Naturalistic Photography* (1889), Emerson was thus implicitly denouncing the unnatural sharpness that characterized the photographs of Robinson.[5]

Emerson's theories are visualized in his photographs of the Norfolk landscape. Unlike the artificial constructions that are the hallmarks of Robinson's work, Emerson's images are peopled by labourers who appear more 'natural', thus offering a seemingly uncontrived representation of the Norfolk rural working classes. *Life and Landscape on the Norfolk Broads* (1886) is a fascinating visual record of aspects of rural life. Emerson and the little-known artist Thomas Frederick Goodall (1857–1944), an old schoolfriend of La Thangue, produced the photographs for *Life and Landscape*, and these were accompanied by a detailed account of what was happening in each picture,

Fig. 6.1 *Coming Home from the Marshes* (1886) by Peter Henry Emerson

the combination of image and words providing the reader with 'a complete Naturalistic experience'.[6] Emerson's focus on Norfolk rural life chronicles almost a whole decade, between 1886 and 1895: *Life and Landscape on the Norfolk Broads* was followed by *Idylls of the Norfolk Broads* (1886), *Pictures from Life in Field and Fen* (1888), *Pictures of East Anglian Life* (1888), *Wild Life on a Tidal Water* (1890), *On English Lagoons* (1893) and *Marsh Leaves* (1895).

Unlike the 'snapshot' approach adopted by George Clausen (discussed below), Emerson often spent several days finding a landscape, suggesting 'not only an educated eye but the considerable time and money that such sophistication requires'.[7] Rather than using middle- or upper-class models for his photographs, he actively sought the company of the local people who figure in his work, but at the same time he believed in a traditional rural hierarchy in which landlords, farmers and landless labourers each had their place in the order of things. Holding the tourist in contempt, he was opposed to the influx of the lower-middle classes into the countryside, setting himself up as a 'guardian of the old order'. His underlying motive was to 'preserve' the land 'in pictures and texts for the future'.[8]

Emerson had strong views on the clothing suitable for the villagers who were to appear in his photographs. In an article written for *Amateur Photographer* in 1886, he described how he persuaded a man and woman into

Fig. 6.2 *Haymaker with Rake* (1888) by Peter Henry Emerson

more appropriate clothing: from the village shop, 'the man came out in a hideous new hat, and the girl also was got up in the villagers' latest fashion. It was only after much talking and begging that they were persuaded to change and equip themselves in less pretentious manner, and then they were etched in silver, for better, for worse.'[9] Thus, while Emerson did not determine the clothing for his subjects in the manner adopted by Robinson, he clearly exerted a strong influence on 'choice' of attire to represent his idea of what rural life should be. Like an agreed code, clothing could do that more effectively and emotively perhaps than anything else. In his writing, Emerson often expressed the contrast between the corrupt town and the innocent countryside, presenting contrasting values through different clothing styles. In *On English Lagoons*, the story of two children and their respective spiritual sickness and health is told through descriptions of their bodies and clothes: the 'country-bred child [...] turned her dear, strong eyes curiously upon us for a moment [...] her dress swinging loosely and gracefully from her swelling hips'. By contrast, the 'town-bred girl' was 'clad in a bright red dress, all puffed and puckered, fantastically distorted to hide her ill-developed little body'.[10] The association of the countryside with tradition, health and authenticity and that of the town with fashion, sickliness and artificiality became familiar ones. As John Taylor observes in *A Dream of England*:

> When 'natives' began to look like townspeople, taking on the materi-alist values of the despised, urban classes, he [Emerson] was evidently shocked. By abandoning the appearance of authentic country peasants for modern dress, they had broken out of the distant time, untouched by history, where he had been used to placing them. Fashion could not exist in a society of caste and rank. When the 'natives' dressed in fashion, then the once clear signs of class (and class itself) had become confused. He begged them to dress in their everyday clothes, and not to change. When he fixed the peasants in time, he could demonstrate that the old values which supported him could still exist.[11]

So for all Emerson's insistence on photography's role in capturing 'truth to nature', his images are more complex, less objective than at first they might appear to be. We might ask whether such a project can ever be neutral: the county-record and county-survey photographers of the late nineteenth century, who recorded in a scientific way country landscapes and buildings for the benefit of posterity, were, in fact, 'concerned about ways of life which were vanishing: from their positions in the middle class, they regretted the disappearance of what they considered to be the quaint, unspoilt lifestyles of different and lower-class people.'[12] Their stated objective may have been to make a total and unbiased record illustrating the archaeology, architecture, landscape and scenery, ethnology, botany, geology and town life of the county, but a cursory look at diary accounts left by, for example, the photographers for the Warwickshire Photographic Survey (begun in 1890) reveals 'that the duty to survey according to the ideal "scientific" approach of record work was unrealizable':

> [The diaries] betray the impurity of the scheme, the fact that it was always tied to the surveyors' own ideological perspectives of what was 'quaint' or 'historical'. The 'claim' to objectivity was only ever a part of the 'rhetoric of discovery' and 'the picturesque was [...] used to reassure people that England was as beautiful as ever.[13]

THE INFLUENCE OF REALISM AND NATURALISM ON THE REPRESENTATION OF THE RURAL LABOURER

Agricultural landscape scenes of the late eighteenth and early nineteenth centuries had largely been bought by members of the aristocracy or gentry, but over the course of the nineteenth century buyers like the Mitchell family, who were the long-standing patrons of Henry Herbert La Thangue, were increasingly likely to have made their wealth in manufacturing and industry. The popularity of rural images among middle-class town-dwellers illustrates increasing polarization between country and town, and that the gaze on the country was that of the town. 'The countryside', observes Christiana Payne, 'was contrasted, not just with the corrupt city, but also with the new industrial towns, with their horrific living and working conditions and their irreligious and riotous populations.'[14] At the same time, while the tendency of agricultural landscape painting, up to and including the last quarter of the nineteenth century, had been towards a mythologized representation of the countryside and of rural work, alternative naturalistic interpretations were gradually being accepted, desired even, by the world of art criticism and by popular audiences. George Clausen,[15] and to a lesser extent Henry Herbert La Thangue, were the most successful exponents of the rural naturalist school; it is rare to see smocks or sunbonnets depicted in their work, and although their treatment of rural life is not straightforward, their landscapes and the labourers in them, and the latter's clothing, as we shall see, are strikingly different from the images considered up to this point.

The term 'naturalism' in art has been used since classical times in different ways, but it refers here to the depiction of actual, as opposed to imaginary or supernatural, subject matter, and suggests that the artist has attempted to observe and faithfully record the world rather than idealizing it. For the nineteenth century, the term describes best the work of the French artist Jules Bastien-Lepage (1848–84) and his followers. In England, Clausen and La Thangue questioned the traditional relationship between art and the representation of the countryside, just as Jean-François Millet had done in France, and their work came subsequently to characterize what has been described as a 'counter-myth' in the painting of agricultural landscape of the late nineteenth century.[16] Stronger in literature than in art, the counter-myth emphasized the hardships of the labourer's life and questioned some of the poetic illusions surrounding it. It veered away from what in 1856 the novelist

George Eliot referred to as 'the influence of idyllic literature [...] which has always expressed the imagination of the cultivated and town-bred, rather than the truth of rustic life'.[17] By the 1880s, when much of Clausen's most influential work was done, a significant body of literature, including, for example, the later novels of Thomas Hardy, questioned the rural stereotype, and in so doing focused on the daily reality of the agricultural labourer's life.

The work of the British rural naturalists owed a debt to a number of influences. Evolving naturally from the development of agricultural land-scape painting in England, it also represented a radical departure from the latter's idealizing tendencies and emphasized the relationship between the labourer, including his or her clothing, and the landscape that was the set-ting. It also emerged from the Pre-Raphaelite interest in close observation of the natural world, with the artist often working out-of-doors, return-ing to the same scene repeatedly if necessary – in the case of Ford Madox Brown's creation of *Pretty Baa Lambs* (1851), enduring the elements for five months – in order to achieve the desired detailed representation of the natural world and the requisite 'outdoor effect'. Perhaps of greater signifi-cance in this context than the Pre-Raphaelites, in terms both of subject mat-ter and the scale on which the human figure is represented, is the work of social realist artists, in particular, that of Frank Holl (1845–85), Luke Fildes (1843–1927) and Hubert von Herkomer (1849–1914). These artists docu-mented the lives of the contemporary urban, and sometimes rural, poor and paved the way for a more radical, more realist approach. Julian Treuherz has chronicled the ways in which poor people became subject matter for this new kind of art in the later nineteenth century: 'social conscience was combined with a documentary interest in accurate recording'; there was an attempt at 'an art which sought not just to represent things naturalisti-cally, but to depict the lowly and commonplace, correcting the historical bias in art towards the grand and spectacular; and social realism sought to do both in relation to modern social problems'.[18] Helping to disseminate social realist images, in a number of cases the illustrations that these artists undertook for the weekly news magazine the *Graphic* then became the basis for oil paintings shown at the Royal Academy. Nevertheless, consciously evading harshness and brutality, 'the subjects they didn't paint were perhaps as significant as those they did',[19] so that, still, choices were being made, and the result was not neutral.

French artists had a marked impact on changing attitudes to the rep-resentation of the rural labourer in England from the 1880s onwards. In the 1870s, Clausen painted works influenced strongly by Dutch genre scenes, and 'sub-Whistler portraits'.[20] In 1880, however, he saw exhibited in London's Grosvenor Gallery a collection of nine paintings by the leading French naturalist painter Jules Bastien-Lepage, whose controversial picture of resting haymakers, Les Foins (1878), in which the girl stares disconcertingly out of the canvas at the viewer, 'was to change Clausen's attitude to what he had been doing'.[21] Visiting London each summer from 1879 to 1882, Bastien-Lepage formed friendships with both Edward Burne-Jones and Clausen.[22] Although Clausen declared that he moved to Childwick Green, in Hertfordshire, because living was cheaper in the country, it is likely that he was partly motivated by the example of Bastien-Lepage, who had moved back to his native Damvillers in 1876 where he painted the inhabitants of the village and its environs, the work he produced before his premature death in 1884 having an enormous influence on the way British artists subsequently approached the subject of the rural labourer.

Bastien-Lepage's radical approach can be summarized as follows: he presents the labourer in monumental format and in a way that directly 'confronts' the spectator; his intense observation of the natural world is achieved by working en plein air; he acknowledges aspects of photography, including focusing on a near subject, usually the labourer, with distant objects or distant landscapes appearing out of focus.[23] Bastien-Lepage's work can be seen in the context of developments in French art over the preceding decades, in particular the realist movement with its insistence that art should reflect the contemporary world in an objective manner and that it should be 'of its time': 'Il faut être de son temps' became the rallying cry of the militant realist movement.[24] This emphasis on objectivity was an element of Bastien-Lepage's work expressly admired by Clausen, who commented in The Scottish Art Review in 1888: 'All his personages are placed before us in the most satisfying completeness, without the appearance of artifice, but as they live; and without comment, as far as possible, on the author's part.'[25] In his attempts to show through art the world 'as it really is', as well as in his choice of subject matter, Bastien-Lepage owed a particular debt to the work of Gustave Courbet (1819–77). The latter's treatment of unconventional topics, such as the funeral of a humble peasant presented on a monumental scale in his Burial at Ornans (1849–50), exhibited in 1851 in the Paris Salon, caused a furore, elevating as it did peasant life to a status previously reserved for historical, religious and classical subjects. Jean-François Millet (1814–75) was also a powerful influence: from a relatively prosperous peasant background himself, Millet moved to the village of Barbizon in the Forest of Fontainebleau, where he worked on paintings such as The Sower and The Winnower (1847–8), in which monumental peasant figures dwarf the landscape. These images are a far cry from the rural scenes of the late eighteenth and early nineteenth centuries, in which, as we have seen, the landscape generally dwarfs the figures. Although Clausen was strongly affected by the work of Bastien-Lepage in the 1880s, it was ultimately the work of Millet that had the most lasting influence on him. In the course of his lectures on painting delivered to art students at the Royal Academy, and speaking on the subject of 'Landscape and Open Air Painting', Clausen was to say that Millet presented 'the type and the action' while Bastien-Lepage's work represented 'the individual and his surroundings'. He pointed out that although 'the sentiment was the same, in this Millet was stronger'.[26] Consistent with this critique of the two French artists, Clausen also wrote that 'with Millet the interest always centres in the subject, in Lepage it centres in the individual'.[27]

Access to the work of French artists by British painters increased as a result of a number of factors: in 1853, the French Gallery opened in Pall Mall in London and held annual exhibitions of contemporary French artists, while the Franco–Prussian war of 1870–1 led to an influx of French art and artists into London. The French art dealer Paul Durand-Ruel (1831–1922) exiled himself in London where between 1870 and 1875 he held a total of ten exhibitions of French artists' work.[28] Not only did British artists have access to French art of the period in London, but many studied and worked in France: for example, La Thangue studied at the atelier of the successful French artist Jean-Léon Gerôme (1824–1904) in Paris in the early 1880s. He arrived in Paris when the reputation of Bastien-Lepage was probably at its height, spending his summers with his friend the artist Stanhope Forbes painting in artists' colonies in Brittany, such as Cancale (there were also well-established colonies in Concarneau, Pont Aven and Quimperlé), while in his later years he spent time in Provence, as well as in Italy and Spain. By this time it was, however, his quest for traditional scenes of rural life, increasingly difficult to find in England, that drove La Thangue abroad.[29] Clausen, meanwhile, who between 1873 and 1875 had won a scholarship to the National Art Training School (informally known as the South Kensington Schools because of its location), visited Holland and Belgium in 1875, studying briefly at the Royal Academy of Fine Arts in Antwerp; he then tried, unsuccessfully, to enter Gerôme's Paris atelier in 1876, but continued to make regular summer expeditions to the continent.

In the last two decades of the nineteenth century, artists were drawn to working in France in the belief that they would find there more 'traditional' peasant life – along with accompanying customs and clothing – than could by this time be seen in England. Helen Zimmern observed in *The Magazine of Art* in 1885:

> The English peasant, who has dropped such distinctive costume as he ever wore, and arrays himself instead in a shabby genteel imitation of his social superior, is far removed from the picturesque. But the foreign peasant has not yet doffed his national costume; he has still enough left of the proper pride that makes him prefer being well and appropriately dressed in his own sphere to being shabbily and inappropriately costumed out of it; and though a tendency to cast aside national costume is increasing in those portions of the continent infested by the tourist, the movement is far from universal.[30]

Such observations – that English labourers had cast aside traditional styles that marked them out as being 'distinctive' in favour of 'a shabby genteel imitation' of their social superiors – was a common one, similar comments being made by Thomas Hardy in his essay 'The Dorsetshire Labourer' (Chapter 7).

Not surprisingly, clothing was an important consideration in monumental images of labourers, occupying as it did a considerable area of the canvas as well as constituting part of their picturesqueness: in the artists' colonies of Brittany painters were attracted not least by the traditional dress still worn by many Breton peasants. Although change was also taking place in France, it was less rapid than across the Channel. George Thomson articulated the motivation of artists like La Thangue who spent much of their time working in France, observing: 'The clothing of the country people too frequently comes from the towns; but nevertheless they in their varied occupations afford an abundance of picturesque material to one who looks for it.'[31] In England, on the other hand, there was little in the rural wardrobe by the 1880s and 1890s that could be said to constitute part of a 'folk' culture. For all their claims about objectivity and realism, British artists' interest in painting French labourers in their 'picturesque' traditional dress, rather than their own countrymen dressed up in tacky fashionable clothes borrowed from the towns, shows how firmly rooted, but also how problematic, had become the notion that 'traditional' rural clothing was the manifestation of an authentic rural culture.

Just as the legacy of Bastien-Lepage and Millet was profound in relation to the representation of the French 'peasant', so also was their influence on the work of the British rural naturalist artists. Clausen did for the English rural labourer what Bastien-Lepage and Millet achieved in the French context. And even if he did not afford rural labour the heroic status and dignity we see in Millet's work, Clausen's figures always appear to dominate the landscape, often confront the spectator directly, and usually impart details of some aspect of their working life. Not only are labour and occupation frequently represented, but during the 1880s when Clausen was under the influence of Bastien-Lepage and photography – relatively short-lived though that period was – the rendering of details of the clothing of his subjects represents a radical departure from the mostly small-scale, partial and frequently idealized representations of rural working-class dress so far discussed.

DRESS IN THE WORK OF GEORGE CLAUSEN

So pervasive was the image of the landscape and its yeomanry, and so central was this painter to the visual reading of English fields that he became the voice for the aims and ideals of an entire generation of British artists.
(Kenneth McKonkey, *George Clausen and the Picture of English Rural Life*)[32]

We have considered how some artists and photographers saw in the depiction of particular clothing the potential for perpetuating a sense of tradition during a period of rapid change. But, unlike Helen Allingham's paintings of the 1880s, where young boys and women are, respectively, dressed in smocks and sun-bonnets, neither garment is seen with any frequency in the paintings of George Clausen or Henry Herbert La Thangue, where they are worn exclusively by elderly labourers. A smock is worn by an old man in Clausen's *The Villager* (1882) and in La Thangue's *The Shepherd* (c.1880–9: see colour plate 7), while Clausen's *An Old Woman* (1887) wears a sun-bonnet. The sitters appear to have held on to the familiar styles of their youth but, as in Robinson's photographs *When the Day's Work is Done* (1877) and *Dawn and Sunset* (1885), smocks worn by old men have become symbols, representing tradition and longevity.

Often praised for his objectivity and realism in the representation of the rural labourer, according to *The Magazine of Art* in 1881–2 Clausen 'shows us a little company of the poor not in picturesque rags but in garments of fact, gleaning modern English fields'.[33] A *Times* critic wrote of his work retrospectively, in 1928: 'Poetical realism, irrespective of subject, is perhaps the best general description of the character prevailing in Sir George Clausen's work.'[34] So did Clausen depict labourers in the 'garments of fact', rather than in the garments of the past, or of his own imagination? Of course, this is difficult to answer definitively, but the question can be discussed fruitfully with reference to the influences upon, and sources for, Clausen's work. With the exceptions noted above, Clausen rarely chose to clothe his labourers either in garments associated with an idealized past or, alternatively, in the 'picturesque rags' seen in paintings of a century earlier, such as Gainsborough's *Cottage Girl with Dog and Pitcher*. Rather what we see in his work of the 1880s are observations from life combined with some artistic borrowings from Jules Bastien-Lepage.

Just as Bastien-Lepage had moved to Damvillers, a rural village in northeastern France, in 1881 Clausen moved to the Hertfordshire village of Childwick Green, approximately 25 miles from his London birthplace. (La Thangue, who came from a comfortable middle-class background, made a similar move away from London, settling at Bosham, a fishing village on Chichester Harbour in West Sussex.) At about the same time, Clausen also bought a 1½-inch-square-plate camera and began to take a number of 'snapshots' of the labourers working on the surrounding farms (Figs 6.3–6.9). Considered to be among the earliest un-posed photographs of labourers at work in the fields, these extraordinary images supported rather than replaced sketches done by the artist on the spot.[35] The use of both sketches and photographs in this way imitated the methods of the French naturalist painters.[36]

The Royal Academy of Arts in London has among its collections some wonderful figure studies by Clausen entitled simply 'St Alban's Peasants'. It is fascinating to compare his drawings and photographs with the paintings he did at around the same time. Of particular note is the woman in the photograph *Woman in a Turnip Field* (Fig. 6.3) who reappears – down to the last detail of her clothing – in *December* (colour plate 8), the latter used as a *plein-air* study for *Winter Work* (1883). In *The Stone Pickers* (colour plate 9), the same woman appears, stooping at her work in the background on the right. By searching local records, Anna Gruetzner Robins has linked this woman to one of Clausen's figure studies, annotated 'Susan Chapman, 60'. The 1881 census identifies Susan as living alone in Childwick Green and lists her as a straw-plaiter, although this cannot necessarily be used as a reliable guide to her sole occupation: we have seen how field labour at this time was often temporary, marginal work. In April, when the census was taken, few women would have been working in the fields, but when they did they continued to do back-breaking tasks like pulling, topping and tailing mangolds or turnips, stone-picking, hoeing and weeding, just as we see in the photographs.[37]

In each image the woman (Susan) appears to be wearing a rough, working dress underneath a man's coat; a large apron; a checked (tartan) shawl; hat (not a 'picturesque' sun-bonnet!) and heavy boots. Clausen, observes

Fig. 6.3 *Woman in a Turnip Field* by George Clausen

Anna Gruetzner Robins, has here 'followed the precepts of French naturalism in recording the details of her clothing with meticulous care'.[38] If comparison is made between the depiction of the apron in the photograph with that in *December*, it is clear that Clausen has introduced some artistic licence by making the hem frayed and uneven (similarly the hem on the male labourer's jacket). Clausen used this method frequently at this period: see, for example, *The Stone Pickers* and *Ploughing* (colour plates 9 and 10). The effect was probably achieved by painting with a square, flat brush, a technique also adopted by La Thangue and reportedly used by Bastien-Lepage. According to *The Scottish*

Fig. 6.4 *Man and Woman Stone Picking* by George Clausen

Art Review (1889), 'those who practise it in its simplest form leave the brush-marks, and do not smooth away the evidence of method.'[39]

A comparison between the techniques of Clausen and Bastien-Lepage can be made by looking more closely at Clausen's *The Stone Pickers* and Bastien-Lepage's well-known image, *Pauvre Fauvette* (1881). 'If Bastien-Lepage's influence upon Clausen were to be condensed into a single image,' suggests Kenneth McConkey, 'that image would surely be *The Stone Pickers*.'[40] Peyton Skipworth explains how *Pauvre Fauvette* was one of the few paintings by Bastien-Lepage exhibited in London rather than in Paris. It thus 'became a key picture in terms of its influence on British painting, both in subject matter and technique'.[41] The similarities are particularly close in respective representations of fabric. The piece of sackcloth worn as an apron by the girl in *The Stone Pickers* is similar to that worn as a large shawl by the girl in *Pauvre*

Fig. 6.5 *Man Stone Picking* by George Clausen

Fauvette. Some contemporaries saw the resemblances between the two artists' work as unacceptable. For example, in 1887 Sir James Linton wrote of the British rural naturalists:

> The outward imitation is often so close that the style of costume is adhered to as much as possible without making it altogether incorrect [...] The light and shade, the key of colour, the general character impress the spectator as belonging to Normandy not to England – that is the Normandy essentially of Millet, of Breton, of Bastien-Lepage.[42]

Fig. 6.6 *Man Hoeing* by George Clausen

Nevertheless, Clausen may in fact have been depicting reality: for a worker to turn a sack into an apron (by tying it round the waist with a piece of string) for the purpose of collecting stones was a cheap way of making a useful garment. The young boy in *Ploughing* (1889) also wears a makeshift garment; there are similarities between this picture and Bastien-Lepage's *Pauvre Fauvette* in terms of subject matter, clothing and artistic technique. Some years earlier, the 1867 parliamentary commissioners referred to women in Culham in Oxfordshire engaged in spudding thistles, 'dressed in men's coats with shawls over and guano sacks as aprons'.[43] The image described is remarkably similar to Clausen's *Woman in a Turnip Field*.

Significantly, the dress of the girl in *The Stone Pickers* – a plain, pale-blue gown with tightly fitting bodice fastened down the front and a small collar – is similar in style to the blue-and-white checked dress worn by Clausen's model, his family's nursemaid Polly Baldwin, in the well-known painting *The Girl at the Gate* (1889), and the pale-pink one worn by La Thangue's female model in *The Return of the Reapers* (1886). Each of the girls in the latter two paintings wears a white apron, and the bodices of all three gowns are strikingly similar in style to a rare cotton printed bodice kept at the Gallery of English Costume at Platt Hall, Manchester (cat. no 1960/228) and thought to have

Fig. 6.7 *Farm Labourer* by George Clausen

belonged to a farm labourer (Chapter 8). A further example of this style of simple bodice is worn in Clausen's painting *A Girl's Head* (colour plate 11).

In contrast to such soft pastel shades, in Clausen's *December*, the colours of the clothing worn by the woman, like that of the male labourer to her left, are of natural brown and muted tones, mirroring the colours of the winter landscape. Her male companion wears jacket, trousers, loose leggings, heavy boots and a hat. The only colourful addition is a red cravat worn round his neck. McConkey suggests that the use of red contrasted with the rest of the clothes is employed as artistic device: 'Clausen has worked out the essential

Fig. 6.8 *Man Hoeing* by George Clausen

colour harmonies. The dramatic red handkerchief around the neck [...] helps to throw the muted tones of the rest of the picture into relief.'[44] The young boy in *Ploughing* also wears one, just visible beneath his makeshift 'jacket'. While Clausen was undoubtedly aware of the artistic merits of adding this splash of colour to otherwise muted tones, a number of red neckerchiefs survive at the Museum of English Rural Life, University of Reading, revealing that they were not figments of the artistic imagination.

A number of Clausen's paintings of the 1880s were not at first well received by the critics: *Winter Work* remained unsold after it was first

Fig. 6.9 *Two Men Hoeing* by George Clausen

exhibited. Clausen later added to the scene of unremitting toil a young girl with a hoop, perhaps, points out Christiana Payne, 'in an attempt to make the painting less of a stark comment on rural hardship and to suggest a family group'.[45] Gruetzner Robins identifies the young girl with her satchel as a schoolgirl.[46] Clausen's paintings of the early 1880s with 'their ageing figures in bulky, inelegant clothing, engaged in monotonous tasks in bleak landscapes […] offer a striking contrast to the lively, sunny, harvest fields of earlier and even contemporary artists'.[47] However, by the end of the decade Clausen had abandoned this style of realism, possibly in response to unfavourable comments from patrons. And by December 1884 he had also abandoned his plan of living the simple country life and was resident in St Albans, shortly after this moving to Cookham Dene in Berkshire before later settling in Essex. Clausen's images of Susan Chapman as a field worker had contradicted the acceptable and picturesque view of rural life that is represented in the work of Birket Foster, Allingham, Robinson and, to some degree, Emerson. His work represents a much starker view of the country-side than we have seen hitherto. However, if we expect to see unremittingly realist images of the countryside then we will be disappointed. The period from the 1880s represents something of a transition, perhaps, but the ideal-ization of the countryside and of rural life remains a constant and persistent thread right through the nineteenth century and beyond.

By the 1890s, both Clausen and La Thangue were becoming more inter-ested in impressionist techniques, and the labourer was depicted in a more generalized way than in the previous decade. For example, *The Mowers* (1891), which was a re-working of a watercolour of 1885 on the same theme, reflects this shift of emphasis and the changing priorities in Clausen's art, in which the play of sunlight and shade on the folds of the workers' white shirts and natural-coloured trousers is more significant than the details of seams and patches or the laces on shoes. This impressionistic manner of depicting the clothing of his subjects seemed more desirable now than rendering its detail; Clausen, it would appear, was increasingly preoccupied by atmosphere and action.[48] George Moore's comparison between Stanhope Forbes's *Forging the Anchor* (1892) and Clausen's *The Mowers* (exhibited at the Royal Academy the same year) pays attention to the artists' different treatment of clothing, and goes further in dismissing the clothing itself as uninteresting: 'Mr Clausen [...] overcame the difficulty of trousers by generalization. Mr Stanhope Forbes copied the trousers seam by seam, patch by patch; and the ugliness of the garment bores you in the picture, exactly as it would in nature.'[49] The art world did not require precise details of working dress.

But Clausen was not losing interest in his subject matter; rather, he was using different techniques to determine how his subject would be repre-sented. Two paintings with the same theme but painted in different decades and styles serve to demonstrate this point admirably: *Bird Scaring* (1887) and *Bird Scaring – March*, painted nine years later (1896). Apart from the large piece of fabric draped and tied round the boy's neck and worn over the jacket in the later painting, the items of individual clothing worn by the boy are almost identical in both pictures: brown jacket and trousers, red cravat, leggings or gaiters and heavy boots. Both paintings illustrate what a working-class boy engaged in such an occupation would have worn in the 1880s and 1890s. However, in the earlier painting, the details of the garments are clearly delineated, from the buttons on the waistcoat and tears in the pocket of the jacket down to the pieces of string tied round the make-shift leggings (made from strips of fabric) and the laces and eyelets on the boots. But no such detail is visible in the later painting. The earlier painting is incidentally more useful as a record, in terms of the clothing detail it portrays, but this is a consequence of the artist's technique and of what was considered acceptable, desirable and saleable.

La Thangue and Clausen both had their loyal patrons throughout the 1880s and 1890s. One of Clausen's was Sharpely Bainbridge (the founder of the chain of department stores, Bainbridge Ltd, and a Lincoln JP), who purchased The Mowers. La Thangue's The Return of the Reapers was bought by the Mitchell family, wealthy Bradford industrialists. The change in direction by both artists may have been determined partly by the venues at which their work could be exhibited. In the 1880s, both had become supporters of the New English Art Club, founded largely by naturalist artists who had trained and worked in France and who wanted to establish a system of exhibitions along French lines in which paintings were selected by a vote of all exhibiting artists rather than, as at the Royal Academy, by a select committee. The first show of the New English Art Club was opened on 12 April 1886, with 50 members exhibiting 58 pictures and two sculptures. Clausen showed The Shepherdess (1885). He also exhibited his work at the Grosvenor Gallery, though this closed at the end of 1890. Reconsidering his position in relation to the Royal Academy in the late 1890s, Clausen was elected an associate. Appointed Professor of Painting at the Royal Academy Schools in 1903, he delivered his first lectures to large audiences the following year. So, having adopted a radical approach to painting in his early career, he thus became part of the art establishment.

The representation of the rural labourer in the nineteenth century, along with the clothing depicted, not only varied according to artist or photographer, but, as exemplified by the work of Clausen, it also changed over time in response to the artist's own development and changing tastes and evolving markets and/or patrons. The public, whether members of the aristocracy or of the new middle classes, who purchased these paintings helped shape the representation of the rural. As Karen Sayer observes, 'their influence was unconscious, but effective nonetheless; they belonged to the discourse of art as much as the artists themselves.'[50] In the case of the celebratory paintings of the harvest referred to in Chapter 4, these can be considered in the light of fear of social disorder and anxiety in response to the changing economic role of the Victorian countryside. By the 1870s and 1880s, the idealizing and mythologizing of the countryside, and the desire to record remnants of a vanishing world, its villages and cottages and artefacts, including clothes, is evident in the images discussed over the past three chapters. In particular, we have seen how the representation of the rural past, where depictions of setting and people and the work they did and the clothes they wore could be employed, and re-interpreted, like a dying language that is used less and less, and less and less 'accurately'; that representation was never going to be neutral. These images helped to perpetuate the traditions, albeit mostly in people's imagination, that were being threatened by the joint forces of urbanization and the slow decline in the economic role of agriculture. But as David Matless has observed, 'even that which seems most obviously nostalgic and conservative, turns out to have a complexity, either through exhibiting non-nostalgic/conservative traits, or, because neither nostalgia nor conservatism are simple phenomena.'[51] And conversely that which might seem radical contains nostalgic or contrary elements, as exemplified by the work of Emerson.

So here is one aspect of the complexity of signification of the work of art. On one level the paintings of George Clausen and, to a lesser extent, Henry Herbert La Thangue, along with the photographs of Emerson, seem to stand out as uniquely realist in terms of the labour represented and the clothing worn. For Clausen, it has been argued that 'in identifying with the peasant, he was examining the very roots of Englishness'.[52] His interest in the truth afforded to the image by the influence of photography, both as a general attitude in his work but specifically in the snapshots at Childwick Green, takes us perhaps as near as we will ever get to an objective view of the countryside and its workers in Victorian England. But of course, such objectivity is not straightforward or without complexity: Clausen's work of the 1880s can be seen as a working-out in the English context of the ideals of Bastien-Lepage. And neither is photography an objective medium of representation. The paintings and photographs discussed here are in fact valuable both for what they reveal, for what they distort, and for what they obscure, and what is learnt as a result of close study resides somewhere in the margins between the known and unknown. This negotiated no-mans-land between past representation and present understanding is a theme for the following chapter.

7

THOMAS HARDY
Tradition, fashion and the approach of modernity

> How dry it was on a far-back day
> When straws hung the hedge and around,
> When amid the sheaves in amorous play
> In curtained bonnets and light array
> Bloomed a bevy now underground!
> (Thomas Hardy, 'At Middle-Field
> Gate in February')[1]

Not surprisingly, parallels were drawn by their contemporaries between the representations of 'peasants' in the writing of the novelist and poet Thomas Hardy (1840–1928) and those in the paintings of rural naturalist artists, Clausen in particular.[2] In a review of Clausen's retrospective exhibition at Barbizon House in 1928 (the year that Hardy died), Hardy and Clausen were compared directly by a critic in *The Times*: 'It is very seldom pure landscape that Sir George Clausen paints, but nearly always landscape in relation to human labour, or rest from it, rather on the lines of Thomas Hardy in literature, but with a more cheerful acceptance of the common lot.'[3] Elsewhere Clausen was described as 'the Thomas Hardy of Painting'.[4] Both the writer and the artist recreated in their depictions the haunting beauty of people seen labouring in an often bleak yet lovely, and in many cases disappearing, landscape; these images evoked the contradictions between the brutality and the dignity of human labour in close proximity to the soil, and were especially poignant when viewed as part of a way of life that was vanishing as increasing numbers of rural dwellers moved to towns and cities or went into domestic service.

In *The Return of the Native*, Hardy makes Egdon Heath – an area, near the county town of Dorchester, that is both realistically and figuratively created in the novel – the setting for the action. Having himself returned from a very different environment, the rapidly expanding metropolis of London, Hardy in his late thirties saw in Egdon the stability of his childhood. *The Return of the Native* is set in the 1840s when, beyond this tract of Dorset, England, as we know, was already undergoing rapid change, but whether the narrator, in contemplating the landscape of Egdon, is doing so from the perspective of the 1840s, when the novel is set, or that of the late 1870s, when it was published, the heath is the same, while change, just over the horizon, is unstoppable:

> To recline on a stump of thorn in the central valley of Egdon, between afternoon and night, as now, where the eye could reach nothing of the world outside the summits and shoulders of heathland which filled the whole circumference of its glance, and to know that everything around and underneath had been from prehistoric times as unaltered as the stars overhead, gave ballast to the mind adrift on change, and harassed by the irrepressible New.[5]

Read as a series alongside his other writings in prose and verse, Hardy's Wessex novels constitute 'a profound analysis as well as an unrivalled representation of nineteenth-century rural life and landscape'.[6] Perhaps uniquely placed, as a 'native' of Dorset who had 'returned', to observe the changes in the agricultural world that are narrated so intricately in his writing, Hardy is sometimes labelled as 'nostalgic' and 'pessimistic'. However, such judgements oversimplify the complexity of his position in relation to a past, a present and a future in which he seems to have struggled to balance the competing claims of two ideas to which he often referred – 'progress' versus 'picturesqueness'. These diametrically opposed concepts operate as a dialectic in his work, particularly from the 1880s.

In his final novel, *Jude the Obscure*, we see this tension played out in Jude's restlessness – in his literal wanderings in geographical terms and his frustration because of limitations imposed by his own past and by society in its hindering of equal educational opportunity, social mobility and freedom in marital and sexual relations. Writing about Edward Thomas in *The Old Ways*, Robert Macfarlane has observed that 'modernity's most distinctive tensions would be between mobility and displacement on the one hand, and dwelling and belonging on the other – with the former becoming ubiquitous and the latter becoming lost (if ever it had been possible) and reconfigured as nostalgia. He [Thomas] experienced that tension between roaming and homing even as it was first forming [...] "It is hard to make anything like a truce between these two incompatible desires," Thomas wrote in 1909, "the one for going on and on over the earth, the other that would settle for ever in one place, as in a grave and have nothing to do with change."'[7] Thomas seems to have penetrated to the heart of his own dilemma, and perhaps also of Hardy's.

CLOTHING IN FICTION

'Why', asks dress historian Anne Buck, 'should we turn to fiction when we have fact?' Buck's response to the question she sets at the beginning of a reflective article is that a novel can give 'factual and descriptive evidence', but also, 'where dress is used to express character and illuminate social attitudes and relationships, it can give more. It then shows dress in action within the novelist's world.' Furthermore, 'the novelist's evidence may reveal the influences and ways of life which are expressed through dress.'[8] A number of scholars have since explored the role played by dress within the novel itself as a text, and as a means of furthering understanding of the culture and society in which it was written or in which it is set, or both. For example, Clair Hughes says of her exploration of dress in the work of novelists of the eighteenth and nineteenth centuries, including Daniel Defoe, William Thackeray, George Eliot and Henry James: 'My intention is not to prove that dress is the hidden key to all the mysteries of these texts, but to show how an exploration of dress and its accessories can illuminate the structure of that text, its values, its meanings or its symbolic pattern.'[9] To this I would add that a novel highlights 'unspoken assumptions and attitudes towards dress which exist within the society for which the author is writing'.[10]

Reading fiction as history perhaps blurs the traditional boundaries of historical knowledge. While acknowledging challenges encountered in close reading and analysis of literary texts, Daniel Roche proposes in his study of dress and fashion in the *ancien régime* that we should accept the meaning delivered by the texts, since, like the artist, 'the novelist provides information about ways of life because he places objects in a context, so conferring on them a different truth from that discovered by the deciphering of archives [...] fiction achieves authentic effects both by the truth of the descriptions and by their location within a history which has a logic which reveals forms of reasoning and structures of the imagination of an age.'[11] This chapter explores the potential of Hardy's novels, and, to a lesser extent, his poetry, in enabling a deeper understanding of clothing in Victorian society.[12] It considers the ways in which Hardy's views enable us to negotiate past representation and present understanding. Elsewhere I discuss Hardy's descriptions of modes of dress in relation to visual material, including relevant photographs and surviving garments in museums, in order to attempt to confirm those descriptions in relation to actual clothing.[13] But here I explore the ways in which we can use fictional literature in its own right, taking into account meanwhile the agendas that lie on or beneath the surface of the texts. Like leitmotifs in a musical composition, Hardy's preoccupations were frequently veiled in references to clothing.

From the perspective of literary studies, Simon Gatrell has discussed the wide range of functions performed by clothing in Hardy's novels, short stories and poetry. His analysis includes themes such as the interconnections between dress, body and sexuality, the gendering of dress and cross-dressing and the symbolism of colour in clothes and dress conventions relating to death. Gatrell argues that the relationship of dress to identity 'is perhaps the one Hardy addresses with most persistence throughout his writing'.[14] For Gatrell, 'reading [*Jude the Obscure*] through dress brought into focus aspects of what Hardy achieved in it that I could have seen in no other way; it changed my understanding of the whole work.'[15] Clothing can thus denote much more than outward appearance: of *The Mayor of Casterbridge*, J. B. Bullen writes: 'Within the text, the discussion of fashions, the numerous references to details of dress, and the persistent allusions to the sartorial appearance of other characters act as a constant reminder to the reader that clothing here has a significance which lies beyond appearances.'[16] Hardy's responses are to a society in rapid transition from one broadly characterized by rural values to an increasingly urban culture – which for us, as twenty-first century readers, is so much more familiar than the one that it replaced.

A DISCOURSE OF CHANGE

In 'Domicilium', thought to be one of his very first poems, Hardy describes the cottage in Higher Bockhampton, near Dorchester, where he was born on 2 June 1840, and where he spent the formative years of his life. About half-way through the poem, he recalls walking with his paternal grandmother, asking her what the landscape was like when she and Hardy's grandfather first settled there. Her response – 'Fifty years / Have passed since then, my child, and change has marked / The face of all things'[17] – seems to form the context for much of Hardy's later writing. Indeed, the fact that Hardy was born a short distance from Tolpuddle a few years after the deportation of farm labourers who had come together to form a trades union (Chapter 1) should remind us, as Raymond Williams observes, that Hardy was born into 'a changing and struggling rural society, rather than the timeless backwater to which he is so often deported':

> The Hardy country is of course Wessex: that is to say mainly Dorset and its neighbouring counties. But the real Hardy country, we soon come to see, is that border country so many of us have been living in: between custom and education, between work and ideas, between love of place and an experience of change. There can be no doubt at all of Hardy's commitment to his own country, and in a natural way to its past, as we can see in his naming of Wessex. But his novels, increasingly, are concerned with change.[18]

Extending over the boundaries, as they are configured today, of nine counties, and embracing a rich variety of countryside, from coast to bare upland to sheltered and fertile vales, Wessex is, in fact, a rural microscosm, and so it can be said that Hardy's writings 'constitute the most important comprehensive presentation in literature of the nineteenth century countryside'.[19] The settings and/or publication dates for Hardy's best-known works, including *Under the Greenwood Tree* (1872), *Far from the Madding Crowd* (1874), *The Return of the Native* (1878), *The Mayor of Casterbridge* (1886), *The Woodlanders* (1887), *Tess of the d'Urbervilles* (1891) and *Jude the Obscure* (1896), cover almost the entire Victorian period. The exception is the historical novel *The Trumpet Major*, set in the period of the Napoleonic wars. The earlier novels, *Under the Greenwood Tree* and *Far from the Madding Crowd*, are noticeably retrospective and sometimes nostalgic in tone and often seem to refer to the period of Hardy's childhood, whereas his later novels, *Tess of the d'Urbervilles* and *Jude the Obscure*, engage with contemporary issues of the 1880s and 1890s and the complex consequences of agricultural, economic and social change that have been discussed over the course of preceding chapters.

In *Tess of the d'Urbervilles*, Hardy recreates the precariousness of the living conditions of agricultural labourers, their insecurity of tenure and their starvation wages, and the encroachment of machinery into traditional rural tasks. In *Jude the Obscure* he chronicles the incessant search for home, and its shifting physical and psychological parameters as a result of the dissolution of traditional village communities in favour of urbanism and suburbanism. But not only was this restlessness the result of new work patterns and of the slow decline of agricultural employment; it was also a symptom of changing social aspirations and the quest for education. Hardy articulated here more forcefully than hitherto the tensions between traditional values and the shock of the new. In his ostensibly factual essay 'The Dorsetshire Labourer' (1883), he pitched picturesque notions of traditional village life against its reality, alongside the dawning prospects offered to agricultural labourers by modernity with its potential for education and 'mental equality':

> The artistic merit of their old condition is scarcely a reason why they should have continued in it when other communities were marching on so vigorously towards uniformity and mental equality. It is only the old story that progress and picturesqueness do not harmonize. They are losing their individuality but they are widening the range of their ideas, and gaining in freedom. It is too much to expect them to remain stagnant and old-fashioned for the pleasure of romantic spectators.[20]

One of Hardy's biographers, Michael Millgate, reflects that Hardy in his mature years was rarely tempted to indulge in indiscriminate nostalgia for the past: 'He was always deeply conscious, however, of the process of change itself and of the many relics, good and bad, of earlier days and ways which were constantly being swept away.'[21] This tension between the desire for stability and a personal remembered past on the one hand and the witnessing and experiencing of change on the other preoccupied Hardy, just as it did contemporaries like George Millin (in the *Daily News* survey of 1891).

But it is the *perception* of change that is all-important here. Chronicling shifting styles of non-élite clothing is difficult, but correlating the casting off of older styles and the adoption of new ones with broader social change can offer a new perspective on the past. Hardy understood the strong physical, aesthetic and symbolic qualities of clothing, and could express the tensions created as the countryside, where change had always been slow and the way of life seemed permanent, was increasingly subjected to the influence of urban culture. And he describes real working-class dress and its significance in Victorian society. Janus-like, Hardy surveyed the past as well as the future, offering fascinating perspectives on faltering steps towards modernity, demonstrating, observes Andrew Radford, an 'abiding interest in remaking the parochial past; rendering it coterminous with the modern moment as well as a foretaste of the future'.[22]

In his 1912 General Preface to the Wessex Edition of the novels, Hardy states: 'At the dates represented in the various narrations things were like that in Wessex: the inhabitants lived in certain ways, engaged in certain occupations, kept alive certain customs, just as they are shown doing in these pages [...] I have instituted inquiries to correct tricks of memory, and striven against temptations to exaggerate, in order to preserve for my own satisfaction a fairly true record of a vanishing life.'[23] Of course we cannot accept, unquestioningly, everything Hardy wrote about the rural society he observed or ignore the potential pitfalls of citing a novel or poem when seeking in them a more nuanced narrative of the history of dress. Susan Pearce argues that 'the distinction between narrative as "historical" writing, which claims to "tell the truth about the past", and narrative which is "fiction", like a novel or a poem, becomes increasingly flimsy the harder it is looked at.' Rather, 'both are equally "true" in the sense that they set out a view of the human social past as conceived by the writer in his day.'[24]

Hardy, writes Merryn Williams, was 'the first writer to achieve the necessary range and realism of the novel of English country life'.[25] The historian Keith Snell, on the other hand, rejects in the main 'the accounts which stress Hardy's originality as lying in his "realism" and social verisimilitude', questioning the methodology that uses literary texts without caution:

Social historians traditionally have been dependent on various forms of literary evidence, but have made virtually no attempts to set the bounds to what a writer may know and be able to express of his society and its social structure: to understand in what areas his knowledge is likely to be limited, occluded or distorted, and for what reasons. Nor is it always appreciated that some literary texts cannot be forced to yield information or 'evidence' that they do not intend, and are unable of themselves to give.[26]

Snell is severe in his criticism of the over-reliance by social historians on literary sources without 'independent confirmation from other sources and a defined or properly limited social focus'. Rather, he calls for an approach that 'cross-verifies' quantitative and empirical evidence with literary statement, exploring the 'specific "questions" to which a literary work was [...] addressed', the 'senses in which the work formed a dialogue with its own history'.[27] However, even if 'Hardy by-passed many of the important but transient rural issues of his day,' Snell argues that, in his 'choice of signification, and in his artistic emphasis on problems of personal alienation and marital estrangement', he was 'firmly embedded in and responsive to the social history of the period':[28] and his personal response to what he witnessed is part of that history.

RURAL DRESS, 'FASHION' AND THE URBAN

In the novels, Hardy often uses a description of clothing to set a scene or provide a contemporary or historical context. Descriptions of garments and accessories are also employed for characterization, and to emphasize either individuality or adherence to convention, to denote occupation or relate the latter to mental state and mood.[29] In *Tess of the d'Urbervilles* (1891), for example, Tess's optimism and well-being at Talbothays (a dairy farm) are contrasted with her mental suffering and physical degradation later at Flintcomb-Ash (an arable farm). Hardy is exploiting a common perception of the differences in status and clothing in relation to occupation. As a dairymaid at idyllic Talbothays, Tess wears 'picturesque' clothing, but having been deserted by her husband, she becomes a poverty-stricken 'field woman' at 'starve-acre' Flintcomb Ash. Surely the metaphorical and symbolic import of Hardy's respective locations for Tess's story would not have been lost on his readers in the economic context of the novel's setting – Dorset in the 1880s. Hardy was not especially interested in shifts in fashionable dress *per se* and 'didn't put changes in fashion to much significant work in his writing'.[30] But if we pay close attention to clothing references over the body of his work as a whole, and take into account the dates at which individual novels are set, we will see that he often narrated change by referring to clothing.

In the novels set during the period that was in fact Hardy's own childhood and early adulthood (the 1840s and 1850s), *Under the Greenwood Tree* and *Far from the Madding Crowd*, clothing is relatively static in style, Hardy observing that 'Five decades hardly modified the cut of a gaiter, the embroidery of a smock-frock, by the breadth of a hair.'[31] He describes 'snow-white smock-frocks, embroidered upon the shoulders and breasts in ornamental forms of hearts, diamonds and zig-zags'.[32] Of the labourers on Bathsheba Everdene's farm coming to receive their wages, 'some were, as usual, in snow-white smock-frocks of Russia duck, and some in whitey-brown ones of drabbet – marked on the wrists, breasts, backs and sleeves in honeycomb work.'[33] Fine linen ('Russia duck') and, in particular, drabbet (a coarser, twilled fabric, either of cotton, or a cotton and linen mixture) were the usual fabrics used for smocks in the period. Hardy had first-hand knowledge of traditional smocks, including those worn by his father; in 1918, he lent his father's working smocks to the boys in the 'Mellstock' cast, a group of local amateur players, for a production based on *Under the Greenwood Tree*.[34]

In those of his later novels that are set in the latter decades of the nineteenth century, Hardy refers to change by chronicling the replacing of one style of clothing with another, a process which he saw occurring over the course of his own lifetime, following, as he thought, a long period of stability. Clearly his own personal preference was for 'traditional' rural life, which he associated with the time of his childhood before the onset of change that he experienced in his adult years. It is as if the period of Hardy's childhood – and even the period preceding it about which he learnt from his grandmother – became the measure against which later experience was gauged, symptomatic perhaps of the natural tendency to look back nostalgically to one's formative years. Hardy thus viewed the evolution of styles of clothing and fabric as part of broader, far-reaching changes in society and his observations are shaped by what he saw around him: the result was an emphasis on transformations occurring in his own lifetime rather than on the longer historical perspective. But his views about the dissolution of tradition are veiled with ambivalence. While it may be overstating the case to speak of his having a philosophy of dress, some of his personal preferences often came into play, through which he engages with wider issues of the day and his words form 'a dialogue with their own history': for example, although it was first published nearly two decades previously, to the proof copy of the later 1895 edition of *Far from the Madding Crowd* Hardy specifically added a reference to smocks: 'The practice of divination by Bible and key, the regarding of valentines as things of serious import, the shearing supper, *the long smock-frocks* [my italics] and the harvest-home, have, too, nearly disappeared in the wake of the old houses.'[35]

In 'The Dorsetshire Labourer', Hardy describes changes in clothing styles in his observations of the hiring fair 'of recent years', an event that was in fact becoming obsolete. Significantly, he makes a comparison with the hiring fair of the 1850s and 1860s:

The hiring-fair of recent years presents an appearance unlike that of former times. A glance up the high street of the town on a Candlemas-fair twenty or thirty years ago revealed a crowd whose general colour was whity-brown [sic] flecked with white. Black was almost absent, the few farmers who wore that shade being hardly discernible. Now the crowd is as dark as a London crowd. This is owing to the rage for cloth clothes which possess the labourers of to-day. Formerly they came in smock-frocks and gaiters, the shepherds with their crooks, the carters with a zone of whipcord round their hats, thatchers with a straw tucked into the brim, and so on. Now, with the exception of an occasional old shepherd, there is no mark of speciality in the groups, who might be tailors or undertakers' men, for what they exhibit externally. Out of a group of eight, for example, who talk together in the middle of the road, only one wears corduroy trousers. Two wear cloth pilot-coats and black trousers, two patterned tweed suits with black canvas overalls, the remaining four suits being of faded broadcloth. To a great extent these are their Sunday suits; but the genuine white smock-frock of Russia duck and the whity-brown one of drabbet, are rarely seen now afield except on the shoulders of old men […] That peculiarity of the English urban poor […] – their preference for the cast-off clothes of a richer class to a special attire of their own – has, in fact, reached the Dorset farm folk. Like the men, the women are, pictorially, less interesting than they used to be. Instead of the wing bonnet like the tilt of the wagon, cotton gown, bright-hued neckerchief, and strong flat boots and shoes, they (the younger ones at least) wear shabby millinery bonnets and hats with beads and feathers, 'material' dresses, and boot-heels almost as foolishly shaped as those of ladies of highest education.[36]

Hardy's comments, in particular those regarding the demise of the smock and the sun-bonnet (or, as he called it, 'wing bonnet'), accord with the observations made by other writers and commentators. Born in the same decade as Hardy, the naturalist Richard Jefferies made a similar point about the decline in the wearing of smocks, commenting, 'If the race of men have not changed they have altered their costume; the smock-frock lingered longest, but even that is going.'[37] Likewise, W. H. Hudson, describing the 'usual type' of Hampshire labourers in 1902, observed that 'the one change they have made is, alas! in their dress – the rusty black coat for the smock-frock'.[38] In his fictional writing, Hardy uses this change to sinister effect when Alec d'Urberville appears on Tess's village allotments dressed in a smock. This particular disguise, in the sequence of disguises Hardy has Alec adopt as one reinvention of himself follows another, exploits the popular visual association between the (authentic) agricultural labourer and the smock. Alec's superficial attempt to communicate with Tess on her terms fails: his understanding of Tess, and of the agricultural world that she inhabits, is flawed, and literally so: he has not noticed that the smock is now being worn only by older men. Hardy thus creates a sense of sinister irony:

> The unexpectedness of his presence, the grotesqueness of his appearance in a gathered smock-frock, such as was now worn only by the most old-fashioned of the labourers, had a ghastly comicality that chilled her [Tess] as to its bearing. D'Urberville emitted a low, long laugh.[39]

The sinister and comic impact of the passage upon the reader depends on an appreciation of the fact that Alec looks grotesque because at the time the novel was set – probably no earlier than the 1880s – young labourers would no longer be wearing smocks; his casting of himself as a traditional agricultural labourer is as ridiculous, and as phoney, as his earlier casting of himself as a born-again preacher.

Hardy's comments regarding the demise of the sun-bonnet are similarly enlightening. This change in style can be explained to some extent by the shift away from agricultural employment into domestic service. As we have seen, the sun-bonnet was becoming increasingly obsolete as a result of changes in work and in taste, combined with the fact that women no longer needed the protection to their faces from the sun that the bonnet afforded during outdoor work.[40] Describing the Oxfordshire hamlet of Lark Rise in the 1880s, Flora Thompson observed that only the older women wore sun-bonnets away from the fields. Old 'Queenie', for example, 'represented another phase of [the hamlet's] life which had also ended and been forgotten by most people [...] She seemed very old to the children, for she was a little, wrinkled, yellow-faced old woman in a sun-bonnet.'[41] While noting their decline, Hardy also acknowledged their picturesque quality when referring to Tess the dairymaid in 'the print gown of no date or fashion and the cotton bonnet drooping on her brow', and in Alec's threatening taunt to Tess: ' "You field girls should never wear those bonnets if you wish to keep out of danger." '[42]

But beneath the surface of what seems straightforwardly descriptive, Hardy constructs a dialectic between perceptions of modernity and older values which reflect his own ambivalent attitude as expressed in 'The Dorsetshire Labourer' and elsewhere, and his comparisons are described specifically in clothing terms. In the extract quoted above, Hardy compares the labourers at the contemporary hiring fair with a 'London crowd' because their clothing is 'as dark', observing that there is no longer any 'mark of speciality in the groups', such as 'the shepherds with their crooks, the carters with a zone of whipcord round their hats, thatchers with a straw tucked into the brim, and so on'. Alluding to the 'rage for cloth clothes' and the preference of the English urban poor for 'the cast-off clothes of a richer class to a special attire of their own', he is referring to ready-made versions or imitations of middle-class styles and fabrics and suggesting that the desire for these has filtered down to working people in villages and small or provincial town communities. This process, of the emulation of one class by another, was undoubtedly assisted by improved communications brought about by the coming of the railways and new trends in advertising.

In making the comparison with London crowds, Hardy was drawing on his own personal experience, having lived and worked in London in his early to mid-twenties (1862–7), and as a newly married man (1874–5). He continued to make frequent visits to London even after he moved back to Dorset permanently. For Hardy, London was the quintessence of urbanism, although by the end of the nineteenth century it was very different from northern urban centres whose recent growth was associated predominantly with manufacturing and industrialization. In 'The Dorsetshire Labourer', the essential point made is that agricultural workers were imitating 'urban' trends, thereby denying the individuality in dress that had distinguished specific groups in the past. This suggests an implied criticism of the new processes of the making and manufacture of clothing, and, although he does not refer to it by name, it amounts to a critique of the ready-to-wear system, which, by the late nineteenth century, had made possible the production of 'mass fashion'. Hardy saw this as running counter to individual style and to clothing related directly to a person's occupation. Flora Thompson would appear to agree:

> The smock-frock was still worn by the older men, who declared that one well-made smock would outlast twenty of the new machine-made suits the younger men were buying. The smock, with its elaborately stitched yoke and snow-white home laundering, was certainly more artistic than the coarse, badly-fitting 'reach-me-downs', as they were sometimes called.[43]

But Hardy takes the description of clothing much further than Thompson, insisting, for example, that clothes should in some way be related to the wearer. Thus, in The Woodlanders, Hardy laments that 'there can be hardly anything less connected with a woman's personality than drapery which she has neither designed, manufactured, cut, sewed, nor even seen'.[44] This is a reaction to the complex changes described above and in particular to the mass-produced, ready-made clothing that was becoming more easily available from retailers in provincial towns. But it can also be construed as a belief in the importance of what links the individual – physically and psychologically – to their environment. Clothing, Hardy suggests, should be related to the wearer as an expression not only of herself or himself, but of the environment of which she or he is a part; this connection between the wearer and the wearer's physical environment means that an aspect of the landscape or the natural world is represented as clothing and vice versa. At the same time, Hardy emphasizes the psychological need of the individual to be at one with that landscape. For example, Tess is 'a figure which is part of the landscape; a field woman pure and simple, in winter guise'.[45] In *The Return of the Native*, Clym Yeobright, having taken to furze-cutting on Egdon Heath, 'appeared of a russet hue, not more distinguishable from the scene around him than the green caterpillar from the leaf it feeds on'.[46] The atmosphere, the trees and vegetation, the fields, can all be described in terms of their likeness to fabrics and garments: the gloom in *The Return of the Native* is presented as 'funereal: all nature seemed clothed in crape';[47] in *The Woodlanders*, the trees are dressed in 'jackets of lichen and stockings of moss';[48] in *Far from the Madding Crowd* Hardy likened 'soft brown mosses' to 'faded velveteen',[49] and in *Jude the Obscure* the fresh harrow lines of a field 'seemed to stretch like the channellings in a piece of new corduroy'.[50]

These descriptions operate as more than just literary device. In Hardy's memorable depiction of Egdon Heath in *The Return of the Native*, the narrator moves from portraying the heath in an 'antique brown dress' with its 'venerable one coat' (at odds with 'a person on a heath in raiment of modern cut and colours') to adopting a philosophical stance about how we should dress in such an environment – 'in the oldest and simplest human clothing'. The clothes metaphor developed in this depiction was inspired by Thomas Carlyle's *Sartor Resartus*:[51]

> Civilization was its enemy; and ever since the beginning of vegetation its soil had worn the same antique brown dress, the natural and invariable garment of the particular formation. In its venerable one coat lay a certain vein of satire on human vanity in clothes. A person on a heath in raiment of modern cut and colours has more or less an anomalous look. We seem to want the oldest and simplest human clothing where the clothing of the earth is so primitive.[52]

Thus Hardy suggests that the wearing of modern or fashionable dress by working-class people indicates that they are at odds with their environment, and, more importantly, with themselves. In *The Mayor of Casterbridge*, Lucetta's acquisition of a fashionable Parisian appearance betrays her artful and devious character.[53] Meanwhile in *The Woodlanders* Grace Melbury's 'modern attire look[ed] odd where everything else was old-fashioned'.[54] Moreover, the appearance of country girls dressing 'above their station' is criticized, not from the desire to keep the classes in their 'rightful' place that had been the primary motivation behind sumptuary legislation of the past or that determined the 'choices' of middle-class do-gooders (controlling clothing clubs) on behalf of their social 'inferiors', but because Hardy is contemptuous of the fashions that were being imitated, and of imitation itself. References to fine clothing worn by country girls suggest that they have lost their innocence, or, at worst, been raped. After her time at Trantridge, Tess returns home to have her baby and makes clothes for her sisters and brothers 'out of some finery which d'Urberville had given her, and she had put by with contempt'.[55] Then, towards the end of the novel, believing that her husband Angel has abandoned her forever and having been worn down by the attentions of Alec d'Urberville, she is represented as a lady of fashion living at Sandbourne (Bournemouth). When Angel finally tracks her down, she tells him that 'these clothes are what he's put upon me: I didn't care what he did wi' me!'[56] Tess's fashionable clothing here is symbolic of her ultimate moral degradation; dressed up like this, she conforms to society's, and literature's, image of a 'fallen woman', which of course Hardy sets in the context of his construction of Tess as 'pure'; out of desperation and in moral reparation for her past wrong-doings, as she sees them, and as society would see them, she has succumbed to the desires of someone she loathes, and the reader is forced to decide if Tess is 'guilty'. In his poem 'The Ruined Maid', probably conceived when living in London in the 1860s, Hardy explored a similar theme:

> 'O Melia, my dear, this does everything crown!
> Who should have supposed I should meet you in town?
> And whence such fair garments, such prosperi-ty?'
> 'O didn't you know I'd been ruined?' said she.
>
> 'You left us in tatters, without shoes or socks,
> Tired of digging potatoes, and spudding up docks;
> And now you've gay bracelets and bright feathers three!'
> 'Yes: that's how we dress when we're ruined,' said she.

With bitter irony, Melia's interlocutor replies:

> 'I wish I had feathers, a fine sweeping gown,
> And a delicate face, and could strut about Town!'
> 'My dear – a raw country girl, such as you be,
> Cannot quite expect that. You ain't ruined,' said she.[57]

The superficial gaiety, created by the jaunty metre and language of the poem, and the irony created by Hardy through the interlocutor's innocent envy of the ruined girl, make even more poignant the tragedy of what was considered to be the moral ruin of country girls who, like Tess, were exploited by their employers in domestic service, or fell victim to the attractions and materialism of the town. Daniel Roche's study of eighteenth-century French literature highlights how 'clothing evokes dissolute seduction, sexual display and the dangers of city life for virtuous girls.'[58] In 'The Ruined Maid', Hardy, with characteristic brilliance, develops a similar theme.

Hardy also expresses his contempt for fashionable, town clothing in 'The Dorsetshire Labourer'. We have seen how he describes young country women of the early 1880s as 'pictorially, less interesting than they used to be', wearing 'shabby millinery bonnets and hats with beads and feathers, "material" dresses, and boot-heels almost as foolishly shaped as those of ladies of highest education.'[59] Conversely, Hardy asked derisively of London high-society women, 'if put into rough wrappers in a turnip-field, where would their beauty be?'[60] And one is reminded of George Clausen's images of Susan Chapman (see Chapter 6). Conversely, the transformative power of elegant clothes is illustrated by the descriptions of Tess as a lady of fashion, and we are asked to consider their possibilities in *Jude the Obscure*, with reference to Sue Bridehead's plain clothes: 'a matter of ten pounds spent in a drapery-shop which had no connection with her real life or real self, would have set all Melchester staring.'[61] In fact, a complex dialectic of the values of the countryside versus those of the town, the traditional versus the modern, echo throughout this, his final novel. This dialectic is complex indeed: Sue, as a 'modern woman', and Jude, trapped by the limitations of his social background and by a past relationship, both suffer as a result of certain traditions and conventions that are not at all 'picturesque' – which, of course, Hardy appears to condemn, as he does in *Tess*. Despite the shock-value of some of his ideas, Hardy had the preoccupations of his essentially middle-class urban readership in mind and he captures and plays upon the general ambivalence and concern seen elsewhere about urban values replacing those of the countryside. As Michael Millgate observes, 'Hardy saw clearly that his career as a writer was founded upon his capacity to mediate between essentially rural material and a predominantly urban audience.'[62] As a mature writer, Hardy acknowledged that 'the town man finds what he seeks in novels of the country.'[63]

Nevertheless, Hardy's negative comments about the corruptive influence symbolized by urban fashions, while they fed, and responded to, contemporary anxieties, were more extreme than his readership found acceptable. After his marriage to Arabella, Jude discovers, to his horror, that his wife wears false hair:

> A little chill overspread him at her first unrobing. A long tail of hair, which Arabella wore twisted up in an enormous knob at the back of her head, was deliberately unfastened, stroked out, and hung upon the looking-glass which he had bought her.
>
> 'What – it wasn't your own?' he said, with a sudden distaste for her.
>
> 'O no – it never is nowadays with the better class.'
>
> 'Nonsense! Perhaps not in towns. But in the country it is supposed to be different. Besides, you've enough of your own, surely?'
>
> 'Yes, enough as country notions go. But in towns the men expect more.'[64]

Here and elsewhere, Hardy associates fashion with 'artfulness' and scheming. Arabella's deception of Jude by wearing false hair indicates her deeper dishonesty: her leading Jude to believe she is carrying his child in order that he make – superficially – an 'honest woman' of her by marrying her. In Hardy's work, as J. B. Bullen observes, '"art" – whether it is the art of the fashion-designer or even the skill of the painter – is always associated with "artfulness", with false appearances, personal cunning, and ultimately, moral duplicity.'[65] Furthermore, in *Jude the Obscure*, the weakest and most superficial character, Arabella, generally conforms to what were, or had become, conventional dress codes, but the most complex and intelligent – and 'modern' – character, Sue Bridehead, does not. Hardy offers a thinly veiled challenge to the rigid Victorian etiquette of mourning, in which fabric, including texture, appearance and colour, was specified depending on the relationship of the deceased to the bereaved and the time that had elapsed since the death.[66] Following the death of her second husband, Mr Cartlett, Arabella wears the most conventional and popular of mourning fabric, black crape, made into a 'sombre suit of pronounced cut'.[67] Jude, after the death of his three children, also wears black crape. Sue, however, does not conform to any specified dress code: her 'coloured clothing, which she had never thought of changing for the mourning garb he [Jude] had bought, suggested to the eye a greater grief than the conventional garb of bereavement could express'.[68] We are reminded of the inadequacy of 'correct' clothing in conveying the truth of experience or feeling in Shakespeare's *Hamlet*; Hardy was not the first to articulate suspicion of it in this way: 'But I have that within which passeth show / These but the trappings and the suits of woe'. In 'She at his Funeral', the distraught speaker compares her clothing – 'unchanged' because how can a mere gown do justice to her grief? – with that of other, properly dressed mourners:

> Unchanged my gown of garish dye,
> Though sable-sad is their attire;
> But they stand round with griefless eye,
> Whilst my regret consumes like fire.[69]

Grief is not articulated by clothing so the etiquette of dress is no more than that if worn without genuine sorrow. Perhaps Hardy's comments sound commonplace to a contemporary readership, but to challenge late-Victorian dress codes would have been radical in his own time. On the other hand, by the 1890s there was some loosening of the strictures of Victorian etiquette, and in this respect Hardy was engaging with one of a number of contemporary debates, a debate that forms 'a dialogue with its own history'. Hardy's voice was not a lone one. Dress reformers and followers of the Arts and Crafts Movement also questioned what they saw as the absurdities of fashion, such as the dangerous and constrictive lacing of the female corseted torso.[70] Thus in the context of wider issues relating to dress reform, Hardy's novels are products of their time, engaging both directly and indirectly with current concerns, including the extremes of fashionable dress.

Hardy's perception of radical change occurring in his own lifetime lies at the heart of his representation of rural working-class dress. The social and economic changes of which Hardy was acutely aware account for the disappearance of traditional styles in favour of those influenced by notions of 'fashion' and the availability of mass-produced clothing, which Hardy associated primarily with towns. For him, the influence of urban fashions alienated people from the individuality in dress that formed a link with their environment, and ultimately their own past and wider history. That clothing should play an important part in this transition is significant: not only do we see, to use Anne Buck's words, 'dress in action in the novelist's world', but we also encounter the way in which it became central to the construction of an idealized rural past invested with a recognizable folk culture in England over the second half of the nineteenth century.

The history of rural working-class dress is not limited to a narrative about the changing physical characteristics of clothing. Rather it can encompass responses to more general and far-reaching change, a thread that is woven into the links and disjunctions between the past and present. Always seeing beneath the superficiality of appearances, Hardy recognized fabric and clothing to be a signifier and gauge of many things, not least the cultural and social transformations of the landscape of late Victorian England. Never able fully to resolve the competing claims of progress and picturesqueness that he had explored over the span of his novel-writing years, Hardy in his fifties chose to step away from, and seek to transcend, the limiting contemporaneity of his own time by turning exclusively to writing poetry.

8

RURAL WORKING-CLASS DRESS
Survival, representation and change

'Mute chroniclers of their time …'

(Richard Cobb, *Death in Paris, 1795–1801*)[1]

The role of clothing in addressing the human need for warmth, protection and a search for identity, and the manner in which clothing was made, manufactured or acquired, are influenced by the shifting historical context. But can change be chronicled by the clothing that survives? And if so, how exactly? What precisely do those garments represent that *do* survive down to the present, in the possession of an individual or displayed in the museum context? The relative anonymity of the rural labourer already alluded to, and the obstacles faced in trying to make out, without intervention from others, the voice of the working classes themselves, makes this a fascinating and challenging topic. Traditionally, dress historians have begun with the surviving articles of clothing – artefacts in their own right – as the focus of study. I consider these clothes here, in the final chapter, with specific reference to examples found in a selection of museum collections, in particular the Museum of English Rural Life, University of Reading, in the context of secondary literature. This is not because they are less important than other 'evidence', but because I want to treat them as contributing to our incomplete picture of the past rather than as the 'reality' against which depictions in literature, photographs and paintings are gauged or assessed.

OBSTACLES TO SURVIVAL

For most working men, women and children in the countryside, clothing was a matter of what could be afforded, made, adapted, mended and passed on to the next person, and the intense overall wear and tear to which working clothes were subjected lessened the likelihood of their survival. Richard Cobb's study of Paris suicides in the last decade of the eighteenth century, *Death in Paris*, vividly brings home this point today, when the practice of regular darning and wearing of worn-out clothing is often alien, at least to Western culture. Although it may have lost something in translation, the language used to describe the clothing of the 'suicidés' in documentary and literary evidence is telling:

> 'Torn', 'darned', 'stitched together', 'worn down to the seam', 'holed', 'heel-less', 'out at the elbows', 'out at the knees', 'patched', 'reinforced with leather squares', 'worn through at the seat', 'letting in water' are words that represent, in graphic terms, an economy of fairly desperate expedients, and a daily effort merely to keep going a little longer.[2]

Visual evidence of the wear and tear on clothes (Fig. 8.1) of the rural poor in the Victorian period, and of the repeated attempts 'to keep [it] going a little longer', are provided by a number of the garments kept by museums, many meticulously and skilfully patched and darned (Fig. 8.2), although the quality of work can vary even on the same garment. Probably indicative of a number of different owners over time, these repairs – for example to a linen smock – reflect the undocumented and complex provenances of such garments. We find, too, skilfully mended shoes and boots with hob-nailed soles (Figs 8.3 and 8.4). Given the lengths to which some people went to afford and obtain them, it should not surprise us that clothes were seen as a valuable commodity. In her study of the provincial clothing trade in the first half of the nineteenth century, Alison Toplis looked at the Herefordshire Quarter Session records for the period between 1820 and 1830; these show approximately two-thirds of all cases of clothing theft to have been those of working men stealing workaday clothes such as smocks, shirts and corduroy breeches from men of similar status. To realize its value, stolen clothing had to be sold on as quickly as possible to avoid detection.[3]

Apart from the inevitability of working-class garments getting worn out, other factors determined their longevity and survival: for example, some smocks were treated with linseed oil to make them water-resistant; these

Fig. 8.1 White linen smock

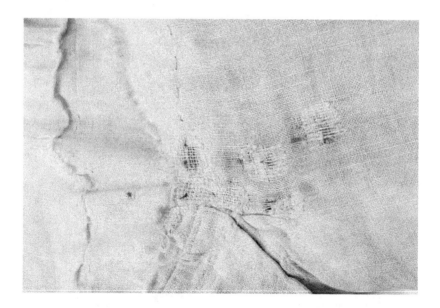

Fig. 8.2 Detail of linen smock

Fig. 8.3 Leather boots: note patches and mends on front right shoe

Fig. 8.4 Hob-nailed boot (sole)

Fig. 8.5 Detail of 'oiled smock'

are rare in museum collections because the oil caused deterioration of the material. So it is difficult to know how common these smocks were; out of a total of over 50 smocks in the collection of the Museum of English Rural Life, only one – in a delicate condition – is an oiled smock (Fig. 8.5), though a number survive at Worthing Museum and Art Gallery, including one of brown linen thought to have a Sussex provenance.[4]

And, while in most cases the lives of clothes and textiles were eked out for as long as possible, there were circumstances in which their destruction was absolute and final: they could be destroyed deliberately to prevent the spread of infection following the outbreak of disease. In his biography of Thomas Hardy, Michael Millgate describes how Hardy 'was to remember all his life the terrible final cholera epidemic in Dorset of 1854 when Henry Moule, vicar of Fordington [at that time the poorest part of Dorchester] ignored personal danger to visit the sick, organize the boiling or burning of clothes and linen of those who had died, and direct various other attempts to prevent the spread of infection'.[5] Or, if they had literally become rags and so were beyond repair, they could even be used for making manure.[6]

Given all these factors militating against its survival, how can we account for the presence of clothing that – so far as we can reasonably assume – would have belonged to working-class people? Do these items survive as a result of 'accidents' of history or a conscious process of collection and preservation? Given the intense wear and tear and exposure to the elements that most clothing would have been subjected to over long periods of time, on one level it seems nothing short of a miracle that anything survives at all. On the other hand, for men and women on low incomes, clothing not only played a practical role, but also – as we have seen – had the potential to confer respectability or might have strong sentimental value. If an item of working-class clothing survived repeated wear and was subsequently passed down from one family member or generation to another, it must have meant something important – perhaps because of the original cost of the fabric, or the work that went into its making, or the significance of the occasion(s) on which it was worn, or all of these factors.

REPRESENTATIONS OF RURAL WORKING-CLASS DRESS AND MUSEUM COLLECTIONS

Whilst the last decades of the twentieth century have seen the appearance of museums of fashion, a phenomenon by definition short-lived, historians have yet to think how to write about something other than these sumptuous and insubstantial phantoms.

(Daniel Roche, *The Culture of Clothing: Dress and Fashion in the Ancien Régime*)[7]

In comparison with items with known provenances linked to wealthier owners, the relative scarcity of extant examples of rural working-class dress has, unsurprisingly, influenced the way the subject has been studied. While the prevailing focus by dress historians has shifted away from élite dress, along with its communication of status, wealth and spectacle, this move has been reflected only infrequently in either temporary exhibitions or permanent displays, with some notable exceptions.

The dress collection at the Gallery of English Costume at Platt Hall in Manchester was established in 1947 as Britain's first dedicated museum of dress history; it originated in the personal collection of husband and wife Christopher and Phillis Cunnington, avid collectors of historic dress. Concerned with 'mass-psychology, not with the psychology of the individual', their intention was to collect the clothes of 'ordinary folk'.[8] Christopher Cunnington's undisguised lack of interest in the provenances of the clothing they collected presented later difficulties in documenting the collection for the museum's first curator, Anne Buck, who pioneered major policies for the collection, as well as for the conservation and display of dress in Britain as a whole. At Platt Hall, she resolved to collect English dress representing all social levels, both urban and rural and, as Lou Taylor explains, she 'researched the manufacture and consumption of farm workers' smocks, red woollen country cloaks and mid-nineteenth-century mill girls' shawls just as enthusiastically as the grandest of ball-gowns'.[9] Although based in Manchester, the collection at Platt Hall is not restricted to garments with a known local provenance.

Simon Knell observes that it is the 'changing world' that 'provides the motivation to collect' and that 'museums were invented to capture and keep against a background of change'.[10] It is in this context that the Museum of English Rural Life (MERL) was established by the University of Reading in 1951, the brainchild of John Higgs (1923–86), a specialist in agricultural technology, who recognized the need to preserve England's rural heritage. The first public displays opened in 1955; the collection had 7,000 items. As curator Oliver Douglas has pointed out, this was at a time, like the nineteenth century, when the British countryside was changing particularly rapidly.[11] Some of the first acquisitions were the tools and products of countryside crafts, many of which were in decline. While the museum's policy is to collect artefacts dating from 1750 to the present, relatively few objects with an eighteenth-century provenance have been donated, and the majority date from 1850 to 1950. Among its items of clothing, the collection contains over 50 smocks, the majority of which were acquired in the period 1951–68; headgear (sun-bonnets and billycock hats) and leggings, as well as numerous items of footwear including shoes, boots and pattens. The majority of smocks were gifted to the museum by individual collectors and donors, sometimes – as in the case of the collection bequeathed by Harold John Massingham (1888–1952) – as items in a broader collection of objects related to agriculture, rural crafts and lifestyle.[12]

Research I have carried out in a number of museum collections in England, including those at Manchester and Reading, reveals that the most plentiful examples of nineteenth-century working-class garments are smocks worn by men and sun-bonnets worn by women.[13] While my study is by no means exhaustive, the pattern of survival and collection I have encountered is often repeated in provincial museums. But the potential for open-ended interpretation in relation to the study of such surviving garments is wide. Here is the paradox: the garments that survive in greatest quantity in museums and that,

Fig. 8.6 Detail of white linen smock

as we have seen, were often depicted by Victorian artists and photographers in pursuit of the picturesque, are also those that were going out of general wear by the 1870s and 1880s.

This begs the question, how representative are surviving garments in museum collections of what was commonly or generally worn at a given period? Were they collected precisely because they were (becoming) scarce? And what information can they be said to *contain or communicate*? Even if these questions cannot be answered definitively, consideration of them furthers a more critical methodological approach and assessment. What *is* clear is that if we were to rely on garments alone to construct a narrative of rural working-class dress, this would give an incomplete or distorted view, just as if we looked at the work of one artist or one photographer in isolation. The garments that survive beyond the period in which they were worn, and which continue to have a life beyond their original context, may be considered 'representations' in a not entirely different way from depictions of rural dress found in paintings, photographs and literary accounts. If it is the case that a museum's collecting policies reflect an approach that treats objects as facts to be gathered up, this can lead to an overestimation of 'the inherent qualities of the object' and an underestimation of 'the interpretive processes which make sense of the material world'.[14] Susan Pearce describes the terms commonly used to refer to holdings of museums: 'objects', 'things', 'artefacts', encompassed by the collective noun, material culture, or, as Jules Prown defines it, 'the manifestations of culture through material productions'.[15] All these terms can be said to 'share common ground in that they all refer to selected lumps of the physical world to which cultural value has been ascribed'.[16] Pearce adopts a semiotic approach in order to analyse the way in which individual objects accumulate meanings as time passes, arguing that these are not just passive, but both active and passive, and that meaning develops as an interactive process between things and viewer.[17]

The collection of smocks at the Museum of English Rural Life illustrates one aspect of this interactive process between object and viewer. Some were probably made in the first half of the nineteenth century, judging by their fabric (often fine linen) and their exclusively hand-sewn construction (Fig. 8.6). Others are made from cotton twill or drabbet and are very roughly hand-sewn together at the side seams (Figs 8.7 and 8.8).

Still others represent revivalist movements, such as that of the Bere Regis Arts and Crafts Association in the early twentieth century, and appear to have

Fig. 8.7 'Drabbet' smock

Fig. 8.8 Detail of 'drabbet' smock, showing side seam roughly sewn together

Fig. 8.9 Detail of hand-smocking and embroidery on a white linen smock

Fig. 8.10 Detail of a hand-stitched side seam and hem on a white linen smock

been made as a specific response to the demise of smocks in general wear, and where the interaction of the 'viewer' (in this case the makers of the revival smocks) with the earlier 'genuine' smocks – a knowledge of which would most probably be derived from extant examples – stimulated the making of the revival items (see colour plate 12). The latter in their turn, and as time passes, will have a changing relationship with those who view them. Thus, not only do these smocks accumulate different and complex meanings with the passage of time, but they evidence the interactive process with the viewer as described by Pearce.

To illustrate this process, Pearce analyses the significance of a red coatee (jacket) in the National Army Museum worn by an infantry officer at the battle of Waterloo in June 1815. Adopting the approach of the Swiss linguist and semiotician Ferdinand de Saussure and the critical theory of Roland Barthes, Pearce explains how the jacket becomes a 'signe' (the social construct which members of a group can recognize and understand) uniting the message

(that is, the signified – the body of social understanding which must operate through a social action of some kind) and the physical embodiment
(the signifier).[18] Pearce develops her analogy with reference to the work of
Edmund Leach (1910–89), arguing that objects operate as 'signs' when they
stand for the whole of which they are an intrinsic part (as the coatee does
for the actual events of Waterloo), and as 'symbols' when they are brought
into an arbitrary association with elements to which they bear no intrinsic
relationship: in this case the relationship is said to be metaphoric.[19] Shifting
perceptions of the battle and the coatee were absorbed into the imaginations
of those who continued to live after the battle was over. The coatee therefore
became rich in symbolic possibilities and so is polysemantic – capable of
acting as a signifier for much signification. 'In historical terms the experience of Waterloo, in all its guises, including its physical souvenirs, becomes
part of the collective consciousness, in which it will play its role in bringing
about social change'; the coatee thus becomes a 'sign which carries meaning' and is 'able to do so because, unlike we ourselves who must die, it bears
an "eternal" relationship to the receding past, and it is this that we experience as the power of "the actual object".'[20]

In the same way, the numerous smocks and sun-bonnets located in
museum collections can be interpreted as 'symbols' (in the way Leach defines
them) of a rural culture that, by the last decades of the nineteenth century,
was being eroded. It is in this context of change that they were actively collected or, at least, not thrown away. Lack of precise information relating to
provenance in many cases leads to generalization about the significance of
such items, but it is not chance alone that has led them to be relatively well
represented in museums (even if infrequently *displayed* as part of permanent
collections). And this prompts consideration of broader issues around interpretation, balanced with close observation and research of the individual
items themselves. This is a complex process: the survival of the object (of
clothing) means that it comes to represent a particular perception of the
past, while the application of traditional knowledge and expertise (scholarship or curatorship) to this, or to part of a collection, extends the bound-
ary of understanding. The curator is part of the 'dialectical' process, with
each presentation of an object representing 'a selective narrative'.[21] When we
encounter it directly – or handle it in a museum context – we put ourselves
inside the bodies of those who made, or used, or wore these objects.[22]

Elsewhere in Europe, peasant and regional dress was collected from the
1850s onwards, in many cases to serve the political and ideological purposes of nationalists, artists, designers and utopian socialists, fascists and

communists alike. In this way, dress and textiles played a significant icono-
graphical role in the process of European nation-building.[23] While England
seems to have remained largely outside this trend, there is nevertheless
something of a common thread, even if the political element was less obvi-
ous. Concerns about the consequences of industrialization, the physical
deterioration of the urban classes combined with rural depopulation and a
dying way of life climbed their way up the political agenda in the last three
decades of the nineteenth century.[24] Just as many European countries did
not collect examples of what Lou Taylor describes as transformation clothing (the concept of 'transformation' here meaning the way all aspects of
rural life absorb urban culture), in England, artefacts that showed signs of
strong urban influence were not collected until the 1960s.[25] So attempting
to construct a history of male and female rural working-class clothing in
our period reveals a significant discrepancy – the survival of smocks and the
non-survival of the 'urban' or transformation garments that replaced them.
This factor has influenced the historiography of the subject.

MALE WORKING-CLASS CLOTHING

Of all the garments worn by male agricultural workers, smocks survive in
the greatest variety and quantity. They were worn primarily in the rural midland and southern counties of England. While some surviving examples are
found elsewhere, for example, at the North Cornwall Museum in Camelford,
they were not generally worn where the dominance of the fishing industry explains the popularity of warm knitted Cornish Guernseys or 'knit-
frocks'.[26] Neither were they as extensively worn in Wales,[27] or in the north of
England, the parliamentary commissioners, for example, reporting in 1867
that 'a smock-frock is not to be seen in all Cumberland.'[28] But the smock is
nevertheless the garment that has come to represent nineteeth-century rural
working life: it is in the form of explanatory catalogues of their smock collections, specifically, that much of the published and unpublished work on
rural working-class dress has been written by museum curators of provincial
museums. Smocks are documented in the records of the Old Bailey as early
as the 1770s.[29] William Cobbett recalls wearing one as a child:

I, with two brothers, used occasionally to desport ourselves, as the law-
yers call it, at this sand-hill. Our diversion was this: we used to go to
the top of the hill, which was steeper than the roof of a house; one used

to draw his arms out of the sleeves of his smock-frock, and lay himself down with his arms by his sides; and then the others, one at head and the other at feet, sent him rolling down the hill like a barrel or a log of wood.[30]

One of the earliest visual images of smocks is in George Morland's painting *Outside the Alehouse Door* (1792). By the early nineteenth century, depictions of smocks were commonplace; they are worn by ploughmen, dairymen and shepherds in W. H. Pyne's *Microcosm* (1806), and in numerous paintings of the first half of the nineteenth century, for example in John Linnell's *Shepherd Boy Playing a Flute* (1831). The smock protected and obscured the clothes worn underneath it. Describing the Sussex countryside in the 1820s, William Cobbett observed that when the men and boys did not wear smocks, they always looked 'dirty and comfortless'.[31]

Smocks were typically worn over a linen or cotton shirt and breeches, or, from the 1820s, trousers. Breeches, usually made of leather or corduroy, the former being harder-wearing, continued to be worn in some districts for much of the nineteenth century, Rev. J. C. Atkinson recalling in his memoirs, *Forty Years in a Moorland Parish*, that it was not until the early 1890s that they finally went out of fashion in the village of Danby in Cleveland.[32] Leggings or gaiters and hard-wearing hob-nailed boots completed the typical working outfit. Leggings were used throughout the nineteenth century and even into the twentieth century: a pair made of black hide (now in the Shoe Museum in Street, Somerset, cat. no 34/36), thought to have been worn by Oswald Wyatt, who farmed at Sheephouse Farm in Bruton in Somerset, was worn until the 1940s. A cheaper, makeshift method of keeping trousers protected from mud and dirt was to tie pieces of string, which were then known as 'yarks', just above or below the knees.

The earliest smocks were relatively plain, without the elaborate smocking and embroidery that became characteristic by the 1830s. As Anne Buck observes, none of the (late) eighteenth-century references to smocks mention decoration and no ornamental stitching is shown in early illustrations, although this may represent an omission on the part of the artist.[33] The smocking itself gave a degree of 'elasticity', facilitating comfort and allowing the wearer movement. The increased amounts of embroidery have been linked to a similar trend towards more ornamentation seen in fashionable dress of the 1820s and 1830s, 'the smock sharing this wave of fashion'.[34] Having undertaken a careful study of surviving smocks, Anne Buck concludes that the finest and most intricate embroidery (including the quality of the smocking itself) appears on those made and worn between c.1830 and 1870.[35]

Well-provenanced smocks are rare and it is difficult to be precise about dating.[36] Many smocks were likely to have been handed down from one family member to another over a period of half-a-century at least. So the date of making/manufacture may indicate only the earliest date at which a smock was worn, but gives no idea of its longevity. For example, the donor (aged 71 in 1955) of a smock at the Museum of English Rural Life (see Figs 8.9 and 8.10) recalled her father wearing a smock as 'Sunday best' with a red, knotted handkerchief round his neck. She was a child at the time so this was probably in the late 1880s and, before that, both her grandfather (a cowman) and her great grandfather (a shepherd) had, allegedly, worn the same smock. While such magnificently crafted smocks of fine linen were mostly worn for best – on Sundays or at a wedding – there is a marked distinction between these and those that were likely to have been worn for work, for example a buff-coloured round (that is, with the same front and back) smock of a heavy twilled fabric in the Victoria and Albert Museum (cat. no T.744/1919), thought to have been worn in the first half of the nineteenth century in Bedfordshire. Over time, and as a best smock was worn and gradually deteriorated, it could of course become a working smock.

As mentioned in relation to Thomas Hardy's descriptions, smocks were generally made from fine, bleached linen (Russia duck; see Fig. 8.6) or coarser twilled cotton (drabbet). The latter (see Figs 8.7 and 8.8) was usually the material of later use, by the 1870s being associated with poorly designed and executed, sparser embroidery.[37] Traditionally, many smocks were probably made at home with embroidery patterns passed down from one generation to the next, reflecting the considerable handicraft skill of those who made them. Using stem-stitch, in rope, basket, wave and chevron patterns, with feather-stitch variations, chain-stitch and sometimes French knots for the embroidered panels, the designs were usually based on spirals, diamonds, leaves and floral motifs. There seems little evidence to support the theory that particular designs were specific to the occupation of the wearer.[38] A number of smocks possibly owned by shepherds were examined by Anne Buck but showed no common motif in their embroidery,[39] but, as we have seen, 'much farm work is seasonal, and labourers did different tasks at different times of the year'.[40] On the other hand, there may be a link between design and quality of embroidery and the occasion for which a smock was crafted, for example, one with heart-shaped embroidery at the Museum of English Rural Life is thought to have been worn at a wedding. The same is true of an ornate, beautifully embroidered linen round smock supposed also to have been worn at a wedding (Whitchurch, Warwickshire, c.1840) in the Victoria and Albert Museum (cat. no T.108/1921).

The colour of smocks has sometimes been linked to place: William Howitt, who, in *The Hall and the Hamlet* (1845) refers to smocks as 'slops',[41] believed that colour varied with region, pointing out that in the counties near London, through Hampshire, Berkshire and Wiltshire, smocks were white; in Hertfordshire and Bedfordshire they were olive green; in the Midlands (especially Leicestershire, Derbyshire, Nottinghamshire and Staffordshire), the blue 'Newark frock' was worn.[42] Others have remarked upon the large number of brown smocks kept in museums in the south-east (by the Worthing Museum and Art Gallery, for example). But this geographical distribution was not as simple as Howitt suggests, and 'the colour of a smock could, therefore, be governed by region, locality, occupation of the wearer, or none of these'.[43] In fact what is striking is the *variety* of surviving smocks, which, observes Nicholas Thornton, should surprise only 'those of us who are surrounded by mass-produced, machine-made goods, and commercial conditions which encourage uniformity'.[44]

Even so, there is evidence of a well-established trade in ready-made smocks from as early as the first decades of the nineteenth century. Alison Toplis's study of the provision of clothing in Herefordshire and Worcestershire identifies retailers of ready-made clothing selling smocks. For example, they were sold at 59 Parsons Street, Banbury in Oxfordshire, by a tailor, William Baker, from at least 1813. His account book shows that by 1818 he had developed standardized patterns and sizing for them, with ready-made samples priced at between 8s 9d and 7s (for adults); between 5s and 4s 4d (for youths); and around 3s (for boys). He also sold 'best work' and 'full work' ready-made smocks (presumably with additional embroidery) for 9s 6d and above.[45] According to *The Workwoman's Guide* (1838), smocks 'are to be met with at clothing warehouses, and cost from 9 shillings to 18 shillings each, depending on the quantity and quality of the work put in', a price range representing for the agricultural worker from a week's to a fortnight's wages.[46] These observations seem to substantiate Thomas Hardy's description, in *Far from the Madding Crowd*, of Gabriel Oak exchanging his overcoat for a 'shepherd's regulation smock-frock' in a Casterbridge (Dorchester) shop selling ready-made clothes, 'the owner of which had a large rural connection'.[47] A child's smock in the Luton Museum (cat. no L/4/62) of olive-green linen was sold and possibly made by Henry Hyde of Poluxhill in Bedfordshire, described in the local directories from 1850 to 1890 as a tailor, draper and grocer.[48]

Well-known centres of smock-making included Newark-on-Trent in Nottinghamshire (for the characteristic blue smocks associated with the region); Burberrys of Basingstoke also made smocks on a commercial basis;[49] the firm Gurteens of Haverhill in Suffolk produced smocks as well as the fabric from which they were made. The first documented smock from Gurteens is recorded in 1819, costing 9s 3d, when the company was supplying an Essex shopkeeper (Mr Robert Fox of Bardfield) with ready-made smocks and fabric.[50] Pigot and Company's Royal National and Commercial Directory for September 1839 states: 'The principal trade and manufacture of the town [Haverhill] is the weaving of a coarse description of twilled cotton cloth, called drabbet, used principally for waggoner's frocks.' Seven drabbet manufacturers are listed, one of which was D. Gurteen and Son, which was still manufacturing the fabric in 1922.[51] Drabbet was originally woven for the company on an outwork basis until 1856, but then Gurteens built a factory for the purpose.[52] Even with the advent of the sewing machine, smocks continued, for the most part, to be sewn by hand in the second half of the nineteenth century, with hand-stitched side-seams, tightly oversewn with only minimal seam allowances (there are a few exceptions such as an unworn, machine-stitched smock labelled '1938', one of the last smocks made at the Gurteens factory and possibly suggesting a smock 'revival', though there are no known records telling us for whom this smock was made). And, along with the decline of smocks in the last three decades of the nineteenth century, went the decline of outwork. Even in the late 1860s the parliamentary commissioners commented on the fact that smock-making in some areas was becoming less widely available for outworkers. John Salt, a farm labourer from Bransford in Worcestershire, commented: 'My wife works at smock-frocks and not at gloving, but the smock-frock work is going out. She cannot earn 3 shillings a week at it.'[53]

Noted by contemporaries, the replacement of the smock by cheap, ready-made suits purchased 'off-the-peg' at local retail outlets reflected both technological and cultural changes. The economic historian Stanley Chapman argues that there was a revolution in the manufacture of men's ready-made clothing in the period between 1840 and 1860 that began well before the invention of the sewing machine. For Chapman, economies of scale and specialization are the key to understanding the process of change in the clothing industry. He describes a fall in prices of yarns and fabrics as well as in the cost of labour after 1815. Innovative manufacturing systems were based upon the division of labour and highly effective marketing entrepreneurship practised by such London-based clothing retailers as Elias Moses & Son Ltd and H. D. Nicholl, who also supplied provincial outlets serving rural markets.[54] Although the clothing of the working classes had largely been the realm of the slop-sellers, Moses marketed a *new* product – the ready-made suit for the working man.[55] The London- and Colchester-based dealer of ready-made clothes Hyam Hyams (by 1845 the firm had retail shops in London, Colchester, Manchester, Liverpool, Glasgow, Bristol, Birmingham and Leeds) was advertising a large variety of garments for all rungs of the social ladder by the late 1830s. Apart from smocks, of particular relevance to this study is the clothing at the bottom of the range: an 1828 handbill advertised, amongst other things, men's fustian trousers (3s) and fustian jackets (from 3s 6d).[56] At first, these garments were probably consumed more readily by an urban-based, artisan and manufacturing clientele, but improved transport made possible by the spread of the railway network in the second half of the nineteenth century made them increasingly available in country towns and rural districts.

In addition to the availability of ready-made clothing, mechanization on farms, in particular the adoption of threshing machines, may also have contributed to the decline of smocks; their 'unconfined looseness [...] must have been positively dangerous'.[57] Just as the parliamentary commissioners of 1867 noted a number of accidents caused by voluminous clothing worn in close proximity to farm machinery, in 1861 the Suffolk and Essex Free Press recorded the following incident for 25 January: 'At Belchamp Otten, Will Ginn aged 13 yrs jumped from the threshing machine while it was in motion, he was caught in the spindle by his smock-frock. The accident happened at Mr Edwards farm. Verdict Accidental Death.'[58]

Over the course of the last three decades of the nineteenth century, head-gear also changed: the billycock hat – a soft, felt, 'wide-awake' style worn by working men for much of the nineteenth century – disappeared in favour of smaller felt and straw hats and cloth caps.[59] The hat in Fig. 8.11 is described as a billycock hat but is possibly more rigid and has a narrower brim than a true billycock.

In his *Cottage Life in a Hertfordshire Village* (c.1934), Edwin Grey recalls that, by the end of the 1870s, the younger men had discarded smocks in favour of 'a short sort of jacket, a slop [...] made of strong canvas-looking cloth of a light colour [...] Others wore the fustian jacket and for winter wear, most wore thick, short overcoats of black or navy cloth, called "Pilots or

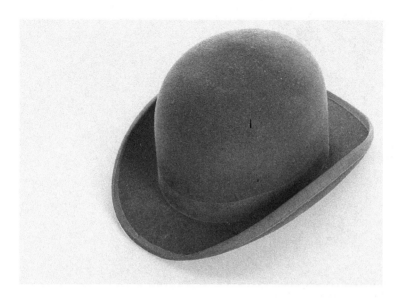

Fig. 8.11 'Billycock' hat (second half of the nineteenth century)

Reefers".'[60] Thomas Hardy's observations in relation to changes in clothing styles have already been mentioned, but noteworthy is his reference to the 'rage' for 'cloth pilot-coats and black trousers', 'canvas overalls', 'suits of faded broad cloth' and 'the mechanic's "slop"'. These new 'fashions' had superseded traditional 'corduroy trousers' and smocks.[61] Alexander Somerville also refers to a dark pilot-coat, although he offers no detailed description.[62]

Fustian, once a term for linens or linen mixtures, by the nineteenth century described heavy cottons like corduroy or moleskin (a kind of velour-like brushed fabric). Fustian clothes were cut loosely and mostly without padding or interlining and their colours ranged from white, buff and yellow to brown and blue. 'Cheap ready-made fustians', observes Sarah Levitt, 'were the characteristic dress of the workman throughout the century.'[63] The term fustian also took on political connotations, becoming associated principally with working-class clothing whereas 'broadcloth' was usually worn by middle-class men, unless passed from the latter to working-class men, as implied by Hardy. While such garments seem rarely to have survived, the Museum of English Rural Life has a jacket purportedly belonging to a Hampshire shepherd when it was bought from him in 1914, the owner apparently glad to exchange it for a 'Burberry' and some cash (Figs 8.12 and 8.13). Made from a double layer of beige fustian, it is interfaced throughout with coarse-woven, hessian-type material, and although worn and roughly mended in

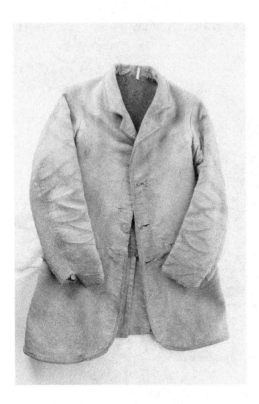

Fig. 8.12 Coat purportedly bought from a Hampshire shepherd in 1914

Fig. 8.13 Detail of coat showing lining and inside pocket

places, it was probably of superior quality compared with other similar jackets that do not survive.

The slops and pilot-coats or 'pilots' referred to by Grey, Hardy and Somerville – examples of Lou Taylor's 'transformation' clothing – do not appear to have survived. Like other items of working dress, we must assume that they were worn out, but, unlike the smock, there was no aesthetic or sentimental reason for keeping them. Yet without secure provenances of the items that do survive or examples of the transformation clothing that replaced them, we have only a partial view of men's rural working-class clothing in our period, though arguably one that suggests a dynamic and changing society.

FEMALE WORKING-CLASS CLOTHING

As with men's clothing, relatively little is known about the individual histories of women's (and children's) clothing, which rarely have a known or undisputed provenance. The final section of this chapter considers the main changes in women's clothing as reflected in a selection of those items that survive. From the end of the eighteenth century and into the early nineteenth century, rural working-class women's dress consisted principally of the bed-gown (a three-quarter-length wrap-over garment) worn over a petticoat and often with a kerchief at the neck. This is probably the garment that is worn by the women in George Stubbs's paintings *Haymakers* and *Reapers* of 1785. The Gallery of English Costume has a rare example of a late-eighteenth-century bed-gown of white cotton with a printed pink design (cat. no 1935/50). Not unlike a 'kimono' in design, the garment is open down the front and has plain, short sleeves. For warmth, red woollen cloaks were worn. This garment can be seen in paintings of the early decades of the nineteenth century, and a rare surviving example of c.1800, with a possible Cheshire provenance, an 'upmarket' version perhaps as the hood is lined with red silk, is also at the Gallery of English Costume (cat. no 1951/114). By the 1830s, however, shawls worn over cotton print dresses or those made of 'stuff' (worsted fabrics of varying quality for warmer wear) were more usual for working women in the countryside. This was partly due to the changing fashion-silhouette, with more voluminous skirts popular from the 1830s, making a shawl more suitable than a cloak or coat. The Scottish (Paisley) shawl industry, famous for imitating Indian patterns, flourished from the late eighteenth century. 'Scotch plaids' were popular for everyday wear.[64]

With regard to footwear, sturdy boots were commonly worn in the countryside. However, pattens (Fig. 8.14), which until the late eighteenth century were adopted both in town and countryside by all classes, were, by the
early nineteenth century, mostly confined to rural areas and to working-class
women. With their tough wooden soles and hardwearing 'irons', pattens
were worn over shoes and protected the latter from rough and muddy roads
and lanes. The Museum of English Rural Life has over a dozen pairs. One is
said to have been in the family of the donor (the vergeress of Winchcomb in
Gloucestershire) since 1750. Although the wooden soles, irons and toe caps
are 'original', the side pieces and leathers have been transferred from another
pair. Like smocks, pattens are likely to have complicated provenances because
they were often worn over many years and repaired many times.

Clogs were more commonly associated with northern counties, becoming well-established items of working-class dress in Cumberland by the
early eighteenth century and in Lancashire by the late eighteenth or early
nineteenth centuries. However, there is no consistent demarcation between
the wearing of clogs in the north and pattens in the south.[65] A notice still
stands in the porch of St Andrew's church in the village of Trent (formerly in
Somerset and now in Dorset) that reads: 'All Persons are requested to take off
Pattens and Clogs before entering the Church'. Pattens and clogs were noisy

Fig. 8.14 Pair of pattens (nineteenth century)

and would make floors muddy! With the increasing manufacture of ready-made boots and shoes from the 1860s, clogs and pattens began to go out of fashion.[66] Like the sun-bonnet, pattens became associated with outmoded, 'quaint' rural styles.

The frequent representation of sun-bonnets in the work of artists and photographers such as Helen Allingham and Henry Peach Robinson is echoed by the relatively abundant survival of sun-bonnets in museum collections. The Gallery of English Costume alone has approximately 30, while the Museum of English Rural Life has in the region of 40 (see colour plates 13 and 14a). Rarely prioritized in permanent museum displays, their survival and collection suggests, however, that they were valued. Miss Waern of High Wycombe in Buckinghamshire donated a sun-bonnet of white cotton to the Museum of English Rural Life in 1960 with the following letter:

Dear Sir,

I read somewhere that you collect old things connected with husbandry in Berkshire. I enclose an old woman's harvesting cap which is genuinely old. It was given to me in 1914 by Mrs Wicksteed, The Old Manor, Childrey, near Wantage who told me she had bought several of these caps as they were going out of fashion. I have worn it myself as it shades your eyes and protects the nape of your neck when working in the fields or garden. I hope you will accept my gift. I want to find a decent home for it in its old age.

Yours truly,

Miss F. M. R. Waern.[67]

Although predominantly associated with the countryside, sun-bonnets were not worn exclusively for field work. Frilled bonnets were worn by canal-women and A. J. Munby saw pit-women and brewery workers wearing cotton bonnets for outdoor work at Wigan in 1860.[68] When sun-bonnets first appeared in the 1840s, they mirrored the shape of the bonnet of fashionable wear, the cording and frilling showing the influence of drawn bonnets of silk and the morning caps of linen or cotton of the 1830s.[69] A hand-stitched white-spotted-muslin and gauze bonnet with elaborate pin-tucking at the Gallery of English Costume (cat. no 1960/46) is thought to date from the early nineteenth century, and, with its large, circular expanse of fabric framing the face, reflects this relationship between fashionable and working-class dress. However, the shape and construction of sun-bonnets evolved in the 1840s and 1850s to become representative of a uniquely rural style, the area encircling the face becoming less pronounced, while the frilling and tucking remaining as decorative features.

Sun-bonnets performed an important practical function, with sides – or 'curtains' as they were referred to – protecting the wearer's face and neck from the harmful rays of the sun, and ties which could be fastened under the chin in windy weather. Made generally from plain or printed cotton in a variety of patterns, the majority that survive are mostly machine-stitched (see colour plate 14b), but often finished (hemmed, and with decorative frills and bows added) and meticulously stitched by hand. They were probably made either at home by people with superior dressmaking skills or by a village dressmaker, an important provider of clothing well into the twentieth century. Sometimes cord or fine cane was threaded through stitched channels on the outer edge (the area framing the face) to give a more substantial structure and to prevent the fabric from falling away in the wind. Others are roughly hand-sewn, demonstrating only basic sewing skills, and are of a simple construction. Cut from semi-circular pieces of fabric, they were shaped by a piece of tape being run through the outer semi-circular edge to draw the fabric into the bonnet shape.[70]

As their practical function became obsolete, sun-bonnets went out of general wear, but retained an important role in the memorializing of rural England. The pattern of wear in the United States, where the sun-bonnet took on a 'unique symbolic role', serves as a telling comparison.[71] Here this garment became emblematic of the United States as an agrarian society, while its disappearance 'parallels American urbanization in the twentieth century'.[72] Whereas in England sun-bonnets were becoming obsolete by the end of the nineteenth century, in the USA machinery began to replace hand-picking of cotton by women only in the late 1940s (with some states such as Texas remaining a majority rural population as late as the 1930s and 1940s), and the sun-bonnet persisted well into the twentieth century in pockets of the rural south, from Virginia to Texas.[73] This was primarily because of its function in keeping sunlight off the wearer's face,[74] accounts of interviewees who had worn sun-bonnets proving their success in giving protection to the skin.[75] But as its functional role became unnecessary, so it became old-fashioned, backward and agrarian in people's minds. Hats, by contrast, were considered modern, sophisticated and urban.[76] The pattern of decline in the USA provides insights into the earlier English experience.

From the 1830s, the silhouette of rural styles reflected generally that of fashionable dress. Although it is unlikely that large numbers of working women wore such 'excesses' as the crinoline or, later, the bustle, modest versions of these styles were probably adopted. *The Cage of Cranford* is the final story in Elizabeth Gaskell's novel *Cranford* (1853), in which the main 'character' is a mysterious present from Paris. The storyteller is a young woman from Manchester, who, by her own admission, 'was rather looked upon in the light of a fast young woman by all the laundresses of Cranford because I had two corded petticoats'. It is the 'little stupid servant maid, Fanny' who first identifies the strange object, only to be scorned and scolded for the idea. But, writes Gaskell, Fanny has her own line of fashion news through the world of the servants' hall and is correct in her identification of the crinoline sent from Paris.[77] In spite of Gaskell's tongue-in-cheek depiction of rural areas as backwaters of fashion, improved communications over the course of the nineteenth century resulted in greater access to a knowledge of fashionable styles and, for men, there was the increased availability of ready-made clothing discussed above. Meanwhile the move into domestic service meant that rural women must have had increased contact with fashion, employers sometimes passing down their clothing to their servants.

Two examples illustrate the relationship between middle- and working-class fashions in the 1880s, in terms of style if not fabric and quality. The first is a bodice of printed cotton at the Gallery of English Costume (cat. no 1960/228) referred to in Chapter 6. The garment is thought to have been worn by the donor's grandmother, possibly a farm labourer, and is a simplified version of contemporary fashionable dress in silhouette. Dated to about 1880–5, it is made of printed cotton with a small floral stripe in two shades of (faded) mauve and black and lined with white cotton. It has a small selvedge-edge frill at the neck and piping at the shoulder seams. By contrast, a dress at the Museum of English Rural Life (colour plate 15a) was donated by Alfred Pool, an agricultural engineer in Somerset, who also took some remarkable photographs of working-class life. Although cut in the fashionable style of the 1880s, what is striking about this garment is the rough brown woollen fabric, the coarse black cotton lace trimming, and the poorly executed stitching (colour plate 15b). The reasons for its survival are unknown but, without the foresight of Alfred Pool and the collecting policy of the Museum of English Rural Life, it is unlikely that it would have survived at all.

The replacement of a distinctive rural working-class style by 'fashion' was frequently a source of concern to commentators over the last three decades of the nineteenth century. But such comments imply that observers at least thought that working-class dress was or had been homogeneous or that working-class people had previously been unaware of fashion. Neither of these observations is necessarily accurate, but can perhaps be understood in the context of anxieties about the influence of urban culture on the rural. While the historical forces of poverty and utility worked against fashion,[78] rather than claim that the countryside suddenly became aware of fashion in the second half of the nineteenth century it is more accurate to say that certain garments were replaced because they were redundant in terms of utility, and therefore outmoded in terms of style; and notions of what was and wasn't fashionable were becoming stronger influences behind changes in rural dress styles, with urban cultures influencing the pace of change. It was the *perception* that things were changing that is important and, with it, the conscious move to keep and collect examples of clothing.

Like the literary and visual representations considered in previous chapters, extant examples in museum collections on their own offer a partial – if fascinating – selection of the clothes that would have been worn at any given time and this 'incompleteness' is compounded by the lack of documentation with regard to who made and wore them and over what period of time. Difficult as it would be to chronicle change from a study of surviving garments alone, the 'over-representation' of certain items and their survival into our present says something of past attitudes towards them. And in the very margins of the known (the unknown even), these amazing items – patched, darned and ragged as they sometimes are – represent something of the process of complex change that was gathering momentum over the Victorian period.

Although in some country towns, such as Banbury in Oxfordshire, makers of bespoke footwear were still very much in evidence,[79] by the 1870s new retailing practices and outlets were gradually taking the place of traditional crafts such as bespoke shoe- and boot-making. A letter to the editor of the *Daily News* in 1891 'from a bootmaker' regretted the disappearance of old village tailors' and shoemakers' shops, and the consequent reduction of the 'openings for the learning of these useful handicrafts'.[80] Joseph Ashby's fourth daughter, Margaret, tells a similar story of how traditional retailing practices were dying, and observes how, by the late nineteenth century, there were fewer pedlars than there used to be, a young 'Tysonian' returning to his village in 1902 and, 'to the general astonishment and admiration', building and opening 'a new shop for drapery and ready-made clothes'.[81]

CONCLUSION
Clothing and landscape

In considering the ways in which a selection of paintings, photographs and different modes of writing, with all their various agendas and apparent contradictions, have represented Victorian rural working-class dress, I hope I have demonstrated how such an exercise can illuminate the story of complex social change. And this particular perspective on change, and of people's attitudes towards it, of course also offers us a glimpse of the important roles clothing plays in people's lives. The study of clothing contributes to our understanding of the past, and, in the case of Victorian rural life, to our understanding of what it was like, and how it was both experienced and perceived. A world can indeed be evoked through a wardrobe[1] – as well, perhaps, as through the lack of one.

In terms of the actual changes in clothing, Daniel Roche observes how 'the major difficulty is to grasp within the same movement stability and change in appearance'.[2] As we have seen there was, for example, no sudden shift from traditional smocks to ready-made suits, but a gradual evolution, in which younger men cast off what they thought was old-fashioned, while an older generation maintained the styles of their youth probably up until their deaths. This explains the large numbers of photographs in museum collections of older men in smocks as late as the 1890s (and even beyond), along with descriptions such as 'Old Henry Parkman [...] who sat in his cottage, always in his old, tall, silk hat, and a smock with fantastic stitching and stiff, bulging folds'.[3]

The sources discussed in the preceding chapters reveal a class-based bias of perspective. The idea of a rural idyll was appropriated and perpetuated by artists, photographers and writers through their work and consumed by a predominantly middle-class urban audience. As Karen Sayer observes, the aristocracy and, increasingly over the course of the nineteenth century, the middle classes, bought art and, 'by purchasing work they found acceptable, this audience shaped the representation of the rural'.[4] And Rosemary Treble points out that 'the profound nostalgia of the urban middle classes for their rural past ensured the survival, in however changed a form, of the English landscape in art'[5] – and, one might add, in photography and literature. While I have included the views of the labouring poor, these are accessible only sporadically – often, of course, when their discontent spilled over into active protest.[6] And the irony is that the representations I have discussed (including the extant garments referred to in Chapter 8) do not always do justice to the importance of working-class history in shaping our perceptions of the Victorian period. On the other hand, the paintings of, say, George Clausen and the novels of Thomas Hardy bear witness to a growing demand for, and acceptance of, monumental representations of the rural labourer in the visual and literary arts in the second half of the nineteenth century.

A series of responses to profound change characterized the transition from an essentially rural to a predominantly urban society, whether these are to be seen in the report of a parliamentary commission of enquiry, or a novel, or a painting by Helen Allingham, or a photograph by Henry Peach Robinson. But in all of these 'narratives', clothing is often connected – sometimes literally, at other times on a metaphorical level – to the idealism, the concern or the angst that informed a particular response to the changing cultural landscape. Paradoxically, and as is the case with other historical sources, it is often the subjectivity of feeling, the bias of opinion, certain agendas, undisguised or implicit, and incomplete representations – what isn't there, as well as what is – from which we can glean the most.

What of clothing in relation to landscape? Not only was landscape itself seen to be under threat, quite literally, as the railways were cut through the countryside and as urban sprawl encroached outwards upon it, but the land, as a symbol of the values that were at the heart of agricultural communities and of human beings' relationship with nature, was also at stake. As Robert Macfarlane puts it: 'Landscape has long offered us keen ways of figuring ourselves to ourselves, strong means of shaping memories and giving form to thought.'[7] If that is the case, then our gradual severance from the landscape (a process that was at a turning point at the end of the nineteenth century as the numbers of people living in towns outnumbered those living in the 'countryside'), along with the combined impact of increasingly accessible railway travel, the motor car and, more recently, digital technology, has distanced us more and more from the natural world, from the subject of Hardy's poem 'Afterwards', where the world is seen by a man 'who used to notice such things'.[8] The progressive and day-by-day loss of the landscape beneath our feet continued to be lamented into the twentieth century. As D. H. Lawrence wrote in 1929, 'the real tragedy of England, as I see it, is the tragedy of ugliness. The country is so lovely; the man-made England is so vile.'[9] Lawrence considered the transition to urbanization to have taken place from 1800, when 'the English people were strictly a rural people − very rural'. From his perspective of the inter-war period, he described the English as 'town-birds through and through, today, as the inevitable result of their complete industrialization'.[10] For us in the twenty-first century, landscape, argues John Stilgoe, has been 'turned out' of our lives.[11]

But as we have seen through the course of this book, clothing maintains a link with the urban dweller's view of the retreating landscape and its associations. The desired vision of the immutability of landscape offers respite − or, to use Hardy's phrase, 'ballast' − to 'the mind adrift on change', with places like Egdon Heath becoming a metaphor for unchanging values, and the clothing of its inhabitants extensions of that landscape. Hardy, as we have seen, often makes this link: a flock of sheep is positioned like a Vandyke lace collar around its wearer's neck; the figure of Tess is 'part of the landscape', in apparently timeless clothing. So when people move away from the landscape or adopt fashions that are 'out of sync' with their environment, individuals may no longer be 'figured to themselves', but instead to something alien and dislocated from their own identity − the new urban and suburban sprawl. So a landscape became the repository of memory and nostalgia, alongside the clothing with which it associated itself: in his *Rural Rides*, William Cobbett compares himself with a young boy, a public-house landlady's son, whom he meets in Billingshurst in Sussex: 'he was just such a chap as I was at his age, and dressed just in the same sort of way, his main garment being a blue smock-frock, faded from wear, and mended with pieces of *new* stuff, and of course, not faded. The sight of this smock-frock brought to my recollection many things very dear to me.'[12]

The memory of wearing a particular item of clothing has a special quality of taking the imagination into the past. And this operated collectively. Nostalgia was manifested in picturesque representations of rural dress, albeit worn sometimes by models outside a 'genuine' context, or else collected by individuals and museums, thereby constructing and perpetuating a particular view of history. For clothing in which time has been invested in making and mending, memories of it can be especially poignant. Extant garments originating from the Victorian period, along with their different representations, continue to inspire us, their interactive relationship with the present evolving, and meanings accumulating as time passes. This memorialization of dress can be performed in various ways, both on an individual and a collective level: by, for example, William Morris wearing and being photographed in his working smock (c.1876); by the revival of smock-making in the Dorset village of Bere Regis in the early twentieth century; or by the success of Laura Ashley dresses and prints in the 1970s. Such style appropriations have their cultural origins in the late Victorian period, when 'the dream of living in the country became implanted in the national consciousness'.[13]

Aside from William Morris's adoption of a smock, the perceived association between smocks and the concept of the individually hand-crafted item may account for the ways they were adapted by middle-class followers (and their children) of the Arts and Crafts Movement. Kate Greenaway's illustrations of children wearing smocks in rural settings in her popular *Under the Window* (1878), and the popularity of smocking embroidery on children's 'Kate Greenaway dresses' sold by the costume department at Liberty's from the 1880s,[14] exemplify how smocks were taken outside the context in which they were originally worn. In the twentieth century, revivals of smock-making evidenced the nostalgic symbolism attached to these garments. The Bere Regis Arts and Crafts Association was formed around 1905 by Sarah Lucy Bere, wife of the Rev. Montague Acland Bere (vicar of Bere Regis from 1905 to 1919), with the object of interesting local workers in the making of raffia baskets and traditional smocks. Mrs Bere's interest was probably aroused initially by the smocks in the Dorset County Museum (Dorchester), of which her uncle, Capt. J. E. Acland, had been curator. Collecting patterns from various sources and locations, the Bere Regis Arts and Crafts Association was made up of 15 or 20 regular workers who met on certain days each week in a special room in the vicarage. Both Rev. and Mrs Bere left for war service in 1916, returning in 1919. Although a few individual workers continued to take orders after that date, the Association ceased as such. The Museum of English Rural Life has a number of examples of Bere Regis smocks (see colour plate 12), distinguishable from nineteenth-century smocks by the fact that they are made from linen in different pastel shades, with finely executed embroidery using coloured threads, and fastened with Dorset buttons (mostly of the crosswheel and cartwheel type).

This study has focused upon the cultural meanings that may be ascribed to different representations of rural working-class dress and the significance of collected items of dress as evidence of the desire to retain emblems of the past. Traditional values were ranged alongside actual garments, the smock and the sun-bonnet the emblems of a vanishing folk culture, exemplifying and elevating traditional hand skills, retail practices and feminine domestic economy. However superficial this interpretation (noting, for example, that smocks were, in fact, often made commercially), this perception characterized the 1890s, continued into the twentieth century, and has persisted well beyond the time-frame of this study. On the other hand, the shoddy ready-made men's suits (Flora Thompson's 'reach-me-downs') and women's 'material' dresses (described by Hardy) that replaced them became synonymous with fashion and the mass-produced and, ultimately, with the rootlessness of modernity. If we could only find examples of these latter garments, then perhaps some of the gaping holes of dress history might begin to be filled.

The complexity of representations of clothing and their relationships with landscape discussed in this book arose from a specific social, cultural and economic historical context. While extant garments are significant cultural objects in their own right, my approach has also referenced art, photographic and literary history. As Lou Taylor observes, 'because of the multi-faceted "levels" at which clothing functions within any society and any culture, clothing provides a powerful analytical tool across many disciplines'.[15] This study has illustrated some of the ways in which rural working-class dress both reflects and defines the cultural history of Victorian England. And the survival of working-class clothing from the nineteenth century – along with its numerous mends and thinning fabric – reflects a very different society from one that mass-produces and consumes fast, throwaway fashion delivered by high-street chains and, increasingly, online, all in competition for market share. In the future, what will be salvaged to shape our associations with and attitudes towards this kind of clothing?

NOTES

Introduction

1 C. F. G. Masterman, *The Condition of England* (London, 1909), p. 16.

2 Francis Pryor, *The Making of the British Landscape* (London, 2010), p. 4.

3 Cited in Hugh Cunningham, *The Children of the Poor: Representations of Childhood since the Seventeenth Century* (Oxford, 1991), p. 56.

4 Alun Howkins, 'Labour history and the rural poor, 1850–1980', *Rural History* 1/1 (1990), p. 116. For the 1891 census, a considerable number of agricultural labourers returned themselves simply as 'labourers' without anything to indicate that they were employed on farms, and these would then have been classified as general labourers. Conversely, many agricultural carters and waggoners were probably accounted for as carters, carriers and hauliers of general traffic: see Alun Howkins, *Reshaping Rural England: A Social History 1850–1925* (London, 1991), p. 10.

5 Raphael Samuel (ed.), *Village Life and Labour* (London and Boston, 1975), p. 3.

6 Alexander Somerville, *The Whistler at the Plough – Containing Travels, Statistics and Descriptions of Scenery and Agricultural Customs in Most Parts of England* (1852; this edn London, 1989), p. 416.

7 Mick Reed, '"Gnawing it out": a new look at economic relations in nineteenth-century rural England', *Rural History* 1/1 (1990), pp. 84–5.

8 See David Morgan, 'The place of harvesters in nineteenth-century village life', in Raphael Samuel (ed.), *Village Life and Labour*, p. 29. However, G. E. Mingay gives a different figure: for England alone, he calculated that in 1851 there were 1,284,000 male and 199,000 female workers in agriculture – see G. E. Mingay, *Rural Life in Victorian England* (Stroud, 1990), p. 71.

9 Mingay, *Rural Life in Victorian England*, p. 19.

10 Howkins, *Reshaping Rural England*, p. 8.

11 William Cobbett, *Rural Rides* (this edn Harmondsworth, 1987), p. 69.

12 Mark Freeman (ed.), *The English Rural Poor, 1850–1914: Vol. I, The Moral and Material Condition of the Mid-Victorian Rural Poor* (London, 2005), p. xii.

13 Gordon E. Cherry and John Sheail, 'The urban impact on the countryside', in E. J. T. Collins (ed.), *The Agrarian History of England and Wales*, Vol. 7, 1850–1914 (Cambridge, 2000), p. 1515.

14 Howkins, *Reshaping Rural England*, p. 290.

15 Jan Marsh, *Back to the Land: The Pastoral Impulse in England, from 1880 to 1914* (London, 1982), p. 4.
16 David Matless, *Landscape and Englishness* (London, 1998), p. 16.

Chapter 1 Change and transition in Victorian England: the rural context

1 Gordon E. Cherry and John Sheail, 'The urban impact on the countryside', in E. J. T. Collins (ed.), *The Agrarian History of England and Wales*, Vol. 7, 1850–1914 (Cambridge, 2000), p. 1515.
2 Mark Freeman, *Social Investigation and Rural England 1870–1914* (Woodbridge, 2003), p. 36.
3 Howard Newby, *Country Life: A Social History of Rural England* (London, 1987), p. 54.
4 Alun Howkins, *Reshaping Rural England: A Social History 1850–1925* (London, 1991), p. 7.
5 However, these figures may under-represent both the extent of rural depopulation as well as urban growth due to the fact that many administrative boundaries did not distinguish between 'rural' and 'urban'. See Cherry and Sheail, 'The urban impact on the countryside', p. 1526.
6 Raymond Williams, *The Country and the City* (1973; this edn London, 1985), p. 1.
7 Elizabeth Gaskell, *Mary Barton* (this edn Harmondsworth, 1985), p. 39.
8 Tim Barringer, *Men at Work: Art and Labour in Victorian Britain* (London and New Haven, 2005), especially p. 103.
9 D. H. Lawrence, *The Rainbow* (this edn Harmondsworth, 1983), p. 458.
10 Elizabeth Gaskell, *North and South* (this edn Harmondsworth, 1994).
11 For example, with reference to the Rebecca Riots of the 1840s in South Wales, historians argue that the collaboration between industrial and agricultural labourers was never to be repeated, and represented the swansong of shared aspirations between what would become the increasingly polarized positions of different social, economic and cultural interests. Andrew Charlesworth argues that scholars, by studying just one major outbreak of social disorder, have caused a historiographical 'separation of industrial and agrarian protests in a way more befitting twentieth-century conceptual dichotomies than eighteenth- and nineteenth-century realities': see 'An agenda for historical studies of rural protest in Britain, 1750–1850', *Rural History* 2/2 (1991), p. 231.
12 Thomas Hardy in his General Preface to the Wessex Edition of the novels (1912).
13 Francis Pryor, *The Making of the British Landscape* (London, 2010), p. 463.
14 W. G. Hoskins, *The Making of the English Landscape* (1955; this edn Harmondsworth, 1981), p. 11.
15 For example, as regards the eastern zone, they ignore the large-scale sheep and cattle pastures of the Yorkshire and Lincolnshire wolds, the sheep lands of the chalk downs and the hitherto rich pastures of fenland meadows.
16 Alun Howkins, *The Death of Rural England – A Social History of the Countryside since 1900*, London, 2003), p. 18.
17 Ibid., p. 26.
18 Barry Reay, *Rural Englands: Labouring Lives in the Nineteenth Century* (Basingstoke, 2004), pp. xii and 21; Alun Howkins, 'The discovery of rural England', in Robert Colls and Phillip Dodd (eds), *Englishness: Politics and Culture* (London, 1986), pp. 62–88.

19 Mark Freeman (ed.), *The English Rural Poor, 1850–1914*: Vol. 1, *The Moral and Material Condition of the Mid-Victorian Rural Poor* (London, 2005), p. x.
20 Ibid., pp. xiv–v.
21 William Cobbett, *Rural Rides* (this edn Harmondsworth, 1987), p. 320.
22 Andrew Charlesworth, 'An agenda for historical studies of rural protest in Britain, 1750–1850', *Rural History* 2/2 (1991), p. 238.
23 G. E. Mingay, *Rural Life in Victorian England* (Stroud, 1990), p. 19. Alun Howkins's figures differ somewhat: 'by the 1900s, only just over 6 per cent of the national income came from agriculture and about 6 per cent of the population was employed in it' (Howkins, *Reshaping Rural England*, p. 4).
24 Ibid., p. 17.
25 Howkins, *Reshaping Rural England*, p. 138.
26 Mingay, *Rural Life in Victorian England*, p. 40.
27 Howkins, *Reshaping Rural England*, p. 143.
28 Ibid., p. 142.
29 Ibid., pp. 167–8.
30 Cherry and Sheail, 'The urban impact on the countryside', pp. 1526–7.
31 Alun Howkins, 'Labour history and the rural poor, 1850–1980', *Rural History* 1/1 (1990), p. 113.
32 Freeman (ed.), *The English Rural Poor 1850–1914*, p. ix.
33 Bronislaw Geremek, *Poverty – A History* (Oxford, 1997), p. 3.
34 Mingay, *Rural Life in Victorian England*, p. 14.
35 Howkins, *Reshaping Rural England*, pp. 94–5.
36 Ibid., p. 113.
37 Parliamentary Papers: *Report of Special Assistant Poor Law Commissioners on the Employment of Women and Children in Agriculture*, 1843 (510), Vol. XII, pp. 6–8.
38 Ibid., pp. 13–15.
39 Ibid., p. 16.
40 Freeman, *Social Investigation and Rural England 1870–1914*, p. 37.
41 Mick Reed, '"Gnawing it out": a new look at economic relations in nineteenth-century rural England', *Rural History* 1/1 (1990), p. 92.
42 Ibid., p. 90.
43 Richard Heath, 'Peasant life in Dorset' (1872), in Keith Dockray (ed.), *The Victorian Peasant by Richard Heath* (Gloucester, 1989), p. 119.
44 Ibid., p. 123.
45 Howkins, 'Labour history and the rural poor, 1850–1980', p. 114.
46 Ibid., p. 115. See also J. L. and Barbara Hammond, *The Village Labourer 1760–1832*, (Stroud, 1987), especially chapters X and XI.
47 Captain Swing was the name given to the mythical leader of the labourers, but, as Eric Hobsbawm and George Rudé point out in their study of the riots, there is no evidence, except in Kent, that any labourers believed themselves to be following any 'Captain Swing'. See E. J. Hobsbawm and George Rudé, *Captain Swing* (1969; this edn Harmondsworth, 1985), p. xviii.
48 Ibid., pp. 163–4.
49 Ibid., p. 258.
50 Ibid., pp. 258–9.
51 Mingay, *Rural Life in Victorian England*, p. 51.

52 Roger Wells, 'Southern Chartism', *Rural History* 2/1 (1991), p. 39.
53 For further discussion of the Poor Law Amendment Act, see Newby, *Country Life: A Social History of Rural England*, p. 48.
54 Ibid., p. 49.
55 Howkins, *Reshaping Rural England*, p. 87.
56 Hobsbawm and Rudé, *Captain Swing*, pp. 242–3.
57 Ian Dyck, 'Towards the "cottage charter": the expressive culture of farm workers in nineteenth-century England', *Rural History* 1/1 (1990), p. 106.
58 Joseph Arch, *Joseph Arch, The Story of His Life. Told by Himself* (1898; this edn London, 1966), p. 41.
59 For further details, see Newby, *Country Life: A Social History of Rural England*, pp. 120–33.
60 Howkins, *Reshaping Rural England*, p. 187.
61 Thomas Hardy, 'The Dorsetshire Labourer', *Longman's Magazine*, Vol. 2 (1883), p. 265.
62 See, for example, Mingay, *Rural Life in Victorian England*, p. 98.
63 Pamela Horn, *Victorian Countrywomen* (Oxford, 1991), p. 141.
64 Parliamentary Papers: *Second Report from the Commissioners on the Employment of Children, Young Persons and Women in Agriculture, with Appendix Part I and Part II*, 1868–9, p. lxvii.
65 Newby, *Country Life: A Social History of Rural England*, p. 136.
66 Horn, *Victorian Countrywomen*, p. 28.
67 Howkins, *The Death of Rural England*, p. 3.
68 Howkins, *Reshaping Rural England*, p. 249.
69 Hammond, *The Village Labourer 1760–1832*, p. viii.
70 See, for example, Pamela Sharpe, 'The women's harvest: straw-plaiting and the representation of labouring women's employment c.1793–1885', *Rural History* 5/2 (1994), pp. 129–42.
71 '[The] study of 'rural history' continues to be rather narrowly defined, confined by an essentially economistic agenda that has excluded much of the most fascinating recent work. Rural history is often seen as synonymous with agricultural history, and although the latter has generated a great deal of valuable and interesting research, its privileging of the economic perspective has tended to preclude the methodological inclusiveness that now seems necessary to foster cross-fertilisation between the disparate areas in which the study of rural history is being pursued [...] The time seems right for the founding of a journal that can stimulate investigation of the whole concept of the rural, by overcoming the disciplinary boundaries that have been so integral to the academic edifice': Liz Bellamy, K. D. M. Snell, Tom Williamson, 'Rural history: the prospect before us', *Rural History* 1/1 (1990), p. 1.
72 Phillis Cunnington and Catherine Lucas, *Occupational Costume in England from the Eleventh Century to 1914* (1967; this edn London, 1976), p. 11.
73 Anne Buck, 'Clothes in fact and fiction 1825–1865', *Costume* 17 (1983), pp. 89–104.
74 Alma Oakes and Margot Hill, *Rural Costume, Its Origin and Development in Western Europe and the British Isles* (London and New York, 1970), pp. 141–7.
75 Buck, 'Clothes in fact and fiction', p. 90.
76 Alison Toplis, *The Clothing Trade in Provincial England 1800–1850* (London, 2011).
77 Peter Jones, 'Clothing the poor in early-nineteenth century England', *Textile History* 37/1 (2006), p. 34.
78 See Steven A. King, *Poverty and Welfare in England 1700–1850: A Regional Perspective* (Manchester, 2000), and Steven A. King, 'Reclothing the English poor, 1750–1840',

Textile History 33/1 (2002), pp. 37–47. For a fuller discussion of some recent work in this field, see Rachel Worth, 'Developing a method for the study of the clothing of the "poor": some themes in the visual representation of rural working-class dress, 1850–1900', *Textile History* 40/1 (2009), pp. 70–96, especially pp. 70–5.

79 John Styles, *The Dress of the People: Everyday Fashion in Eighteenth-Century England* (New Haven and London, 2007).

80 Vivienne Richmond, *Clothing the Poor in Nineteenth Century England* (Cambridge, 2013).

81 Margaret Spufford, *The Great Reclothing of Rural England: Petty Chapman and their Wares in the Seventeenth Century* (London, 1984), pp. 98–9.

82 See, for example, Angela V. John, *By the Sweat of Their Brow: Women Workers at Victorian Coal Mines* (London, 1980), especially p. 26 and pp. 180–7, where she makes interest-ing comparisons between the descriptions of the physical appearance of the female miners of the1840s and of women field workers in the 1860s; and Melanie Tebbutt, *Making Ends Meet: Pawnbroking and Working-Class Credit* (London, 1984).

83 Steven A. King and Christiana Payne (eds), 'The dress of the poor: old and new per-spectives', *Textile History* 33/1 (2002), p. 1.

Chapter 2 Women's work, education and the domesticity of dress: surveying and documenting the rural (I)

1 Alun Howkins gives the following figures in *Reshaping Rural England: A Social History 1850–1925* (London, 1991), p. 11:

Year	No. of Labourers (includes shepherds, horsemen and 'ordinary' labourers)
1851	1,253,786
1861	1,188,768
1871	980,166
1881	870,798

2 Elizabeth Roberts, *Women's Work 1840–1940* (Cambridge, 1995), p. 33.

3 G. E. Mingay, *Rural Life in Victorian England* (Stroud, 1990), p. 60.

4 Karen Sayer, *Women of the Fields: Representations of Rural Women in the Nineteenth Century* (Manchester, 1995), p. 9.

5 Pamela Horn, *Victorian Countrywomen* (Oxford, 1991), p. 6.

6 Roberts, *Women's Work 1840–1940*, p. 9.

7 Ibid., p. 63.

8 Horn, *Victorian Countrywomen*, p. 4.

9 Sayer, *Women of the Fields: Representations of Rural Women*, p. 58.

10 Ibid., p. 152.

11 Pamela Sharpe, 'The women's harvest: straw-plaiting and the representation of labouring women's employment c.1793–1885', *Rural History* 5/2 (1994), p. 138.

12 Jane Rendall, *Women in an Industrializing Society: England 1750–1880* (Oxford, 1990), p. 98.

13 Ibid., p. 102.

14 Ibid., p. 16.

15 Horn, *Victorian Countrywomen*, p. 159.

16 Ibid., p. 2 and p. 133.

17 Liz Bellamy and Tom Williamson (eds), *Life in the Victorian Village: The Daily News Survey of 1891*, Vol. 1 (London, 1999), p. 17.

18 Rendall, *Women in an Industrializing Society*, p. 55.

19 Ibid.

20 Alun Howkins, 'Labour history and the rural poor, 1850–1980', *Rural History* 1/1 (1990), p. 119, acknowledging Edward Higgs, 'Women, occupations and work in the nineteenth-century censuses', *History Workshop Journal* 23 (1987).

21 Parliamentary Papers: *Reports of Special Assistant Poor Law Commissioners on the Employment of Women and Children in Agriculture*, 1843 (510), Vol. XII; Parliamentary Papers: *Second Report from the Commissioners on the Employment of Children, Young Persons and Women in Agriculture, with Appendix Part I and Part II*, 1868–9; Bellamy and Williamson, *Life in the Victorian Village: The Daily News Survey of 1891*.

22 Raphael Samuel, *Village Life and Labour* (London, 1975), p. xvi. Cited in Mark Freeman, *Social Investigation and Rural England, 1870–1914* (Woodbridge, 2003), p. 6.

23 Bellamy and Williamson, *Life in the Victorian Village: The Daily News Survey of 1891*, Vol. 1, p. 10.

24 For example, the publication in May 1842 of the *First Report of the Commission for Inquiry into the Employment and Condition of Children in Mines and Manufacture* and the passing of the Ten Hours Factory Act in 1847 (which, despite its shortcomings, established in principle the notion of a ten-hour working day) illustrate the urgent need for legislative intervention in the regulation of matters of working conditions and employment generally.

25 E. H. Hunt, *Regional Wage Variations in Britain, 1850–1914* (Oxford, 1973), p. 66.

26 Parliamentary Papers: *Reports of Special Assistant Poor Law Commissioners on the Employment of Women and Children in Agriculture*, 1843. The letter acts as a preface to the report (no page number is given). The four commissioners appointed were each allocated one of these four regions as follows: Mr Alfred Austin: Wiltshire, Dorset, Devon and Somerset; Mr Vaughan: Kent, Surrey and Sussex; Mr Stephen Denison: Suffolk, Norfolk and Lincolnshire; Sir Francis Doyle: Yorkshire and Northumberland.

27 Ibid., p. 1.

28 Cited in Mark Freeman, *Social Investigation and Rural England*, p. 23, and referring to Parliamentary Papers: *Reports of Special Assistant Poor Law Commissioners on the Employment of Women and Children in Agriculture*, 1843, p. 1, and appendices to Austin's report.

29 Freeman, *Social Investigation and Rural England*, p. 25.

30 Parliamentary Papers: *Reports of Special Assistant Poor Law Commissioners*, p. 3.

31 Ibid., p. 6.

32 Ibid., p. 28.

33 Ibid., pp. 9–12.

34 Ibid., pp. 13–15.

35 Ibid., pp. 18–19.

36 Ibid., pp. 4–5 and p. 12.

37 Ibid., p. 13.

38 Freeman, *Social Investigation and Rural England*, p. 23.

39 Ibid., p. 11.

40 Parliamentary Papers: *Second Report from the Commissioners on the Employment of Children, Young Persons and Women in Agriculture, with Appendix Part I and Part II*, 1868–9, p. lxiv.

41 Alun Howkins, *Reshaping Rural England*, p. 107.

42 Two reports relating to England were published as a result of the 1867 commission: the first in 1867–8 (C. 4068) and the second in 1868–9 (C. 4202). The majority

of the references here are to the second report. The counties listed below were vis-
ited by the following commissioners: Hon. E. Stanhope: Dorset, Kent, Cheshire,
Shropshire, Staffordshire, Sussex and Rutland; Hon. E. B. Portman: Hampshire,
Devon and Cornwall; F. H. Norman: Surrey, Wiltshire, Warwickshire, Worcestershire
and Herefordshire; G. Culley: Oxfordshire, Berkshire, Derbyshire and Hertfordshire;
R. F. Boyle: Somerset; H. S. Tremenheere: Cumberland, Westmorland and northern
Lancashire.

43 Mark Freeman (ed.), *The English Rural Poor 1850–1914*: Vol. 1, *The Moral and Material
    Condition of the Mid-Victorian Rural Poor* (London, 2005), p. xvii.

44 *Parliamentary Papers: Second Report from the Commissioners*, p. vii.

45 Ibid., *Appendix Part I*, p. 32.

46 Ibid., p. 51. In Surrey 36 questionnaires were distributed and 21 returned complete; in
    Wiltshire, 54 were distributed and 22 returned; in Warwickshire, 43 were distributed and
    17 returned; in Worcestershire, 17 were distributed and 11 returned, and in Herefordshire,
    19 were distributed and 7 returned. The commissioner adds that the amount of informa-
    tion contained in the answers varied greatly, but a representative selection of answers
    (according to the commissioner) is printed in *Appendix II* of the report.

47 Freeman, *Social Investigation and Rural England*, p. 38.

48 Ibid., p. 39.

49 Ibid.

50 Ibid., pp. 40–1.

51 *Parliamentary Papers: Second Report from the Commissioners*, pp. xxxii–ix.

52 Ibid., *Appendix Part I*, p. 14.

53 Ibid., p. 15.

54 Ibid., *Appendix Part II*, p. 84.

55 Ibid., *Appendix Part I*, p. 84.

56 Ibid., *Appendix Part II*, pp. 18–19.

57 Richard Heath, 'The cottage homes of England' (1870), in Keith Dockray (ed.), *The
    Victorian Peasant by Richard Heath* (Gloucester, 1989), p. 57.

58 Bellamy and Williamson, *Life in the Victorian Village: The Daily News Survey of 1891*,
    Vol. 1, p. 1.

59 Henry Mayhew's series of 82 articles, describing (often in the words of those he
    spoke with) the 'condition' of the poor in the metropolis and couched as lengthy
    'letters' in the *Morning Chronicle* in 1849–51 were subsequently published with some
    revisions as *London Labour and the London Poor*.

60 Freeman, *Social Investigation and Rural England*, p. 46.

61 Ibid.

62 Bellamy and Williamson, *Life in the Victorian Village: The Daily News Survey of 1891*, Vol. 2, p. 235.

63 Ibid., Vol. 1, p. 2.

64 *Parliamentary Papers: Second Report from the Commissioners*, *Appendix II*, p. 373.

65 Ibid., *Appendix Part II*, p. 12.

66 Ibid., *Appendix Part I*, p. 33.

67 Ibid., p. 35.

68 Ibid., p. 54.

69 Ibid., *Appendix Part II*, p. 84.

70 Ibid., p. 12.

71 Ibid., p. 27.

72 Ibid., p. 84.

73 Ibid., *Appendix Part I*, p. 112.
74 Ibid., p. 123.
75 In 1840 an act was passed making it an offence for any person under 21 to ascend a flue; the act was widely disregarded, and in the 1850s a new campaign had to be mounted, leading to an act in 1864 which itself required reinforcement in 1875. The 1833 Factory Act limited the work of children under the age of 13 to eight hours per day. For a fuller discussion see Hugh Cunningham, *The Children of the Poor: Representations of Childhood since the Seventeenth Century* (Oxford, 1991), especially p. 64 and p. 79.
76 Cunningham, *The Children of the Poor*, p. 171 and p. 173.
77 Ibid., especially pp. 32–8.
78 Parliamentary Papers: *Second Report from the Commissioners, Appendix Part II*, p. 97.
79 Parliamentary Papers: *Second Report from the Commissioners*, p. lv.
80 Ibid., *Appendix Part I*, p. 36.
81 Ibid., p. 129.
82 Cunningham, *The Children of the Poor*, p. 27.
83 Parliamentary Papers: *Second Report from the Commissioners, Appendix Part II*, p. 469.
84 Ibid., p. 17.
85 Ibid., *Appendix Part I*, p. 23.
86 See the views of Rev. E. Hammond of Sundridge, Kent in Parliamentary Papers, *Second Report from the Commissioners, Appendix Part II*, p. 41.
87 This is the case for a school in Windsor 'supported entirely by the Queen for the benefit of 120 children of persons employed by Her Majesty' (Parliamentary Papers: *Second Report from the Commissioners, Appendix Part II*, pp. 403–4).
88 Ibid., p. 96.
89 Ibid., *Appendix Part I*, p. 68.
90 Vivienne Richmond (ed.), *Clothing, Society and Culture in Nineteenth-Century England*, Vol. 3, *Working-Class Dress* (London, 2013), p. xiv.
91 Parliamentary Papers: *Second Report from the Commissioners, Appendix Part II*, p. 331 and p. 334.
92 Ibid., *Appendix Part I*, p. 141.
93 Ibid., p. 152.
94 Ibid., p. 116.

Chapter 3 Clothing and its acquisition in a changing society: surveying and documenting the rural (II)

1 Raphael Samuel (ed.), *Village Life and Labour* (London and Boston, 1975), p. 3.
2 Mark Freeman, *Social Investigation in Rural England 1870–1914* (Woodbridge, 2003).
3 Steven King has suggested – referring to the period up to 1840 – that those who wore ragged clothing were those who struggled to avoid dependence on parish relief, in 'Reclothing the English poor, 1750–1840', *Textile History* 33/1 (2002), pp. 46–7.
4 Friedrich Engels, *The Condition of the Working Class in England* (1845; first English trans.1892; this edn London, 1982), p. 290.
5 G. E. Fussell, *The English Labourer: His Home, Furniture, Clothing and Food from Tudor to Victorian Times* (London, 1949), p. ix.
6 Ibid., p. 14.

7　Ibid., p. 68.

8　Alexander Somerville, *The Autobiography of a Working Man* (1848; this edn London, 1951), p. 19.

9　Parliamentary Papers: *Reports of Special Assistant Poor Law Commissioners on the Employment of Women and Children in Agriculture*, 1843 (510),Vol. XII, p. 79. See also *Second Report from the Commissioners on the Employment of Children,Young Persons and Women in Agriculture, with Appendix Part I and Part II*, 1868–9: Appendix Part II, p. 209.

10　Quoted in J. Ketteringham, 'Country work girls in nineteenth-century England', in Raphael Samuel, *Village Life and Labour*, p. 82 (source: Kent Record Office, C/ES 408/2, log-book,Yalding National School, 6 October 1873).

11　Parliamentary Papers: *Second Report from the Commissioners*, Appendix Part II, p. 213.

12　Joseph Arch, *Joseph Arch, The Story of His Life.Told by Himself* (1898; this edn London, 1966), p. 30.

13　W. H. Hudson, *Hampshire Days* (1903; this edn Oxford, 1980), p. 180.

14　Fussell, *The English Labourer*, p. 122.

15　AlisonToplis, *The Clothing Trade in Provincial England 1800–1850* (London, 2011), p. 91.

16　Pamela Horn, *Victorian Countrywomen* (Oxford, 1991), p. 155 (source: Mary Lewis (ed.), *Old Days in the Kent Hop Gardens* (Tonbridge, 1962), pp. 22–5: 1868–9 Report: Evidence, p. 43).

17　David Gentleman (ed.), *George Ewart Evans,The Crooked Scythe: An Anthology of Oral History* (London, 1993), p. 15.

18　Parliamentary Papers: *Reports of Special Assistant Poor Law Commissioners*, p. 45.

19　Parliamentary Papers: *Second Report from the Commissioners*, p. xvii.

20　Anne Buck, 'The countryman's smock', *Folk Life: Journal for the Society of Folk Life Studies* 1 (1963), p. 32.

21　Liz Bellamy andTom Williamson (eds.), *Life in theVictorianVillage: The Daily News Survey of* 1891,Vol. 1, p. 189.

22　Parliamentary Papers: *Second Report from the Commissioners,Appendix Part II*, p. 144.

23　Ibid., pp. 13–14.

24　Ibid., p. 15.

25　Bellamy and Williamson, *Life in the Victorian Village: The Daily News Survey of 1891*, Vol. 1, p. 118.

26　Ibid., p. 128.

27　Pamela Horn, *The Changing Countryside* (London, 1984), p. 122.

28　G. E. Mingay, *Rural Life inVictorian England* (Stroud, 1990), p. 83.

29　Parliamentary Papers: *Second Report from the Commissioners*, Appendix Part II, p. 448.

30　Richard Heath, 'Sussex commons and Sussex songs' (1871), in Keith Dockray (ed.), *TheVictorian Peasant by Richard Heath* (Gloucester, 1989), p. 94.

31　Parliamentary Papers: *Second Report from the Commissioners*, Appendix Part I, p. 28.

32　Ibid., *Appendix Part II*, pp. 14–15.

33　Ibid., p. 37.

34　Ibid.

35　Ibid., p. 170.

36　Ibid., *Appendix Part I*, p. 47.

37　Pamela Horn, *The Changing Countryside* (London, 1984), p. 122.

38　Parliamentary Papers: *Second Report from the Commissioners,Appendix Part II*, p. 39.

39　See documentary records relating to smocks belonging to Amalek Old, accession nos. T814 andT815, Dorset County Museum, Dorchester.

40 Parliamentary Papers: *Second Report from the Commissioners, Appendix Part II*, p. 281.
41 The Scottish scheme was adopted in the 1840s in the towns of Edinburgh, Aberdeen and Glasgow; the total cost came to £8 13s 10d, with an allowance of 2s 6d per week given to the host family to cover board, lodging, washing and mending clothes. Clothing was supplied in addition (Parliamentary Papers: *Second Report from the Commissioners, Appendix Part I*, pp. 68–9).
42 Parliamentary Papers: *Second Report from the Commissioners, Appendix Part 1*, pp. 68–9.
43 Ibid., *Appendix Part II*, p. 283.
44 Ibid., p. 180.
45 Alun Howkins, *Reshaping Rural England: A Social History, 1850–1925* (London, 1991), p. 81.
46 G. E. Mingay, *Rural Life in Victorian England* (Stroud, 1990), p. 73.
47 See John Styles, *The Dress of the People: Everyday Fashion in Eighteenth-Century England* (New Haven and London, 2007), p.147 and p. 253.
48 See Vivienne Richmond, ' "Indiscriminate liberality subverts the morals and depraves the habits of the poor": a contribution to the debate on the poor law, parish clothing relief and clothing societies in early nineteenth-century England', *Textile History* 40/1 (2009), pp. 51–69.
49 Parliamentary Papers: *Reports of Special Assistant Poor Law Commissioners*, p. 79.
50 Richmond, 'Indiscriminate liberality subverts the morals and depraves the habits of the poor', p. 60.
51 Samuel Smiles, *Self Help* (1859).
52 Richmond, 'Indiscriminate liberality subverts the morals and depraves the habits of the poor', p. 52.
53 Parliamentary Papers: *Second Report from the Commissioners, Appendix Part II*, p. 449.
54 Bellamy and Williamson, *Life in the Victorian Village: The Daily News Survey of 1891*, Vol. 2, p. 252.
55 Parliamentary Papers: *Second Report from the Commissioners, Appendix Part II*, p. 81.
56 Heath, 'Sussex commons and Sussex songs', p. 94.
57 Richmond, 'Indiscriminate liberality subverts the morals and depraves the habits of the poor', pp. 58–9.
58 Parliamentary Papers: *Reports of Special Assistant Poor Law Commissioners*, p. 22. Some 20 years later, according to an article on the 'Dorsetshire labourer' which appeared in the *Labour Circular* of February 1868, contributions to a coal and clothes club were between 8d and 1s per month, 'which is added to by about the same amount (but in many places only one-third) by the lord of the manor and others. This gives about 4cwt or 6cwt of coal in the winter and some clothes at Christmas' (Parliamentary Papers: *Second Report from the Commissioners, Appendix Part II*, pp. 37–8).
59 Parliamentary Papers: *Reports of Special Assistant Poor Law Commissioners*, p. 22.
60 Ibid., p. 36.
61 Parliamentary Papers: *Second Report from the Commissioners, Appendix Part II*, p. 405.
62 Ibid., pp. 233–4.
63 Ibid., p. 453.
64 Bellamy and Williamson, *Life in the Victorian Village: The Daily News Survey of 1891*, Vol. 2, p. 3. Evidence cited by John Styles suggests that this more 'progressive' view was that of the minority, especially with regard to the early nineteenth century. The Farthingoe clothing society in Northamptonshire operated in the early 1830s under the direction of Rev. Francis Litchfield, who policed both the quality and style of clothing,

Styles arguing that the Farthingoe 'rules' were widely copied and that a clear moral agenda applied (John Styles, *The Dress of the People: Everyday Fashion in Eighteenth-Century England*, p. 254).

65 Styles, *The Dress of the People*, p. 271.

66 See Alison Toplis, *The Clothing Trade in Provincial England 1800–1850* (London, 2011).

67 Bellamy and Williamson, *Life in the Victorian Village: The Daily News Survey of 1891*, Vol. 1, p. 155.

68 Ibid.

69 Ibid., p. 97.

70 Ibid., p. 155.

71 Giorgio Riello, *A Foot in the Past: Consumers, Producers, and Footwear in the Long Eighteenth Century* (Oxford, 2006), p. 126.

72 Toplis, *The Clothing Trade in Provincial England*, p. 37.

73 Parliamentary Papers: *Second Report from the Commissioners, Appendix Part II*, p. 98.

74 Bellamy and Williamson, *Life in the Victorian Village: The Daily News Survey of 1891*, Vol. 2, p. 93.

75 Elizabeth Wilson and Lou Taylor, *Through the Looking Glass* (London, 1989), p. 95.

76 Bellamy and Williamson, *Life in the Victorian Village: The Daily News Survey of 1891*, Vol. 1, pp. 175–6.

77 Ibid., Vol. 2, p. 235.

78 Ibid., p. 8.

79 Cobbett, William, *Rural Rides* (this edn Harmondsworth, 1987), pp. 185–6

80 Bellamy and Williamson, *Life in the Victorian Village: The Daily News Survey of 1891*, Vol. 2, p. 174.

81 Ibid., pp. 116–17.

82 Ibid., p. 235.

83 Arch, Joseph Arch, *The Story of His Life*. For a discussion of working-class writers with a rural perspective such as Thomas Miller, see Owen Ashton and Stephen Roberts, *The Victorian Working-Class Writer* (London and New York, 1999).

84 Alexander Somerville, *The Whistler at the Plough – Containing Travels, Statistics and Descriptions of Scenery and Agricultural Customs in Most Parts of England* (1852; this edn London, 1989), p. i.

85 At the end of the Napoleonic Wars (1793–1815), corn prices fell and a Corn Law was introduced, prohibiting the duty-free import of foreign corn until the price of wheat had reached 80s per quarter. This was subsequently replaced by a sliding scale of duties. The Anti-Corn Law League was founded in 1839 to advocate free trade and the repeal of the Corn Laws in particular. It was based in Manchester and led by Richard Cobden and John Bright, who argued that the Corn Laws kept the price of bread artificially high and served to benefit the landowners rather than the middle classes or labourers.

86 Somerville, *The Whistler at the Plough*, p. xii.

87 Ibid., p. 18.

88 M. K. Ashby, *Joseph Ashby of Tysoe, 1859–1919* (1961; this edn London, 1979), p. 44.

89 Somerville, *The Whistler at the Plough*, p. 319.

90 Ibid.

91 Ibid.

92 Ibid., pp. 402–3.

93 Ibid., p. 405.

94 Ibid., p. 233 and p. 281.

95 Ashby, *Joseph Ashby*, p. 24.

96 Ibid., p. 40.

97 Ibid., p. 26.

98 Somerville, *The Whistler at the Plough*, p. 119.

99 Ashby, *Joseph Ashby*, p. 173.

100 George Sturt, *Change in the Village* (London, 1956), p. 64.

101 Ibid., p. 90.

102 Ashby, *Joseph Ashby*, p. 99 and p. 107.

103 Ibid., p. 104.

104 Ibid., p. 220.

105 Ibid., p. 149.

106 Ibid., p. 220 and p. 217.

107 Ibid., p. 136.

108 Ibid., p. 60.

109 Somerville, *The Whistler at the Plough*, pp. 33–4.

110 Ashby, *Joseph Ashby*, p. 46.

Chapter 4 Painting nostalgia: dress and the vision of a vanishing rural world

1 Rosemary Treble, 'The Victorian picture of the country', in G. E. Mingay (ed.), *The Rural Idyll* (London, 1989), p. 59.

2 Martin Kemp, *Behind the Picture: Art and Evidence in the Italian Renaissance* (New Haven and London, 1997), p. vii.

3 Ibid., p. 7.

4 Tim Barringer, *Men at Work: Art and Labour in Victorian Britain* (New Haven and London, 2005), p. 17. Barringer says that 'to examine form, surface, and technique, is, ultimately, to engage with the question of artistic labour, itself a process constituted within a particular social, economic and political context. The concept of labour – linking the actions of the artist thematically as well as instrumentally with the subject of representation – allows the discussion of content and meaning as inherent – indeed the pre-eminent – elements of visuality' (p. 17).

5 Although they adopt different approaches to the subject, this is broadly the theme in Christiana Payne, *Toil and Plenty: Images of the Agricultural Landscape, 1780–1890* (New Haven and London, 1993) and Christopher Wood, *Paradise Lost: Paintings of English Country Life and Landscape, 1850–1914* (London, 1988).

6 Wood, *Paradise Lost*, pp. 7–8.

7 Payne, *Toil and Plenty*, p. 23.

8 Barringer, *Men at Work*, p. 88.

9 Payne, *Toil and Plenty*, p. 4.

10 Daniel Roche, *The Culture of Clothing: Dress and Fashion in the Ancien Régime* (Cambridge, 1994), p. 9.

11 Payne, *Toil and Plenty*, p. 2; John Barrell, *The Dark Side of the Landscape: The Rural Poor in English Painting 1730–1840* (Cambridge, 1992), p. 20.

12 Barrell, *The Dark Side of the Landscape*, p. 20.

13 See, for example, *This Land is Our Land: Aspects of Agriculture in English Art* (exhibition organized for the Royal Agricultural Society of England by Demelza Spargo, Mall Galleries, London, January 1989).

14 Payne, *Toil and Plenty*, p. 6.

15 Ibid., p. 47.

16 Barrell, *The Dark Side of the Landscape*, p. 1.

17 Ibid.

18 Guiseppe Gatt, *Constable* (London, 1968), p. 26.

19 Martin Postle and Amima Wright, *Pictures of Innocence: Portraits of Children from Hogarth to Lawrence* (Bath, 2005), p. 46.

20 Martin Postle, *Angels and Urchins: The Fancy Picture in Eighteenth Century British Art* (Nottingham, 1998), p. 7.

21 Postle, *Angels and Urchins*, p. 21.

22 Ibid., p. 24.

23 Adrian Jenkins, *Painters and Peasants: Henry La Thangue and British Rural Naturalism, 1880–1905* (Bolton, 2000), p. 14.

24 For a more detailed discussion see Barrell, *The Dark Side of the Landscape*, pp. 25–31, and Neil Mckendrick, John Brewer and J. H. Plumb in *The Birth of a Consumer Society: The Commercialization of Eighteenth Century England* (London, 1982), pp. 60–2.

25 Payne, *Toil and Plenty*, p. 83.

26 Barrell, *The Dark Side of the Landscape*, p. 90.

27 Ibid., pp. 121–2.

28 Ibid., pp. 95–6.

29 Fitzwilliam Museum, Cambridge, no 1564c. See also Nicola Gauld, 'The Field Calls me to Labour': *Watercolours of Nineteenth-Century Rural Britain by Robert Hills and His Contemporaries* (catalogue of exhibition at Fitzwilliam Museum, Cambridge, 28 May–7 September 2008).

30 Payne, *Toil and Plenty*, p. 137.

31 Ibid., p. 194.

32 Ibid., p. 52.

33 M. A. Nattali, *W. H. Pyne: Etchings of Rustic Figures for the Embellishment of Landscape* (London, 1815).

34 Barrell, *The Dark Side of the Landscape*, p. 137. Barrell goes on to explain that this image is one that Constable arrived at 'in the attempt to adapt the old georgic vision of England, as a rich and peaceful land where labour is valued and rewarded, to a time in which that vision was clearly threatened by a new fear of the power of the labouring class'.

35 Payne, *Toil and Plenty*, p. 47.

36 Ibid., p. 45.

37 The Nazarenes offer an early example of an artistic practice that became common in the nineteenth century and which turned its back on the materialism of the present and sought to revive the spirituality of the past.

38 William Vaughan, Elizabeth E. Barker and Colin Harrison (eds), *Samuel Palmer, Vision and Landscape*, (London, 2005), pp. 12–13.

39 In this sense they were not dissimilar to the work of German Caspar David Friedrich (1774–1840), although there is no evidence to suggest that either knew anything of each other's work.

40 Vaughan, Barker and Harrison, *Samuel Palmer*, p. 13.

41 Payne, *Toil and Plenty*, p. 16 and p. 39.

42 Tim Barringer, *Men at Work*, p. 89.

43 For a more detailed discussion, see Alun Howkins, *Reshaping Rural England: A Social History, 1850–1925* (London, 1991), pp. 172–3 and pp. 202–4.

44 Richard Jefferies, *The Life of the Fields* (1884; this edn London, 1947), pp. 163–4.

45 Payne, *Toil and Plenty*, p. 21.

46 Marcus B. Huish, *The Happy England of Helen Allingham* (first published as *Happy England: As Painted by Helen Allingham R.W.S.*, 1903; this edn London, 1985), p. 185 and p. 81.

47 Christopher Wood, *Paradise Lost: Paintings of English Country Life and Landscape, 1850–1914* (London, 1988), pp. 129–31.

48 Huish, *The Happy England*, p. 3.

49 Ibid., p. 193 and p. 102.

50 Ibid., p. 84.

51 Rachel Worth, 'Rural labouring dress, 1850–1900: some problems of representation', *Fashion Theory: The Journal of Dress, Body and Culture* 3/3 (1999), pp. 323–42.

52 Huish, *The Happy England*, p. 119.

53 Ibid., p. 126.

54 Payne, *Toil and Plenty*, p. 115.

55 The association with the Good Shepherd in Christian symbolism is made by Payne, *Toil and Plenty*, p. 102.

Chapter 5 Photography and rural dress: 'work of art' or documentary realism?

1 This section and the discussion of Henry Peach Robinson that follows draws on Rachel Worth, 'Some issues in the representation of rural working-class dress in British nineteenth-century photography', *Revue Belge de Philologie et d'Histoire*, 87/3–4 (2009), pp. 775–91. Published, as a special issue, as Joeri Januarius and Nelleke Teughels (eds), *The Historical Use of Images: Theory, Methods, Practice*.

2 W. C. Brownell, 'Bastien-Lepage: painter and psychologist', *The Magazine of Art*, Vol. 6 (1883), p. 271.

3 John Taylor, *A Dream of England: Landscape, Photography and the Tourist's Imagination* (Manchester and New York, 1994), p. 39.

4 John Tagg, *The Burden of Representation: Essays on Photographs and Histories* (London, 1988), p. 2.

5 Phyllis Rose, 'Milkmaid madonnas: an appreciation of Cameron's portraits of women', in Sylvia Wolf, *Julia Margaret Cameron's Women* (New Haven and London, 1998), p. 14.

6 Ibid., p. 15.

7 Madeleine Ginsburg, *Victorian Dress in Photographs* (London, 1982), p. 10.

8 Catalogue nos DCM T3 and 14660, Dorset County Museum, Dorchester. The Duchy of Cornwall has substantial estates in Dorset, which would explain the choice of design.

9 Elizabeth Edwards, *The Camera as Historian: Amateur Photographers and Historical Imagination 1885–1918* (Durham and London, 2012), pp. 84–5.

10 For this discussion of the caloytpe and daguerreotype, see Malcolm Daniel, 'The state of the art', in Martin Barnes (ed.), *Benjamin Brecknell Turner: Rural England through a Victorian Lens* (London, 2001), p. 8, p. 9 and p. 13.

11 Michael Frizot, 'The truthfulness of the calotype', in Michael Frizot (ed.), *A New History of Photography* (Cologne, 1998), p. 70.

12 Daniel, 'The state of the art', p. 10.

13 Martin Barnes, 'Photographic views from nature', in Barnes (ed.), *Benjamin Brecknell Turner*, p. 38. The resemblance between the effects produced by watercolour paint and the calotype has been noted by Sara Stevenson in her study *Hill and Adamson's The Fishermen and Women of the Firth of Forth* (Edinburgh, 1991), p. 43.

14 Barnes, 'Photographic views from nature', p. 41.

15 Ibid., p. 47.

16 See Stevenson, *Hill and Adamson's The Fishermen and Women of the Firth of Forth*, p. 45. A special portrait session cost the sitter a guinea, while individual prints were 7s 6d, or, if they were produced in quantity as part of the studio's commercial stock, 5s.

17 Margaret Harker, *Henry Peach Robinson, Master of Photographic Art, 1830–1901* (Oxford, 1988), p. 58.

18 Stevenson, *Hill and Adamson's The Fishermen and Women of the Firth of Forth*, p. 45.

19 Ibid., p. 25. Stevenson describes the 'seed and inspiration' for the Newhaven calotypes as lying in 'the three key works of Scotland's greatest and most influential artists': Robert Burns's poem 'The Jolly Beggars', David Wilkie's painting *Distraining for Rent* and Walter Scott's novel *The Antiquary* (pp. 33–6).

20 Ibid., p. 19.

21 Ibid., p. 40.

22 Elizabeth Rigby Eastlake, 'The art of dress', in *Music and the Art of Dress* (essays reprinted from *The Quarterly Review* (1852).

23 Stevenson, *Hill and Adamson's The Fishermen and Women of the Firth of Forth*, p. 41.

24 Ibid., pp. 29–30.

25 Gale's photographs are published in Brian Coe, *A Victorian Country Album: The Photographs of Joseph Gale* (Yeovil, 1986).

26 *Amateur Photographer*, 7 June 1889, pp. 380–2.

27 Harker, *Henry Peach Robinson*, p. 84.

28 Henry Peach Robinson, *The Elements of a Pictorial Photograph* (Bradford and London, 1896), pp. 139–47.

29 Harker, *Henry Peach Robinson*, p. 44. Harker uses the term 'picturesque' in a specific sense and as it relates to the vogue in the late eighteenth and early nineteenth centuries of what Hugh Honour describes as the 'artfully informal landscape park with its sweeping Claudean vistas' in *Romanticism* (Harmondsworth, 1979, p. 110), which went against the aesthetics of writers such as Wordsworth and artists such as Constable. Robinson's own reference to the term in the quotation shows an awareness of it in precisely this context, which distinguishes the 'picturesque' from the artistic categories of the 'sublime' and the 'beautiful'. The picturesque was neither awe-inspiring (like the sublime) nor serene (like the beautiful) but full of variety, curious details, and interesting textures – medieval ruins were, for example, quintessentially picturesque. From this more specific definition, the term is used descriptively for a scene which may be quaint, pretty, and implies something artificial rather than natural.

30 Henry Peach Robinson, *Pictorial Effect in Photography, Being Hints on Composition and Chiaroscuro for Photographers* (London, 1869).

31 Robinson, *Pictorial Effect in Photography*, p. 78.

32 Henry Peach Robinson, 'Composition not patchwork', *British Journal of Photography* (2 July 1860), pp. 189–90.

33 Robinson, *Pictorial Effect in Photography*, p. 109.

34 Harker, *Henry Peach Robinson*, p. 35.

35 Ibid., p. 25.

36 Henry Peach Robinson, *Picture Making by Photography* (London, 1884), p. 54.

37 Ibid., p. 53. Sara Stevenson comments that 'Robinson's was a dressed-up, theatrical reality – real people with the wrong people inside' (*Hill and Adamson's The Fishermen and Women of the Firth of Forth*, p. 31).

38 Harker, *Henry Peach Robinson*, p. 66.

39 Robinson, *Elements of a Pictorial Photograph*, p. 98.

40 Ibid., p. 95.

41 Harker compares Foster's *Young Gleaners Resting by a Stile* (1886) with Robinson's *Autumn* (1863) in terms of picture construction, tonal arrangement, lighting effects and rendition of detail (see Harker, p. 39). In *Picture Making by Photography*, Robinson wrote of Foster that his 'drawings on wood, as illustrations to books, afford grand lessons in the introduction and composition of groups of figures and incidents and light and shade' (Robinson, *Picture Making by Photography*, p. 77).

42 Harker, *Henry Peach Robinson*, p. 76.

43 Ibid.; see also Christiana Payne's *Rustic Simplicity: Scenes of Cottage Life in Nineteenth-Century British Art* (exhibition catalogue published by the Djanogly Art Gallery, University of Nottingham Arts Centre in association with Lund Humphries Publishers, London, 1998).

44 Edwards, *The Camera as Historian*, p. xi.

45 Ibid., p. 2.

46 Ibid., *Appendix*, p. 268.

47 James Leon Williams, *The Home and Haunts of Shakespeare*, an illustrated work with 15 coloured plates of artists' interpretations of Warwickshire scenery, 45 photogravures and more than 150 other photographic illustrations (London, 1892), p. 26. Discussed in John Taylor, *A Dream of England: Landscape, Photography and the Tourist's Imagination* (Manchester and New York, 1994), pp. 80–1.

Chapter 6 Clothing and the 'counter-myth' in images of rural England

1 George Clausen, *Royal Academy Lectures on Painting: 16 Lectures Delivered to the Students of the Royal Academy of Arts, by George Clausen, R.A.* (London, 1913), p. 110.

2 Jozef Gross, 'The broadland paysanniste', *British Journal of Photography*, Issue 50 (12 December 1896), p. 1423.

3 Peter Turner and Richard Wood, *P. H. Emerson, Photographer of Norfolk* (London, 1974), p. 11.

4 Margaret Harker, *Henry Peach Robinson, Master of Photographic Art, 1830–1901* (Oxford, 1988), p. 78; Adrian Jenkins, *Painters and Peasants: Henry La Thangue and British Rural Naturalism, 1880–1905* (Bolton, 2000), p. 86.

5 Peter Henry Emerson, *Naturalistic Photography* (London and Aylesbury, 1889), pp. 170–3.

6 Jenkins, *Painters and Peasants*, p. 89.

7   John Taylor, *A Dream of England: Landscape, Photography and the Tourist's Imagination* (Manchester and New York, 1994), p. 101.

8   Ibid., p. 103.

9   Peter Henry Emerson, 'The log of the "Lucy"', *Amateur Photographer*, supplement to winter issue (10 December 1884), p. 1.

10 Peter Henry Emerson, *On English Lagoons* (London, 1893).

11 Taylor, *A Dream of England*, p. 104.

12 Ibid., p. 51.

13 Ibid., pp. 62–3 and p. 19.

14 Christiana Payne, *Toil and Plenty: Images of the Agricultural Landscape 1780–1890* (New Haven and London, 1993), p. 24.

15 For an analysis of dress in selected work of George Clausen, see also Rachel Worth, 'Developing a method for the study of the clothing of the "poor": some themes in the visual representation of rural dress, 1850–1900', *Textile History* 40/1 (2009), pp. 70–96.

16 Payne (*Toil and Plenty*, p. 42) points out that the term was coined by W. J. Keith in 'The land in Victorian literature', in Gordon E. Mingay (ed.), *The Victorian Countryside* (London, 1981), p. 147.

17 Thomas Pinney (ed.), *Essays of George Eliot* (London, 1963) p. 269.

18 Julian Treuherz, *Hard Times: Social Realism in Victorian Art* (London, 1987), p. 9.

19 Ibid., p. 10.

20 Kenneth McConkey, *Sir George Clausen, R.A. 1852–1944* (Bradford Art Galleries and Museums and Tyne and Wear County Council Museums, 1980), p. 29.

21 Ibid., p. 29.

22 See Alastair Ian Wright, 'Bastien-Lepage and English critical taste' in *Gazette des Beaux Arts*, Vol. CXVI (September 1990), pp. 94–104; also John House and Maryanne Stevens, *Post-Impressionism: Cross-Currents in European Painting* (London, 1979), p. 30. While greatly admired by Clausen, Bastien-Lepage's work was also criticized by contemporary art critics for its lack of sentiment (although, ironically, twentieth-century criticism focused on its inclusion of 'sentiment').

23 Jenkins, *Painters and Peasants*, p. 24.

24 Linda Nochlin, *Realism* (Harmondsworth, 1971).

25 George Clausen, 'Bastien-Lepage and modern realism', *The Scottish Art Review*, Vol. 1 (1888), p. 114.

26 Clausen, *Royal Academy Lectures on Painting*, p. 108.

27 George Clausen, 'Jules Bastien-Lepage as artist', in André Theuriet, *Jules Bastien-Lepage and his Art: A Memoir* (London, 1892), p. 116.

28 Jenkins, *Painters and Peasants*, p. 23.

29 Ibid., p. 154.

30 Helen Zimmern, 'A painter of peasants', *The Magazine of Art*, Vol. 8 (1885), p. 8.

31 George Thomson, 'Henry Herbert La Thangue and his work', *Studio*, Vol. 9 (1896), p. 177.

32 Kenneth McKonkey, *George Clausen and the Picture of English Rural Life* (Edinburgh, 2012), p. 10.

33 *The Magazine of Art*, Vol. 5 (1881–2), p. 438.

34 *The Times*, 16 May 1928, p. 14.

35 McConkey, *Sir George Clausen, R.A.*, p. 29.

36 Anna Gruetzner Robins, 'Living the simple life: George Clausen at Childwick Green', in David Peters Corbett, Ysanne Holt and Fiona Russell (eds), *The Geographies*

of *Englishness: Landscape and the National Past 1880–1940* (New Haven and London, 2002), p. 17.

37 Ibid., p. 15.
38 Ibid., p. 18.
39 Quoted in Jenkins, *Painters and Peasants*, p. 58.
40 McConkey, *Sir George Clausen, R.A.*, p. 46.
41 Peyton Skipworth, *The Rustic Image: Rural Themes in British Painting, 1880–1912* (London, 1979), Introduction.
42 *The Magazine of Art*, Vol. 10 (1887), p. 158.
43 Parliamentary Papers: *Second Report from the Commissioners*, Appendix Part II, pp. 353–4.
44 McConkey, *Sir George Clausen, R.A.*, p. 48.
45 Payne, *Toil and Plenty*, pp. 63–5.
46 Gruetzner Robins, 'Living the simple life: George Clausen at Childwick Green', p. 20.
47 Payne, *Toil and Plenty*, p. 126
48 McKonkey, *George Clausen and the Picture of English Rural Life*, p. 12.
49 George Moore, *Modern Painting* (London, 1893), p. 116.
50 Karen Sayer, *Women of the Fields: Representations of Rural Women in the Nineteenth Century* (Manchester, 1995), p. 17.
51 David Matless, *Landscape and Englishness* (London, 1998), p. 16.
52 McKonkey, *George Clausen and the Picture of English Rural Life*, p. 12.

Chapter 7 Thomas Hardy: tradition, fashion and the approach of modernity

1 Thomas Hardy, from 'At Middle-Field Gate in February', published in *Moments of Vision*, 1917, lines 11–15.
2 Adrian Jenkins, *Painters and Peasants: Henry La Thangue and British Rural Naturalism, 1880–1905* (Bolton, 2000), pp. 89–90.
3 *The Times*, 16 May 1928, p. 14.
4 Hesketh Hubbard, *A Hundred Years of British Painting 1851–1951* (London, 1951), p. 153.
5 Thomas Hardy, *The Return of the Native* (1878; this edn Harmondsworth, 1979), Ch. 1. Note: references to the novels are given by chapter number and/or part or book rather than by page number so that readers can locate them irrespective of which edition they use.
6 W. J. Keith, 'The land in Victorian literature', in G. E. Mingay (ed.), *The Rural Idyll* (London, 1989), p. 87.
7 Robert Macfarlane, *The Old Ways: A Journey on Foot* (London, 2012), p. 323.
8 Anne Buck, 'Clothes in fact and fiction 1825–1865', *Costume* 17 (1983), pp. 89–104; see especially pp. 89–90.
9 Clair Hughes, *Dressed in Fiction* (New York, 2005), p. 6.
10 Rachel Worth, 'Elizabeth Gaskell, clothes and class identity', *Costume* 32 (1998), p. 53.
11 Daniel Roche, *The Culture of Clothing: Dress and Fashion in the Ancien Régime* (Cambridge, 1994), pp. 18–19.
12 The discussion that follows is based in part on Rachel Worth, 'Clothing the landscape: change and the rural vision in the work of Thomas Hardy (1840–1928)', *Rural*

History, Vol. 24, Issue 2 (2013), pp. 199–215. I am grateful for the permission for this work to be published here.

13 Rachel Worth, 'Thomas Hardy and rural dress', *Costume* 29 (1995), pp. 55–67.

14 Simon Gatrell, *Thomas Hardy Writing Dress* (Bern, 2011), p. 5.

15 Ibid., p. 2.

16 J. B. Bullen, *The Expressive Eye: Fiction and Perception in the Work of Thomas Hardy* (Oxford, 1986), p. 147.

17 Thomas Hardy, from 'Domicilium', published in *Wessex Poems* (1898), lines 26–8.

18 Raymond Williams, *The Country and the City* (this edn London, 1985), p. 197.

19 Keith, 'The land in Victorian literature', p. 85.

20 Thomas Hardy, 'The Dorsetshire Labourer', *Longman's Magazine*, Vol. 2 (1883), pp. 252–69, especially pp. 262–3.

21 Michael Millgate, *Thomas Hardy: A Biography* (Oxford, 1982), p. 35.

22 Andrew Radford: *Mapping the Wessex Novel: Landscape, History and the Parochial in British Literature, 1870–1940* (London, 2010), p. 155.

23 Thomas Hardy, General Preface to the Wessex Edition of the novels (1912).

24 Susan M. Pearce, 'Objects as meaning; or narrating the past', in Susan M. Pearce (ed.), *Interpreting Objects and Collections* (London and New York, 1994), p. 28.

25 Merryn Williams, *Thomas Hardy and Rural England* (Colombia, 1972), p. 193.

26 Snell, K. D. M., *Annals of the Labouring Poor: Social Change and Agrarian England, 1660–1900* (Cambridge, 1985), p. 374.

27 Ibid., p. 375.

28 Ibid., p. 410.

29 Worth, 'Thomas Hardy and rural dress', 55–67.

30 Gatrell, *Thomas Hardy Writing Dress*, p. 5.

31 Thomas Hardy, *Far From the Madding Crowd* (1874; this edn Harmondsworth, 1988), Ch. XXII.

32 Thomas Hardy, *Under the Greenwood Tree* (1872; this edn Harmondsworth, 1987), Part I, Ch. IV.

33 Hardy, *Far From the Madding Crowd*, Ch. IX.

34 Claire Tomalin, *Thomas Hardy: The Time Torn Man* (London, 2006), p. 353, and footnote on p. 448 where she ascribes the information to W. G. L. Parsons, *A Mellstock Quire Boy's Recollections of Thomas Hardy* (St Peter Port, 1967).

35 British Library Add. MS 84021, p. vii.

36 Hardy, 'The Dorsetshire Labourer', pp. 258–9.

37 Richard Jefferies, *Wild Life in a Southern County* (Bradford-on-Avon, 1978), p. 136.

38 W. H. Hudson, *Hampshire Days* (1903; this edn Oxford, 1980), p. 148.

39 Thomas Hardy, *Tess of the d'Urbervilles* (1891, this edn London, 1984), Part VI, Ch. L.

40 Rachel Worth, 'Some issues in the representation of rural working-class dress in British nineteenth-century photography', *Revue Belge de Philologie et d'Histoire*, 87/3–4 (2009), pp. 775–91.

41 Flora Thompson, *Lark Rise to Candleford* (1945; this edn Harmondsworth, 1987), p. 81.

42 Hardy, *Tess*, Part IV, Ch. XXX and Part VI, Ch. XLVII.

43 Thompson, *Lark Rise to Candleford*, p. 259.

44 Thomas Hardy, *The Woodlanders* (1887; this edn Harmondsworth, 1981), Ch. V.

45 Hardy, *Tess*, Part V, Ch. XLII.

46 Hardy, *The Return of the Native*, Book IV, Ch. V.

47 Ibid., Book V, Ch. VII.

48 Hardy, *The Woodlanders*, Ch. XLII.

49 Hardy, *Far From the Madding Crowd*, Ch. IX.

50 Thomas Hardy, *Jude the Obscure* (1896; this edn Harmondsworth, 1985), Part I, Ch. II.

51 Bullen, *The Expressive Eye*, pp. 151–2.

52 Hardy, *The Return of the Native*, Book I, Ch. I.

53 Bullen, *The Expressive Eye*, pp. 148–9.

54 Hardy, *The Woodlanders*, Ch. VII.

55 Hardy, *Tess*, Part II, Ch. XV.

56 Ibid., Part VII, Ch. LV.

57 Thomas Hardy, 'The Ruined Maid' (186?), in *Poems of the Past and Present* (1901).

58 Roche, *The Culture of Clothing*, p. 411.

59 Hardy, 'The Dorsetshire Labourer', p. 259.

60 Florence Emily Hardy, *The Early Life of Thomas Hardy, 1840–1891* (London, 1928), p. 293.

61 Hardy, *Jude the Obscure*, Part III, Ch. 2.

62 Michael Millgate, *Thomas Hardy*, p. 265.

63 Thomas Hardy, 'The profitable reading of fiction', *Forum* (New York, March 1888), p. 57.

64 Hardy, *Jude the Obscure*, Part I, Ch. IX.

65 Bullen, *The Expressive Eye*, p. 148.

66 See Lou Taylor, *Mourning Dress: A Costume and Social History* (London, 1983).

67 Hardy, *Jude the Obscure*, Part V, Ch. VII.

68 Ibid., Part VI, Ch. II.

69 Thomas Hardy, 'She at his Funeral' (187?), in *Wessex Poems* (1898).

70 See Stella Mary Newton, *Health, Art and Reason* (London, 1974).

Chapter 8 Rural working-class dress: survival, representation and change

1 Richard Cobb, *Death in Paris, 1795–1801* (Oxford, 1978), p. 102.

2 Ibid., p. 35.

3 Alison Toplis, *The Clothing Trade in Provincial England 1800–1850* (London, 2011).

4 For more information on oiled smocks, see Louise Squire, *The Conservation of a Nineteenth Century Waterproofed Sussex Round Smock-Frock* (unpublished dissertation for Postgraduate Diploma Course, Textile Conservation Centre in affiliation with the Courtauld Institute of Art, University of London, 1996).

5 Michael Millgate, *Thomas Hardy: A Biography* (Oxford, 1985), p. 33.

6 See Parliamentary Papers: *Second Report from the Commissioners on the Employment of Children, Young Persons and Women in Agriculture, Appendix Part II*, p. 7, where reference is made to this practice taking place in the hop-picking areas of Kent.

7 Daniel Roche, *The Culture of Clothing: Dress and Fashion in the Ancien Régime* (Cambridge: Cambridge University Press, 1994), p. 3.

8 C. Willett Cunningham, quoted in Jane Tozer, 'Cunnington's interpretation of dress', *Costume* 20 (1986), p. 3.

9 Lou Taylor, *Establishing Dress History* (Manchester, 2004), p. 136.

10 Simon Knell, *Museums and the Future of Collecting* (Aldershot, 1999), p. 1 and p. 11.

11 *Museum of English Rural Life and Special Collections: A Guide* (University of Reading, 2012), p. 4.

12 See the H. J. Massingham Collection (fonds D MASM 1918–57), containing more than 130 objects, Museum of English Rural Life, University of Reading.

13 Collections consulted and referred to in the course of this chapter include: Dorset County Museum, Dorchester; Gallery of English Costume, Manchester; Gurteens Archive, Haverhill; Luton Museum; Museum of English Rural Life (MERL), University of Reading; Victoria and Albert Museum, London; Worthing Museum and Art Gallery.

14 Knell, *Museums and the Future of Collecting*, p. 13.

15 Jules David Prown, 'The truth of material culture: history or fiction?', in Steven Lubar and W. David Kingery (eds), *History from Things: Essays on Material Culture* (Washington and London, 1993), p. 1.

16 Susan M. Pearce, 'Museum objects', in Susan M. Pearce (ed.), *Interpreting Objects and Collections* (London and New York, 1994), p. 9.

17 Susan M. Pearce, 'Objects as meaning; or narrating the past', in Susan N. Pearce (ed.), *Interpreting Objects and Collections* (London and New York, 1994), p. 19.

18 Ibid., p. 21.

19 Ibid., p. 23.

20 Ibid., p. 25.

21 Ibid., p. 27.

22 Prown, 'The truth of material culture: history or fiction?', p. 17.

23 Taylor, *Establishing Dress History*, pp. 200–1.

24 Mark Freeman, *Social Investigation and Rural England 1870–1914* (Woodbridge, 2003); for a specific discussion of the fears of 'urban degeneration', see p. 76.

25 Taylor, *Establishing Dress History*, pp. 234–5.

26 See Mary Wright, *Cornish Guernseys and Knit-frocks* (London, 1979).

27 'Of the 16 smocks in the St Fagan's collection, four are originally from English sources; of the remaining 12, all but three are provenanced firmly in the border counties. This distribution is echoed in the holdings (or lack of them) of local museums throughout Wales. It is also confirmed by the available literary and pictorial evidence […] Many of the tourists of the late eighteenth and nineteenth centuries published accounts of their travels in Wales, and despite frequent references to the dress of the inhabitants, no mention is made of a smock'. Mair G. Rees and Christine Stevens, 'Smocks in the Welsh Folk Museum Collection', *Medel* 3 (1986), p. 32.

28 Parliamentary Papers: *Second Report from the Commissioners, Appendix Part II*, p. 527.

29 Alison Toplis, 'The manufacture and provision of rural garments 1800–1850: a case study of Herefordshire and Worcestershire', *Textile History*, 40/2 (2009), p. 165. Toplis points out that the term first appears in the Old Bailey Records in 1774, https://www.oldbaileyonline.org

30 William Cobbett, *Rural Rides* (this edn Harmondsworth, 1987), p. 41.

31 Ibid., p. 114.

32 Cited in G. E. Fussell, *The English Labourer: His Home, Furniture, Clothing and Food from Tudor to Victorian Times* (London, 1949), p. 119.

33 Anne Buck, 'The countryman's smock', *Folk Life: Journal for the Society of Folk Life Studies* 1 (1963), p. 19.

34 Ibid., p. 32.

35 Anne Buck, 'Dress as a social record', *Folk Life: Journal for the Society of Folk Life Studies* 14 (1976), p. 14.

36 Buck, 'The countryman's smock', p. 16.

37 Ibid., p. 24.

38 In 1928, Alice Armes observed: 'The designs for the various trades generally included conventionalized representations of the following emblems, though they are sometimes rather difficult to decipher – Waggoners or Carters – Cart-wheels, whip lashes, reins and bits; Woodmen – Trees and leaves; Gardeners – Flowers and leaves; Shepherds – Crooks, sheep-pens, hurdles and sheep; Milkmaids – Churns, butter-pats, hearts, etc.; Gravediggers – crosses; Butchers' smocks are somewhat difficult to decipher and one can only surmise that the objects in the Shropshire butcher's smock represent chopping-blocks, saws and pounds of meat'. See Armes, *English Smocks with Directions for Making Them* (Leicester, 1928), p. 8.

39 Buck, 'The countryman's smock', p. 26.

40 Nicholas Thornton, 'Enigmatic variations: the features of British smocks', *Textile History* 28/2 (1997), p. 177.

41 Toplis, *The Clothing Trade in Provincial England* provides useful information on the derivation of the term slop: 'the clothing required for seamen is the origin of "slop" clothing, "slop" eventually becoming a term meaning a cheap, ready-made garment' (p. 6). Unhelpfully, the term 'slops' can refer to smocks as well as to ready-made clothing (p. 22).

42 Thornton, 'Enigmatic variations', p. 182.

43 Ibid., p. 184.

44 Ibid., p. 183.

45 Toplis, *The Clothing Trade in Provincial England*, p. 22.

46 Buck, 'The countryman's smock', p. 22.

47 Thomas Hardy, *Far from the Madding Crowd*, Ch. VI.

48 Marian Nichols, *Smocks in Luton Museum* (Luton, 1980), p. 11.

49 Information provided by Alison Carter, formerly Senior Keeper of Art and Design at Hampshire County Council Museums Service.

50 Sarah Payne, *The Gurteens of Haverhill: Two Hundred Years of Suffolk Textiles* (Cambridge, 1984), p. 22.

51 Nichols, *Smocks in Luton Museum*, p. 3.

52 The Gurteen Museum can be visited by appointment (tel. 01440 702601 at time of writing).

53 Parliamentary Papers: *Second Report from the Commissioners*, Appendix Part I, p. 299.

54 Stanley Chapman, 'The "revolution" in the manufacture of ready-made clothing, 1840–60', *London Journal*, 29/1 (2004), especially pp. 44–58.

55 Ibid., p. 58.

56 Pamela Sharpe, 'Cheapness and economy: manufacturing and retailing ready-made clothing in London and Essex 1830–1850', *Textile History* 26/2 (1995), p. 208.

57 Margaret U. Jones, 'The vanished smock-frock', *Country Life* (April 1957), p. 720.

58 Suffolk and Essex Free Press Newspaper Archive (online), 1855–1892. See http://www.foxearth.org.uk/1855-1892SuffolkFreePress.html.

59 Phillis Cunnington and Catherine Lucas, *Occupational Costume in England from the Eleventh Century to 1914* (1967; this edn London, 1976), p. 35. See also Buck, 'Dress as a social record', p. 8.

60 Edwin Grey, *Cottage Life in a Hertfordshire Village* (Harpenden, not dated but c.1934), p. 35.

61 Thomas Hardy, 'The Dorsetshire Labourer', *Longman's Magazine*, Vol. 2 (1883), p. 258.

62 Alexander Somerville, *The Whistler at the Plough – Containing Travels, Statistics and Descriptions of Scenery and Agricultural Customs in Most Parts of England* (1852; this edn London, 1989), p. 50.

63 Sarah Levitt, 'Cheap mass-produced men's clothing in the nineteenth and early twentieth centuries', *Textile History* 22/2 (1991) p. 179.

64 Toplis, *The Clothing Trade in Provincial England*, p. 79.

65 See Evelyn Vigeon, 'Clogs or wooden-soled shoes', *Costume* 11 (1977), especially p. 9 and p. 11.

66 Ibid., p. 12.

67 Cat. no 60/179 along with surviving sun-bonnet, Museum of English Rural Life, University of Reading.

68 Derek Hudson, *A. J. Munby, Man of Two Worlds* (London, 1974), p. 76.

69 Anne Buck, 'Clothes in fact and fiction', *Costume* 17 (1983), p. 103.

70 In the USA Butterick sold sun-bonnet patterns in the 1880s. See Rebecca Jumper Matheson, *Sunbonnet: An American Icon in Texas* (Texas, 2009), p. 41.

71 Ibid., p. 14.

72 Ibid., p. 17.

73 Ibid., p. 129.

74 Ibid., p. 44.

75 Ibid., p. 104.

76 Ibid., p. 130.

77 Elizabeth Gaskell, *Cranford* (1853; this edn Oxford, 1972), pp. 175–6.

78 Neil McKendrick, John Brewer and John H. Plumb, *The Birth of a Consumer Society: The Commercialization of Eighteenth-Century England* (London, 1982), p. 36.

79 M. K. Ashby, *Joseph Ashby of Tysoe, 1859–1919* (London, 1979), p. 57.

80 Liz Bellamy and Tom Williamson (eds), *Life in the Victorian Village: The Daily News Survey of 1891*, Vol. 2, p. 90.

81 Ashby, *Joseph Ashby*, pp. 189–90.

Conclusion: clothing and landscape

1 Jenny Uglow, *Elizabeth Gaskell: A Habit of Stories* (London, 1993), p. 47.

2 Daniel Roche, *The Culture of Clothing: Dress and Fashion in the Ancien Régime*, (Cambridge, 1994), p. 43.

3 Mabel Kathleen Ashby, *Joseph Ashby of Tysoe, 1859–1919* (this edn London, 1979), p. 55.

4 Karen Sayer, *Women of the Field: Representations of Rural Women in the Nineteenth Century* (Manchester, 1995), p. 17.

5 Rosemary Treble, 'The Victorian picture of the country' in G. E. Mingay (ed.), *The Rural Idyll* (London, 1989), p. 59.

6 David Vincent, *Bread, Knowledge and Freedom: A Study of Working Class Autobiography* (London and New York, 1982), p. 201.

7 Robert Macfarlane: *The Old Ways: A Journey on Foot* (London, 2012), p. 193.

8 Thomas Hardy, 'Afterwards', in *Moments of Vision* (1917; this edn London, 1981).

9 D. H. Lawrence, 'Nottingham and the mining country' (first published in *The Adelphi* magazine, June–August 1930, and reprinted here in D. H. Lawrence, *Selected Essays with an Introduction by Richard Aldington* (London, 1981), p. 119).

10 Ibid., p. 121.
11 John R. Stilgoe, *What is Landscape?* (Cambridge, MA, 2015).
12 William Cobbett, *Rural Rides* (this edn Harmondsworth, 1987), p. 114.
13 Jan Marsh, *Back to the Land: The Pastoral Impulse in England, from 1880 to 1914* (London, 1982).
14 Alison Adburgham, *Liberty's: A Biography of a Shop* (London, 1975), pp. 53–5 and p. 64.
15 Lou Taylor, *Studying Dress History* (Manchester, 2002), p. 1.

BIBLIOGRAPHY

Adburgham, Alison, *Liberty's: A Biography of a Shop* (George Allen & Unwin, London, 1975).

Arch, Joseph, *Joseph Arch, The Story of His Life. Told by Himself* (1898; this edition MacGibbon & Kee, London, 1966).

Armes, Alice, *English Smocks with Directions for Making Them* (Dryad Handicrafts, Leicester, 1928).

Ashby, Mabel Kathleen, *Joseph Ashby of Tysoe 1859–1919* (1961; this edn Merlin Press, London, 1979).

Ashton, Owen and Stephen Roberts, *The Victorian Working-Class Writer* (Cassell, London and New York, 1999).

Barnes, Martin, 'Photographic views from nature', in Martin Barnes (ed.), *Benjamin Brecknell Turner: Rural England through a Victorian Lens* (V&A Publications, London, 2001).

Barrell, John, *The Dark Side of the Landscape: The Rural Poor in English Painting 1730–1840* (Cambridge University Press, Cambridge, 1992).

Barringer, Tim, *Men at Work: Art and Labour in Victorian Britain* (Yale University Press, New Haven and London, 2005).

Bellamy, Liz, K. D. M. Snell and Tom Williamson, 'Rural history: the prospect before us', *Rural History* 1/1 (1990), pp. 1–4.

Bellamy, Liz and Tom Williamson (eds), *Life in the Victorian Village: The Daily News Survey of 1891* (Caliban Books, London, 1999).

Brownell, W. C., 'Bastien-Lepage: painter and psychologist', *The Magazine of Art* (Vol. 6, 1883).

Buck, Anne, 'The countryman's smock', *Folk Life: Journal for the Society of Folk Life Studies* 1 (1963), pp. 16–34.

——— 'Dress as a social record', *Folk Life: Journal for the Society of Folk Life Studies* 14 (1976), pp. 5–26.

——— 'Clothes in fact and fiction 1825–1865', *Costume* 17 (1983), pp. 89–104.

Bullen, J. B., *The Expressive Eye: Fiction and Perception in the Work of Thomas Hardy* (Clarendon Press, Oxford, 1986).

Chapman, Stanley, 'The "revolution" in the manufacture of ready-made clothing 1840–60', *London Journal* 29/1 (2004), pp. 44–61.

Charlesworth, Andrew, 'An agenda for historical studies of rural protest in Britain, 1750–1850, *Rural History* 2/2 (1991), pp. 231–40.

Cherry, Gordon E. and John Sheail, 'The urban impact on the countryside', in E. J. T. Collins (ed.), *The Agrarian History of England and Wales*, Vol. 7, 1850–1914 (Cambridge University Press, Cambridge, 2000).

Clausen, George, 'Bastien-Lepage and modern realism', *The Scottish Art Review*, Vol. 1, 1888.
——— 'Jules Bastien-Lepage as artist', in André Theuriet, *Jules Bastien-Lepage and his Art: A Memoir* (T. Fisher Unwin, London, 1892).
——— *Royal Academy Lectures on Painting: 16 Lectures Delivered to the Students of the Royal Academy of Arts, by George Clausen, R.A.* (Methuen, London, 1913).
Cobb, Richard, *Death in Paris 1795–1801* (Oxford University Press, Oxford, 1978).
Cobbett, William, *Rural Rides* (1830; this edn Penguin, Harmondsworth, 1987).
Coe, Brian, *A Victorian Country Album: The Photographs of Joseph Gale* (Oxford Illustrated Press, Yeovil, 1986).
Cunningham, Hugh, *The Children of the Poor: Representations of Childhood since the Seventeenth Century* (Basil Blackwell, Oxford, 1991).
Cunnington, Phillis and Catherine Lucas, *Occupational Costume in England from the Eleventh Century to 1914* (1967; this edn A. and C. Black, London, 1976).
Daniel, Malcolm, 'The state of the art', in Martin Barnes (ed.), *Benjamin Brecknell Turner: Rural England through a Victorian Lens* (V & A Publications, London, 2001).
Douglas, Ollie, *Museum of English Rural Life and Special Collections: A Guide* (University of Reading, Reading, 2012).
Dyck, Ian, 'Towards the "cottage charter": the expressive culture of farm workers in nineteenth-century England', *Rural History* 1/1 (1990), pp. 95–112.
Eastlake, Elizabeth Rigby, 'The art of dress', in *Music and the Art of Dress* (essays reprinted from *The Quarterly Review*), 1852.
Edwards, Elizabeth, *The Camera as Historian: Amateur Photographers and Historical Imagination 1885–1918* (Duke University Press, Durham and London, 2012).
Emerson, Peter Henry, 'The log of the "Lucy"', *Amateur Photographer*, 10 December 1884, pp. 1–4 (supplement to winter issue).
——— *Naturalistic Photography* (Hazell, Watson and Viney Ltd, London and Aylesbury, 1889).
——— *On English Lagoons* (David Nutt, London, 1893).
Engels, Friedrich, *The Condition of the Working Class in England* (1845; this edn Granada Publishing, London, 1982).
Freeman, Mark, *Social Investigation and Rural England 1870–1914* (Boydell Press, Woodbridge, 2003).
——— (ed.), *The English Rural Poor 1850–1914: Vol. I: The Moral and Material Condition of the Mid-Victorian Rural Poor* (London: Pickering and Chatto, 2005).
Frizot, Michael, 'The truthfulness of the calotype', in Michael Frizot (ed.), *A New History of Photography* (Könemann, Cologne, 1998).
Fussell, G. E., *The English Labourer: His Home, Furniture, Clothing and Food from Tudor to Victorian Times* (Batchworth Press, London, 1949).
Gaskell, Elizabeth, *Mary Barton* (1848; this edn Penguin Books, Harmondsworth, 1985).
——— *Cranford* (1853; this edn Oxford University Press, Oxford, 1972).
——— *North and South* (1855; this edn Penguin, Harmondsworth, 1994).
Gatrell, Simon, *Thomas Hardy Writing Dress* (Peter Lang, Bern, 2011).
Gatt, Guiseppe, *Constable* (Thames and Hudson, London, 1968).
Gauld, Nicola, *'The Field Calls me to Labour': Watercolours of Nineteenth-Century Rural Britain by Robert Hills and His Contemporaries* (Fitzwilliam Museum, Cambridge, 2008).
Gentleman, David (ed.), *George Ewart Evans, The Crooked Scythe: An Anthology of Oral History* (Faber and Faber, London, 1993).
Geremek, Bronislaw, *Poverty – A History* (Blackwell, Oxford, 1997).

Ginsburg, Madeleine, *Victorian Dress in Photographs* (Batsford, London, 1982).

Gruetzner Robins, Anna, 'Living the simple life: George Clausen at Childwick Green', in David Peters Corbett, Ysanne Holt and Fiona Russell (eds), *The Geographies of Englishness: Landscape and the National Past 1880–1940* (Yale University Press, New Haven and London, 2002).

Gross, Jozef, 'The broadland paysanniste', in *British Journal of Photography*, 12 December 1896, pp. 1420–3.

Hammond, J. L. and Barbara, *The Village Labourer 1760–1832* (1911; this edn Alan Sutton Publishing Ltd, Stroud, 1987).

Hardy, Florence Emily, *The Early Life of Thomas Hardy, 1840–1891* (Macmillan, London, 1928).

Hardy, Thomas, *Under the Greenwood Tree* (1872; this edn Penguin, Harmondsworth, 1987).

——— *Far from the Madding Crowd* (1874; this edn Penguin, Harmondsworth, 1988).

——— *The Return of the Native* (1878; this edn Penguin, Harmondsworth, 1979).

——— 'The Dorsetshire Labourer', *Longman's Magazine* Vol. 2 (1883), pp. 252–69.

——— *The Woodlanders* (1887; this edn, Penguin, Harmondsworth, 1981).

——— 'The Profitable Reading of Fiction', *Forum*, New York, March 1888.

——— *Tess of the d'Urbervilles* (1891; this edn Everyman, London, 1984).

——— *Jude the Obscure* (1896; this edn Penguin, Harmondsworth, 1985).

References to Hardy's poetry are from *The Complete Poems*, New Wessex Edition, edited by James Gibson (Macmillan, London, 1981).

——— 'Domicilium', *Wessex Poems* (1898).

——— 'She at his Funeral', *Wessex Poems* (1898).

——— 'The Ruined Maid', *Poems of the Past and Present* (1901).

——— 'At Middle-Field Gate in February', *Moments of Vision* (1917).

——— 'Afterwards', *Moments of Vision* (1917).

Harker, Margaret, *Henry Peach Robinson, Master of Photographic Art 1830–1901* (Basil Blackwell, Oxford, 1988).

Heath, Richard, 'The cottage homes of England' (1870), in Keith Dockray (ed.), *The Victorian Peasant by Richard Heath* (Alan Sutton Publishing, Gloucester, 1989).

——— 'Sussex commons and Sussex songs (1871), in Keith Dockray, etc.

——— 'Peasant life in Dorset' (1872), in Keith Dockray, etc.

Higgs, Edward, 'Women, occupations and work in the nineteenth-century censuses', *History Workshop Journal* 23 (1987), pp. 59–80.

Hobsbawm, E. J. and George Rudé, *Swing* (1969; this edn Penguin, Harmondsworth, 1985).

Honour, Hugh, *Romanticism* (Penguin, Harmondsworth, 1979).

Horn, Pamela, *The Changing Countryside* (Athlone Press, London, 1984).

——— *Victorian Countrywomen* (Basil Blackwell, Oxford, 1991).

Hoskins, W. G., *The Making of the English Landscape* (1955; this edn Penguin, Harmondsworth, 1981).

House, John and Maryanne Stevens, *Post-Impressionism: Cross-Currents in European Painting* (Royal Academy, London, 1979).

Howkins, Alun, 'The discovery of rural England', in Robert Colls and Phillip Dodd (eds), *Englishness: Politics and Culture* (Croom Helm, London, 1986).

——— 'Labour history and the rural poor 1850–1980', *Rural History* 1/1 (1990), pp. 113–22.

——— *Reshaping Rural England: A Social History 1850–1925* (Harper Collins, London, 1991).

——— The Death of Rural England – A Social History of the Countryside since 1900 (Routledge, London, 2003).

Hubbard, Hesketh, A Hundred Years of British Painting 1851–1951 (Longmans, Green and Co., London, 1951).

Hudson, Derek, A. J. Munby, Man of Two Worlds (Sphere Books, London, 1974).

Hudson, W. H., Hampshire Days (1903; this edn Oxford University Press, Oxford, 1980).

Hughes, Clair, Dressed in Fiction (Berg, New York, 2005).

Huish, Marcus B., The Happy England of Helen Allingham (first published as Happy England: As Painted by Helen Allingham R.W.S., 1903; this edn Bracken Books, London, 1985).

Hunt, E. H. Regional Wage Variations in Britain, 1850–1914 (Clarendon Press, Oxford, 1973).

Jefferies, Richard, The Life of the Fields (1884; this edn Lutterworth Press, London, 1947).

———Wild Life in a Southern County (Moonraker Press, Bradford-on-Avon, 1978).

Jenkins, Adrian, Painters and Peasants: Henry La Thangue and British Rural Naturalism, 1880–1905 (Bolton Museum and Art Gallery, 2000).

John, Angela V., By the Sweat of Their Brow: Women Workers at Victorian Coal Mines (Croom Helm, London, 1980).

Jones, Peter, 'Clothing the poor in early nineteenth-century England', Textile History 37/1 (2006), pp. 17–37.

Jumper Matheson, Rebecca, Sunbonnet: An American Icon in Texas (Texas Tech University Press, Texas, 2009).

Keith, W. J., 'The land in Victorian literature', in G. E. Mingay (ed.), The Rural Idyll (Routledge, London, 1989).

Kemp, Martin, Behind the Picture: Art and Evidence in the Italian Renaissance (Yale University Press, New Haven and London, 1997).

Ketteringham, J., 'Country work girls in nineteenth-century England', in Raphael Samuel, Village Life and Labour (Routledge and Kegan Paul, London and Boston, 1975).

King, Steven A., Poverty and Welfare in England 1700–1850: A Regional Perspective (Manchester University Press, Manchester, 2000).

——— 'Reclothing the English poor, 1750–1840', Textile History 33/1 (2002), pp. 37–47.

King, Steven A. and Christiana Payne (eds), 'The dress of the poor: old and new perspectives', special issue of Textile History 33/1 (2002).

Knell, Simon, Museums and the Future of Collecting (Ashgate, Aldershot, 1999).

Lawrence, D. H., The Rainbow (1915; this edn Penguin, Harmondsworth, 1983).

——— 'Nottingham and the mining country' (first published in The New Adelphi, June–August 1930, reprinted in D. H. Lawrence, Selected Essays with an Introduction by Richard Aldington (Penguin, London, 1981).

Levitt, Sarah, 'Cheap mass-produced men's clothing in the nineteenth and early twentieth centuries', Textile History 22/2 (1991), pp. 179–92.

Macfarlane, Robert, The Old Ways: A Journey on Foot (Penguin, London, 2012).

Magazine of Art, Vol. 5 (1881–2) and Vol. 10 (1887).

Marsh, Jan, Back to the Land: The Pastoral Impulse in England, from 1880 to 1914 (Quartet Books, London, 1982).

Masterman, C. F. G., The Condition of England (Methuen, London, 1909).

Matless, David, Landscape and Englishness (Reaktion, London, 1998).

McConkey, Kenneth, Sir George Clausen, R. A. 1852–1944 (Bradford Art Galleries and Museums and Tyne and Wear County Council Museums, 1980).

——— George Clausen and the Picture of English Rural Life (Atelier Books, Edinburgh, 2012).

McKendrick, Neil, John Brewer and J. H. Plumb, *The Birth of a Consumer Society: The Commercialization of Eighteenth Century England* (Europa Publications, London, 1982).

Millgate, Michael, *Thomas Hardy: A Biography* (Oxford University Press, Oxford, 1982).

Mingay, G. E., *Rural Life in Victorian England* (Alan Sutton Publishing, Stroud, 1990).

Moore, George, *Modern Painting* (Walter Scott Limited, London, 1893).

Morgan, David, 'The place of harvesters in nineteenth-century village life', in Raphael Samuel (ed.), *Village Life and Labour* (Routledge and Kegan Paul, London and Boston, 1975).

Nattali, M. A., *W. H. Pyne: Etchings of Rustic Figures for the Embellishment of Landscape* (London, 1815).

Newton, Stella Mary, *Health, Art and Reason* (John Murray, London, 1974).

Nichols, Marian, *Smocks in Luton Museum* (Borough of Luton Museum and Art Gallery, 1980).

Nochlin, Linda, *Realism* (Penguin, Harmondsworth, 1971).

Newby, Howard, *Country Life: A Social History of Rural England* (Weidenfeld and Nicolson, London, 1987).

Oakes, Alma and Margot Hill, *Rural Costume, Its Origin and Development in Western Europe and the British Isles* (B. T. Batsford, London, and Van Nostrand Reinhold Co., New York, 1970).

Oliver, Tina, *Smocks at the Rural History Centre: A Guide to the Collection* (University of Reading, 2000).

Parliamentary Papers: *Employment of Women and Children in Agriculture*, 1843 (510), Vol. XII: *Reports of Special Assistant Poor Law Commissioners on the Employment of Women and Children in Agriculture (Wiltshire, Dorset, Devon and Somerset)*; Parliamentary Papers: *Second Report from the Commissioners on the Employment of Children, Young Persons and Women in Agriculture, with Appendix Part I and Part II*, 1868–9. Note: Two reports relating to England were published as a result of the 1867 commission: the first in 1867–8 (C. 4068) and the second in 1868–9 (C. 4202). The majority of the references here are to the second report, 1868–9.

Payne, Christiana, *Toil and Plenty: Images of the Agricultural Landscape 1780–1890* (Yale University Press, New Haven and London, 1993).

———— *Rustic Simplicity: Scenes of Cottage Life in Nineteenth-Century British Art* (Djanogly Art Gallery, University of Nottingham Arts Centre in association with Lund Humphries Publishers, Nottingham and London, 1998).

Payne, Sarah, *The Gurteens of Haverhill: Two Hundred Years of Suffolk Textiles* (Woodhead Faulkner, Cambridge, 1984).

Pearce, Susan M., 'Museum objects', in Susan M. Pearce (ed.), *Interpreting Objects and Collections* (Routledge, London and New York, 1994).

———— 'Objects as meaning; or narrating the past', in Susan M. Pearce, etc.

Pinney, Thomas (ed.), *Essays of George Eliot* (Routledge and Kegan Paul, London, 1963).

Postle, Martin, *Angels and Urchins: The Fancy Picture in Eighteenth Century British Art* (Djanogly Art Gallery, Nottingham, 1998).

Postle, Martin and Amima Wright, *Pictures of Innocence: Portraits of Children from Hogarth to Lawrence* (Holbourne Museum of Art, Bath, 2005).

Prown, Jules David, 'The truth of material culture: history or fiction?' in Steven Lubar and W. David Kingery (eds), *History from Things: Essays on Material Culture* (Smithsonian Institution Press, Washington and London, 1993).

Pryor, Francis, *The Making of the British Landscape* (Penguin, London, 2010).

Radford, Andrew, *Mapping the Wessex Novel: Landscape, History and the Parochial in British Literature 1870–1940* (Continuum Literary Studies, London, 2010).

Reay, Barry, *Rural Englands: Labouring Lives in the Nineteenth Century* (Palgrave, Basingstoke, 2004).

Reed, Mick, ' "Gnawing it out": a new look at economic relations in nineteenth-century rural England', *Rural History* 1/1 (1990), pp. 83–94.

Rees, Mair G. and Christine Stevens, 'Smocks in the Welsh folk museum collection', *Medel* 3 (1986), pp. 32–8.

Rendall, Jane, *Women in an Industrializing Society: England 1750–1880* (Basil Blackwell, Oxford, 1990).

Richmond, Vivienne, ' "Indiscriminate liberality subverts the morals and depraves the habits of the poor": a contribution to the debate on the poor law, parish clothing relief and clothing societies in early nineteenth century England', *Textile History* 40/1 (2009), pp. 51–69.

——— *Clothing the Poor in Nineteenth Century England* (Cambridge University Press, Cambridge, 2013).

Richmond, Vivienne (ed.), *Clothing, Society and Culture in Nineteenth-Century England*, Vol. 3: *Working Class Dress* (Pickering and Chatto, London, 2013).

Riello, Giorgio, *A Foot in the Past: Consumers, Producers, and Footwear in the Long Eighteenth Century* (Oxford University Press, Oxford / Pasold Research Trust, 2006).

Roberts, Elizabeth, *Women's Work 1840–1940* (Cambridge University Press, Cambridge, 1995).

Robinson, Henry Peach, 'Composition not patchwork', *British Journal of Photography*, 2 July 1860.

——— *Pictorial Effect in Photography, Being Hints on Composition and Chiaroscuro for Photographers* (Piper and Carter, London, 1869).

——— *Picture Making by Photography* (Piper and Carter, London, 1884).

——— *The Elements of a Pictorial Photograph* (Percy Lund & Company of Bradford and London, 1896).

Roche, Daniel, *The Culture of Clothing: Dress and Fashion in the Ancien Régime* (Cambridge University Press, Cambridge, 1994).

Rose, Phyllis, 'Milkmaid Madonnas: an appreciation of Cameron's portraits of women', in Sylvia Wolf (ed.), *Julia Margaret Cameron's Women* (Yale University Press, New Haven and London, 1998).

Samuel, Raphael (ed.), *Village Life and Labour* (Routledge and Kegan Paul, London and Boston, 1975).

Sayer, Karen, *Women of the Fields: Representations of Rural Women in the Nineteenth Century* (Manchester University Press, Manchester, 1995).

Sharpe, Pamela, 'The women's harvest: straw-plaiting and the representation of labouring women's employment c.1793–1885', *Rural History* 5/2 (1994), pp. 129–42.

——— 'Cheapness and economy: manufacturing and retailing ready-made clothing in London and Essex 1830–1850', *Textile History* 26/2 (1995), pp. 203–13.

Skipworth, Peyton, *The Rustic Image: Rural Themes in British Painting 1880–1912* (Fine Art Society, London, 1979).

Snell, K. D. M., *Annals of the Labouring Poor: Social Change and Agrarian England, 1660–1900* (Cambridge University Press, Cambridge, 1985).

Somerville, Alexander, *The Autobiography of a Working Man*, (1848; this edn Turnstile Press, London, 1951).

——— *The Whistler at the Plough – Containing Travels, Statistics and Descriptions of Scenery and Agricultural Customs in Most Parts of England* (1852; this edn Merlin Press, London, 1989).

Spargo, Demelza, *This Land is Our Land: Aspects of Agriculture in English Art* (Royal Agricultural Society of England / Mall Galleries, London, 1989).

Spufford, Margaret, *The Great Reclothing of Rural England: Petty Chapman and their Wares in the Seventeenth Century* (Hambledon Press, London, 1984).

Squire, Louise, *The Conservation of a Nineteenth Century Waterproofed Sussex Round Smock-Frock* (unpublished dissertation, Textile Conservation Centre / Courtauld Institute of Art, University of London, 1996).

Stevenson, Sara, *Hill and Adamson's The Fishermen and Women of the Firth of Forth* (Scottish National Portrait Gallery, Edinburgh, 1991).

Stilgoe, John R., *What is Landscape?* (MIT Press, Cambridge MA, 2015)

Sturt, George, *Change in the Village* (The County Book Club, London, 1956).

Styles, John, *The Dress of the People: Everyday Fashion in Eighteenth-Century England* (Yale University Press, New Haven and London, 2007).

Tagg, John, *The Burden of Representation: Essays on Photographs and Histories* (Macmillan, London, 1988).

Taylor, John, *A Dream of England: Landscape, Photography and the Tourist's Imagination* (Manchester University Press, Manchester and New York, 1994).

Taylor, Lou, *Mourning Dress: A Costume and Social History* (George Allen & Unwin, London, 1983).

———— *Studying Dress History* (Manchester University Press, Manchester, 2002).

———— *Establishing Dress History* (Manchester University Press, Manchester, 2004).

Tebbutt, Melanie, *Making Ends Meet: Pawnbroking and Working-Class Credit* (Methuen, London, 1984).

Thompson, Flora, *Lark Rise to Candleford* (1945; this edn Penguin, Harmondsworth, 1987).

Thomson, George, 'Henry Herbert La Thangue and his work', *Studio*, Vol. 9, 1896.

Thornton, Nicholas, 'Enigmatic variations: the features of British smocks', *Textile History* 28/2 (1997), pp. 176–84.

Tomalin, Claire, *Thomas Hardy: The Time Torn Man* (Penguin/Viking, London, 2006).

Toplis, Alison, 'The manufacture and provision of rural garments 1800–1850: a case study of Herefordshire and Worcestershire', *Textile History* 40/2 (2009), pp. 152–69.

———— *The Clothing Trade in Provincial England 1800–1850* (Pickering and Chatto, London, 2011).

Tozer, Jane, 'Cunnington's interpretation of dress', *Costume* 20 (1986), pp. 1–17.

Treble, Rosemary, 'The Victorian picture of the country', in G. E. Mingay (ed.), *The Rural Idyll* (Routledge, London, 1989).

Treuherz, Julian, *Hard Times: Social Realism in Victorian Art* (Lund Humphries in association with City of Manchester Art Galleries, London, 1987).

Turner, Peter and Richard Wood, *P. H. Emerson, Photographer of Norfolk* (Gordon Fraser, London, 1974).

Uglow, Jenny, *Elizabeth Gaskell: A Habit of Stories* (Faber and Faber, London, 1993).

Vaughan, William, Elizabeth E. Barker and Colin Harrison (eds), *Samuel Palmer, Vision and Landscape* (The British Museum Press, London, 2005).

Vigeon, Evelyn, 'Clogs or wooden-soled shoes', *Costume* 11 (1977), pp. 1–27.

Wells, Roger, 'Southern Chartism', *Rural History* 2/1 (1991), pp. 37–59.

Williams, James Leon, *The Home and Haunts of Shakespeare* (Sampson Low, Marston & Co. Ltd., London, 1892).

Williams, Merryn, *Thomas Hardy and Rural England* (Colombia University Press, Colombia, 1972).

Williams, Raymond, *The Country and the City* (1973; this edn Hogarth Press, London, 1985).

Wilson, Elizabeth and Lou Taylor, *Through the Looking Glass* (BBC Books, London, 1989).

Wood, Christopher, *Paradise Lost: Paintings of English Country Life and Landscape, 1850–1914* (Barrie and Jenkins, London, 1988).

Worth, Rachel, 'Thomas Hardy and rural dress', *Costume* 29 (1995), pp. 55–67.

———— 'Elizabeth Gaskell, clothes and class identity', *Costume* 32 (1998), pp. 52–9.

———— 'Rural labouring dress 1850–1900: some problems of representation', *Fashion Theory: The Journal of Dress, Body and Culture* 3/3 (1999), pp. 323–42.

———— 'Developing a method for the study of the clothing of the "poor": some themes in the visual representation of rural working-class dress, 1850–1900', *Textile History* 40/1 (2009), pp. 70–96.

———— 'Some issues in the representation of rural working-class dress in British nineteenth-century photography', *Revue Belge de Philologie et d'Histoire*, 87/3–4 (2009), pp. 775–91. Published as a special issue, Joeri Januarius and Nelleke Teughels (eds), *The Historical Use of Images: Theory, Methods, Practice*.

———— 'Clothing the landscape: change and the rural vision in the work of Thomas Hardy (1840–1928)', *Rural History*, 24/2 (2013) pp. 199–215.

Wright, Alastair Ian, 'Bastien-Lepage and English critical taste', *Gazette des Beaux Arts*, Vol. 116, September 1990, pp. 94–104.

Wright, Mary, *Cornish Guernseys and Knit-frocks* (Ethnographica, London, 1979).

Zimmern, Helen, 'A painter of peasants', *The Magazine of Art*, Vol. 8, 1885.

INDEX

Plate 1 *The Farmer's Children* (pencil and watercolour on paper) by Robert Hills

Plate 2 *A Rustic Scene* (1823; pen and brush in sepia) by Samuel Palmer

Plate 3 *Washing Day at Sandhills, Witley* (watercolour on paper) by Helen Allingham

Plate 4 *A Dorsetshire Cottage* (watercolour on paper) by Helen Allingham

Plate 5 *Portrait of a Girl in a Pink Bonnet* (watercolour on paper) by Helen Allingham

Plate 6 *Washing Day* (pencil and watercolour) by Helen Allingham

Plate 7 *The Shepherd* (oil on canvas) by Henry Herbert La Thangue

Plate 8 *December* (*c.*1882; oil on panel) by George Clausen

Plate 9 *The Stone Pickers* (1887; oil on canvas) by George Clausen

Plate 10 *Ploughing* (1889; oil on canvas) by George Clausen

Plate 11 *A Girl's Head* (1886; oil on canvas) by George Clausen

Plate 12 Bere Regis (Dorset) 'revival' smock (early twentieth century)

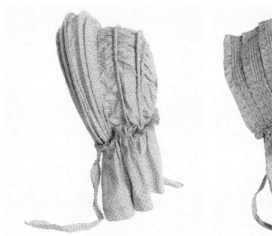
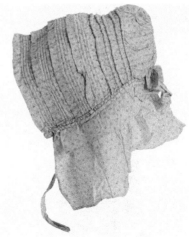

Plate 13 Sun-bonnet of printed cotton
(second half of the nineteenth century)

Plate 14a Sun-bonnet of printed cotton
(second half of the nineteenth century)

Plate 14b Detail of sun-bonnet of printed cotton (second half of the nineteenth century)

Plate 15a Dress (late nineteenth century)

Plate 15b Detail of dress (late nineteenth century)

9 781350 122840